BIBLIOGRAPHY on DEAFNESS

A Selected Index

The Volta Review
1899- 1965

The American Annals of the Deaf
1847- 1965

George W. Fellendorf
Editor

Alexander Graham Bell Association for the Deaf, Inc.
Headquarters: The Volta Bureau, Washington, D.C.

Copyright © 1966

By the Alexander Graham Bell Association for the Deaf, Inc.

First Edition

Library of Congress Catalog Card No. 66–29884

Printed in the United States of America

CONTENTS

Subject Index

Aphasia	1
Arithmetic	1
Audiology & Auditory Training	4
Bell Family	12
Day Schools	14
Deaf-Blind	14
Education	17
Foreign	34
Hard of Hearing	37
Hearing Aids	38
Heredity	42
Language	43
Manual Communication	57
Miscellaneous	59
Multiply Handicapped	59
Music, Rhythm and Art	61
Parents	63
Preschool	68
Psychological	72
Reading	83
Religion	88
Science Studies	89
Social Studies	90
Speech	93
Speechreading	106
Teacher Training	119
Visual Aids	121
Vocational—Rehabilitation	123

Author Index 129

Editors, *The Volta Review*

Frank W. Booth	1899–1910
F. K. Noyes	1910–1912
Ernest Gregory	1912–1914
Fred DeLand	1914–1920
Josephine Timberlake	1920–1953
Alice Dunlap	1953–1957
Jeanette Johnson	1957–1963
George W. Fellendorf	1963–

Editors, *The American Annals of the Deaf*

Luzerne Rae	1847–1854
Samuel Porter	1855–1861
Lewellyn Pratt	1868–1870
Edward A. Fay	1870–1920
Irving S. Fusfeld	1920–1943
Ignatius Bjorlee	1943–1944
Leonard M. Elstad	1945–1948
Powrie V. Doctor	1948–

Foreword

Although *The Volta Review* and *The American Annals of the Deaf* are the two most important and oldest journals in the field of education of the deaf, this is the first cumulative, selected index of these publications.

The American Annals of the Deaf, official journal of the Conference of Executives of American Schools for the Deaf, and the American Instructors of the Deaf, is the oldest educational journal in the United States still in existence. It was founded in 1847 by faculty members at the American School for the Deaf, Hartford, Connecticut. For 118 years the Annals has recorded the practices and thinking of educators of the deaf, as well as presenting statistical information about schools and teachers. Until 1956, cumulative indexes were published every ten years. Since then, annual indexes have been published in November.

The Volta Review, official journal of the Alexander Graham Bell Association for the Deaf, began publication in 1899 under the name The Association Review. It has served to combine the interests of educators and teachers, hearing impaired adults, and the parents of deaf children. The special mission of this journal has been to promote the teaching of speech and lipreading to the deaf, and to encourage training in the use of residual hearing.

Indexing *The American Annals of the Deaf* was a comparatively simple task, since its subject matter has always been directed to a readership of professionals. Indexing *The Volta Review* presented a more difficult problem, due to the broad scope of its readership and contents over the years.

Years ago, when the Alexander Graham Bell Association for the Deaf was closely affiliated with the American Hearing Society, *The Volta Review* gave a great deal of space to stories written by hard of hearing adult readers who reported interesting personal experiences, including their travels abroad. A few of these features have been listed under the Speechreading category, while hundreds of others were not considered of sufficient educational significance for indexing.

Articles listed for *The Volta Review* include those believed by the editor and his associates to be related primarily to educational aspects of deafness.

Some articles that should have been indexed may have been left out. Conversely, there may be articles included in the index that should have been omitted. The editor used his best judgment and assumes full responsibility for errors of omission or commission.

No effort was made to eliminate any controversial articles from the selected index. On the contrary, special attempt was made to include all articles reflecting such controversies as residential versus day schools, manual versus oral communication, deaf versus hearing teachers, and natural versus structured language.

The editor is grateful to many persons who contributed toward this publication. Miss Josephine Carr, while doing graduate work at the University of Illinois, prepared a selected reading list of *The Volta Review* and *The American Annals of the Deaf* which was most helpful in initiating the indexing project.

Margaret Rostel Hayer, former editor of *Hearing News*, served as an efficient assistant editor of this unique publication.

Esther Stovall, assistant editor of *The Volta Review*; Marjorie Desmarais and Harold Wieland, librarians at the Volta Bureau, 1964–1966; and Ada M. Hill, retired American Hearing Society staff member, worked diligently in selecting, checking and editing the thousands of entries in the index.

Special acknowledgment is also due John A. Gough, Chief, Captioned Films for the Deaf, U.S. Office of Education, Department of Health, Education, and Welfare, whose initial interest and eventual support in the distribution of copies helped make this publication possible.

November 1, 1966

George W. Fellendorf,
Executive Director of the
Alexander Graham Bell Association
for the Deaf, and
Editor, *The Volta Review*

Guide for Using the Bibliography

A. Subject Index

1. Signed articles are listed alphabetically according to name of author, followed by title, year of publication, volume number and pages. Unsigned articles are listed alphabetically, using key words in the title as a guide to sequence:

> Adams, Bradford C.; The Independent Study Plan for the Deaf Student at College (with discussion by Jerry A. Pierce); 1933, *35*, 445-475
>
> ─────────; Analysis of the Annals Statistics (pupils and teachers in American Schools for the Deaf, 1893 through 1910); 1911, *12*, 719-720

2. Each article is listed only once; there are no cross-references.
3. Research findings and reports are listed under the category related to the subject of research.
4. Under the Education category are general articles which do not specifically fit into any of the other categories.
5. Of historical interest to students, teachers and researchers in education of the deaf are numerous *Volta Review* articles by or about Alexander Graham Bell, his father Alexander Melville Bell, his wife Mabel and other members of the famous family. If primarily historical in content, these will be found under the category Bell Family. If specific to one of the particular subjects, articles by a member of the Bell family are listed under the appropriate category.
6. Under the category Hearing Aids are articles relating to individual rather than group hearing aids. Articles about group hearing aids are listed in the Audiology and Auditory Training category, as are articles concerning the use of the telephone by deaf persons.
7. Articles on the subject of television are indexed under Visual Aids.
8. Articles on the medical aspects of deafness are included in the Heredity category.
9. *The American Annals of the Deaf* has published annually in the January issue a listing of American and Canadian schools for the deaf and

a directory of American instructors of the deaf. Although not indexed here, this statistical presentation, now occupying a major part of the January issue, gives tabulated information on the following:

Teaching training centers; teachers in training; teachers of the deaf; public residential schools; public day schools; denominational and private schools and classes; schools for the multiply handicapped; schools for the deaf in Canada; state departments of education having a conservation of hearing program; state societies of the National Society for Crippled Children and Adults having speech and hearing programs; speech and hearing clinics in colleges and universities in the U.S. and Canada; speech and hearing clinics in hospitals in the U.S. and Canada; speech and hearing clinics in schools for the deaf in the U.S. and Canada; and speech and hearing services in medical schools.

10. In general, articles of less than two pages in length are not included in this bibliography.

B. Author Index

The numbers following the authors' names indicate the pages where their writings are listed in the Subject Index.

APHASIA

Volta Review

DiCarlo, Louis M.; Differential Diagnosis of Congenital Aphasia; 1960, *62*, 361-364
Elkan, Dorothea; Development of an Aphasic Child; 1955, *57*, 71-72
Kleffner, Frank R.; Teaching Speech and Language to Aphasic Children; 1958, *60*, 326-328
Lloyd, James H.; Sensory Aphasia, Associated with Right Lateral Homonymous Hemianopsia; 1919, *21*, 24-26
McGinnis, Mildred A., et al.; Teaching Aphasic Children; 1956, *58*, 239-244
Monsees, Edna K.; Aphasia in Children—Diagnosis and Education; 1957, *59*, 392-401; 414
Myklebust, Helmer R.; Training Aphasic Children; 1955, *57*, 149-157
Philbrick, William A.; Implications of State Legislation for Aphasic Children; 1958, *60*, 428-430; 463
Rooney, Alice G.; An Aphasic Child in a School for the Deaf; 1945, *47*, 559-562
Scott, Mrs. Elmer W.; Childhood Aphasia: A Reminiscence; 1963, *65*, 592-594
Sweet, Marie E.; The Association Method for Aphasics—Its Application to the Deaf; 1955, *57*, 13-15

Annals of the Deaf

Myklebust, Helmer R.; Language Training: A Comparison Between Children with Aphasia and Those with Deafness; 1956, *101*, 240-244

ARITHMETIC

Volta Review

Acker, Lela; Devices to Make Arithmetic Interesting; 1936, *38*, 11-13; 61
Acker, Lela; Making Arithmetic Attractive; 1934, *36*, 709-711; 762
Adams, Ida H.; Arithmetic Taught by Constructive Measuring; 1906, *8*, 238-241
Archer, Tunis V.; Some Points to Emphasize in Teaching Arithmetic; 1912, *14*, 25-30
——————; Arithmetic; 1925, *27*, 40-47
Booth, Frank W.; Teaching Arithmetic Objectively; 1926, *28*, 606-613

ARITHMETIC—*continued*

Volta Review

Bower, Dolores; Summer Fun with Numbers; 1961, *63*, 284-286
Christian, Harvey T.; Beginning Algebra Taught Objectively; 1929, *31*, 117-120
Cobb, Jennie; Beginning Arithmetic; 1912, *14*, 679-680
Downing, A. U.; Arithmetic—The Equation Method; 1907, *9*, 191-198
Driscoll, Anita; Arithmetic; 1928, *30*, 630-632
Driscoll, Anita; Arithmetic in the Lexington Avenue School; 1926, *28*, 303-304
Elliott, C. Evangeline; Arithmetic in the Elementary Grades; 1933, *35*, 374-376
Haynes, Carrie A.; Problem Analysis; 1926, *28*, 591-592
Hembrook, Margaret; The Use of the Model Store; 1930, *32*, 576-577
Kent, Eliza; Primary Work in Arithmetic; 1907, *9*, 104-110
Lewis, Sarah E.; Primary Number Work; 1926, *28*, 587-588
Long, E. Florence; The Logical Way of Teaching Arithmetic; 1930, *32*, 413-414
McLaughlin, Clayton L.; Practical Mathematics; 1927, *29*, 463-465
McMillan, K.; Work with Number Combinations in the Alabama School; 1928, *30*, 227-228
Morris, Dorothy; Mathematics in the Grammar School; 1926, *28*, 148-149
Newlee, Clara E.; The Cleveland Arithmetic Test; 1918, *20*, 212-222
Numbers, Leona P.; The Teaching of Arithmetic in the Primary and Intermediate Grades; 1958, *60*, 210-212; 226-227
O'Neill, Veronica; Number Fun at Home; 1955, *57*, 257-259; 275
Poulos, Thomas H.; Needs and Objectives in Teaching Arithmetic to the Deaf; 1953, *55*, 452-455
Sensenig, Barton; Equational Methods; 1911, *13*, 91-95
Sensenig, Barton; Methods in Arithmetic; 1903, *5*, 132-139
Sensenig, Barton; An Outline in Arithmetic and Methods of Presenting the Subject; 1914, *16*, 21-26; 60-64
Sensenig, Barton; An Outline of Third-Year Work in Arithmetic, with Methods; 1914, *16*, 154-159
Sensenig, Barton; Training for Number Work; 1920, *22*, 767-778
Taylor, Annah S.; A Helpful Device for Teaching the Formal Skills of Arithmetic; 1919, *21*, 554-555
Taylor, Annah S.; A Project for Eighth Grade Mathematics; 1921, *23*, 297-299
Welty, Harry L.; The Teaching of Numbers; 1929, *31*, 312-320

Annals of the Deaf

Andrews, Harriet E.; Primary Arithmetic; 1922, *67*, 232-235
Bemis, Luna M.; Early Steps in Number Work for Deaf Children; 1916, *61*, 134-136
Bird, William L.; Preparatory Drill in Figures; 1879, *24*, 1-9
Booth, F. W.; Primary Arithmetic: The Notation of Money; 1893, *38*, 1-4
Caldwell, Wm. A.; A Device for Teaching Numeration; 1926, *71*, 268-270
Deem, Harriet, L.; Primary Arithmetic; 1922, *67*, 112-116
Denison, James; A New Arithmetical Device; 1891, *36*, 129-136
Eddy, Jonathan H.; Arithmetic in the Education of the Deaf; 1887, *32*, 93-98
Freeman, Samuel M.; Addition and Subtraction for Beginners; 1901, *46*, 159-166
Fullington, Angeline; Primary Arithmetic; 1908, *53*, 137-141
Glenn, Sallie; Some Devices in Arithmetic; 1928, *73*, 249-251
Greenberger, D.; Arithmetic; 1882, *27*, 12-28
Greenberger, D.; Form Study; 1888, *32*, 234-241
Harvey, A., et al.; Arithmetic in the Intermediate and Advanced Departments of the Pennsylvania Institution; 1909, *54*, 197-237
Haskins, C. N.; Mental Arithmetic; 1887, *32*, 156-161
Jenkins, Weston G.; The Teaching of Arithmetic; 1892, *37*, 9-14
Keep, John R.; Addition, How It May be Taught; 1856, *8*, 110-113
Kent, Eliza; Primary Arithmetic; 1906, *51*, 315-320
Mossel, Max N.; Dealing with Zeros in the Minuend; 1938, *83*, 218-224
Newman, Lawrence; Meaningful Mathematical Problem Work for the Deaf; 1957, *102*, 293-299
O'Donnell, Francis H.; Four Arithmetic Formulas; 1922, *67*, 117-124
Reed, Katharine F.; Devices for Primary Number Work; 1905, *50*, 173-177
Sensenig, Barton; Errors in Arithmetical Methods; 1906, *51*, 370-375
Sensenig, Barton; Practical Arithmetic; 1923, *68*, 287-300
Smith, J. L., et al.; A Course in Arithmetic; 1888, *33*, 197-199
Smith, James L.; "Too Much Arithmetic?;" 1934, *79*, 205-209
Sowell, James W.; Arithmetic; 1905, *50*, 279-293
Stafford, May M.; Some Possibilities of Arithmetic; 1901, *46*, 526-531
Storrs, Richard S.; Arithmetic for Deaf-Mutes; 1871, *16*, 143-160
Vermillion, Frances F.; A Key to the Language of Arithmetic—An Aid in Teaching the Fundamental Processes; 1936, *81*, 209-211
Wait, Selah; Method of Teaching the Fundamental Rules of Arithmetic; 1869, *14*, 239-245
Walker, S. Tefft; The Teaching of Numbers; 1882, *27*, 224-227
Wolach, Marvin; Visualizing the Units of Measure; 1952, *97*, 341-347

AUDIOLOGY & AUDITORY TRAINING

Volta Review

Anderson, J. Scott; Development of the Hearing; 1910, *12*, 175-176

Anselmini, Andrew A.; Auditory Training: Design for Growth, Basic Considerations; 1959, *61*, 322-323; 342

Anselmini, Andrew A., and Wallin, Margaret K.; Auditory Training: Design for Growth, Instructional Techniques; 1959, *61*, 461-466; 486

Asals, Frances B., and Ruthven, Henrietta C.; Acoustic Training for the Primary Grades; 1948, *50*, 498-510

Asals, Frances B., and Ruthven, Henrietta C.; Auditory Training for the Primary Grades; 1956, *58*, 205-207

Bangs, Tina E.; Methodology in Auditory Training; 1954, *56*, 159-164

Barley, Kenneth; Hearing, Discrimination and Interpretation; 1939, *41*, 69-70

Barrows, C. M.; A Method of Teaching Hearing to the Deaf; 1905, *7*, 332-342

Beebe, Helen H.; Direct Tone Introduction Test and the Chewing Method; 1954, *56*, 19-23

Bellefleur, Philip A., and McMenamin, Sayre B.; Problems of Inductance Loop Amplification; 1965, *67*, 559-563; 579

Bender, Ruth E.; The Discovery and Training of Hearing in Young Deaf Children; 1948, *50*, 572-574; 592-594

Berry, Amelia E.; Audiometer Testing and Auricular Training with the Audiophone; 1929, *31*, 780-782

Berry, Gordon; Auditory Symptoms from Dental Bite, (a review); 1947, *49*, 509; 530

Blake, Clarence John; The Fatigue of Deafness; 1918, *20*, 302-305

Bodycomb, Margaret; The Auricular Program at Mt. Airy; 1937, *39*, 202-204; 246

Bollbach, Betty L.; Enriching Deaf Children's Experience Through Auditory Training; 1958; *60*, 411-413

Bollbach, Betty L., and Crane, Norman W.; A Meaningful Approach to Auditory Training; 1957, *59*, 243-247

Braddock, Mary J.; Teaching the Use of the Telephone to the Severely Hard of Hearing; 1957, *59*, 442-444

Braly, Kenneth, et al.; Some Aspects of Acoustic Work; 1938, *40*, 325-327

Broderick, Thomas G. and Kranz, Fred W.; The New ISO Audiometric Standard Zero Reference; 1965, *67*, 570-571

Buchanan, Nancy; Not More Learning but Better Hearing; 1920, *22*, 2-4

Calvert, Donald R.; A Comparison of Auditory Amplifiers in the Classroom in a School for the Deaf; 1964, *66*, 544-547

Coakley, Estelle L.; Auditory Training at Northwestern; 1950, *52*, 23-25; 40

Collins, Helen M.; The 4-A Audiometer and the C.W.A. in Florida; 1934, *36*, 294-295; 310-311

Costello, Mary Rose; Changing Concepts in Audiology; 1958, *60*, 395-398
Cotton, Jack C., and Hall, Jayne; Administration of 6-A Audiometer Tests to Kindergarten and First Grade Children; 1939, *41*, 291-292; 312-314
Cox, Jerome R., Schoenfeld, Sidney L. and Totoki, Akira; Evaluation of the Acoustical Environments for Group Hearing Aids; 1957, *59*, 383-385
Cuddy, Nelle M.; Auricular Training in Our Schools; 1930, *32*, 173-174
Davies, Gladys B.; Testing for the Hard of Hearing Child; 1932, *34*, 399-400; 423-424
DiCarlo, Louis M.; Auditory Training for the Adult; 1948, *50*, 490-498
DiCarlo, Louis M.; The Effect of Hearing One's Voice Among Children with Impaired Hearing; 1958, *60*, 306-314
Doerfler, Leo G. (moderator, panel discussion); Auditory Training; 1954, *56*, 350-354; 368; 393-396; 402-407
Doyle, F. W.; Oakland's Acoustic Program; 1941, *43*, 517-520; 566-567
Doyle, John B., et al.; Electrical Stimulation in Eighth Nerve Deafness; 1965, *67*, 82-84
Elliott, Sarah L.; Auricular Possibilities in Classes with Varying Hearing Percentages; 1936, *38*, 389-390; 428
Elliott, Sarah L.; A Questionnaire on Acoustic Training; 1942, *44*, 73-75
Elstad, Leonard M.; Auricular Training; 1928, *30*, 276-278
Elstad, Leonard M.; The Use of the Audiophone No. 10-A in the Wright Oral School; 1926, *28*, 675-677
Empey, Margaret; Pure Tone Audiometry with Young Children; 1953, *55*, 439-442
Ferreri, Giulio; The Audiphone-Stroboscope; 1934, *36*, 133-139
Ferreri, Giulio; Systematic Acoustic Exercises; 1911, *13*, 5-8; 228-230; 1912, *13*, 473-476
Field, Lois G.; All They Need Is a Boost From You; 1956, *58*, 197-199
Fitzgerald, Margaret H.; Auditory Training in Schools for the Deaf; 1955, *57*, 167-170
Fletcher, Harvey; Audiometric Measurement and Their Uses; 1924, *26*, 10-14
Fletcher, Harvey; The Progress of Hearing Tests in Public Schools of the United States; 1930, *32*, 1-4
Fletcher, Harvey; The Science of Hearing; 1948, *50*, 351-352; 386
Forrester, T. C.; The Problems of Training the Remnants of Auditory Perception; 1928, *30*, 136-140
Fort, Berneice; My Experience with Auditory Training; 1957, *59*, 214-215
Frueh, Frank; The Audiologist in the Residential School; 1958, *60*, 405-408

AUDIOLOGY & AUDITORY TRAINING—continued

Volta Review

Gardner, W. Morton; Getting Results in Hearing Tests; 1934, *36*, 359-361; 374

Gardner, Warren H.; Audiometer Testing in Iowa Schools; 1936, *38*, 727; 749-750

Gardner, Warren H.; Hearing Tests in 37 Iowa School Systems; 1937, *39*, 699-701; 722

Gardner, Warren H.; Testing Kindergarten Children With the 4-A Audiometer; 1937, *39*, 229-231; 247

Gentilli, Amadeo; An Automatic Recorder of Speech; 1911, *13*, 19-22

Gile, Ben C.; What Is Hearing?; 1917, *19*, 47-53

Gill, Dorothy; Auricular Work; 1933, *35*, 420-422

Goldstein, Max A.; An Acoustic Method; 1920, *22*, 716-719

Goldstein, Max A.; Demonstration: Auricular Training; 1919, *21*, 157-160

Goldstein, Robert; Detection and Assessment of Auditory Disorders in Children Less Than Three Years Old; 1955, *57*, 215-219

Graves, Frank P.; The Use and Abuse of Intelligence Tests; 1925, *27*, 73-75

Griffiths, Ciwa; The Auditory Approach for Preschool Deaf Children; 1964, *66*, 387-397

———; Group Hearing Aids in the Schools; 1956, *58*, 208-212

Guilder, Ruth P., and Hopkins, Louise A.; The Importance of Auditory Function Studies in the Educational Program for the Auditorially Handicapped Child; 1936, *38*, 69-74; 116-117; 149-155; 180-181

Guilder, Ruth P., and Hopkins, Louise A.; Program for the Testing and Training of Auditory Function in the Small Deaf Child During Preschool Years; 1935, *37*, 5-11; 79-84

Haeseler, Charlotte; Auricular Work with a Group Aid, Building a Hearing Vocabulary; 1933, *35*, 211-212

Hardy, William G.; Modern Audiology: Version of 1862; 1955, *57*, 98-100

Harris, Grace; An Acoustic Training Program for Severely Deaf Children; 1946, *48*, 557-560; 606-612; 767-769; 790-796; 1947, *49*, 29-31; 48-52

Heider, Fritz; Acoustic Training Helps Lip Reading; 1943, *45*, 135; 180

Herrick, Helen; An Auditory Training Program for Nursery Schools; 1950, *52*, 448-451; 482-484; 497-499; 528-530

Hudgins, Clarence V., and Ross, D. A.; The Measurement of Hearing; 1947, *49*, 128-130; 146; 173-174; 196-198

Hudgins, Clarence V.; Auditory Training—Its Possibilities and Limitations; 1954, *56*, 339-349

Hudgins, Clarence V.; A Rationale for Acoustic Training; 1948, *50*, 484-490

Hutton, Charles; Combined Auditory and Visual Stimuli in Aural Rehabilitation; 1959, *61*, 316-319

Johnson, Marion C.; Auricular Exercises; 1917, *19*, 657-660

Jones, Miss Ogwen; Auricular or Acoustic Training; 1925, *27*, 8-10

Keaster, Jacqueline; Quantitative Hearing Tests for Young Children; 1948, *50*, 465-468

Kelly, J. B.; Audiometer Technique in the Public Schools; 1929, *31*, 629-633

Kelly, J. B.; Physical Factors Affecting the Instrumental Utilization of Residual Hearing in the Education of the Deaf; 1930, *32*, 561-565

Kendall, David C., The Audiological Examination of Young Children; 1964, *66*, 734-740; 795

Kennedy, Mildred; Learn to Listen; 1947, *49*, 21; 52-54

Kennedy, Mildred; Re-education of Hearing: Try Taking It Seriously; 1944, *46*, 30; 54

Kerr, A. M.; Values and Limitations of the Audiometer; 1929, *31*, 621-626

Kling, Gertrude N.; Auricular Work; 1946, *48*, 83; 114-15

Koch, Albert; Industrial Audiology; 1956, *58*, 28-31

LaBenz, Paul J.; Potentialities of Auditory Perception for Various Levels of Hearing Loss; 1956, *58*, 397-402

LaCrosse, Edwin L.; The Value of Auricular Training; 1921, *23*, 356-357

Lamb, Marion H.; Listening In (With the First Auricular Class at Mt. Airy); 1936, *38*, 197-199; 250

Larsen, Laila L.; Recordings for Auditory Training; 1949, *51*, 461-462; 472-474

Lynndelle, Vivian; Hearing Conservation in a School System; 1940, *42*, 29-32; 59-61

Macfarlan, Douglas; The Next Step in the Problem of Defective Hearing; 1930, *32*, 51-52

Macfarlan, Douglas; The Report of the Committee Appointed to Survey the Instrumental Aids to Hearing; 1927, *29*, 592-629

McConnell, Freeman; The Child with a High Frequency Hearing Loss; 1951, *53*, 295-297; 328

McGee, T. Manford; Research in Hearing; 1962, *64*, 460-464

McGroskey, Robert L., and Bell, Marian M.; An Annotated Bibliography of Publications on Testing the Hearing of Infants; 1965, *67*, 548-558

McKenzie, Lilla B.; Physiological and Psychological Factors to be Considered When Building a Program of Acoustic Education; 1932, *34*, 522-525

McKenzie, Lilla B.; Stimulating the Language Centers Through Auditory Channels; 1919, *21*, 725-732

McManaway, H. M.; Report of the Use of Standard Tests in the Virginia School for the Deaf; 1923, *25*, 407-416

Madden, Anne M.; A New World of Sound; 1949, *51*, 551-553; 578

Marage, R.; Measurement and Development of Hearing Power in the Deaf; 1904, *6*, 127-129

AUDIOLOGY & AUDITORY TRAINING—*continued*

Volta Review

Mason, Marie K.; A Laboratory Method of Measuring Visual Hearing Ability; 1932, *34,* 510-516

Merkl, W.; Employment of the Partial Hearing of Pupils; 1903, *5,* 101-111

Merklein, Richard A., and Briskey, Robert J.; Audiometric Findings in Children Referred to a Program for Language Disorders; 1962, *64,* 294-298

Miller, Alfred L.; Light—An Unconditioned Stimulus in EDR Audiometry; 1965, *67,* 494-499

Montague, Harriet A.; A Class for the Conservation of Hearing; 1931, *33,* 197-199; 232-233

Moore, Lucile M.; Time—and the Hearing Ear; 1937, *39,* 500-502; 533-534

Morgan, Lucia C.; Effect of Temperature and Humidity on Hearing Acuity; 1960, *62,* 364-368

Morley, D. E.; Rationalism in Testing the Hearing of Children; 1948, *50,* 468-478

Murphy, Margaret; Unit of Work in Connection with Hygiene; 1933, *35,* 247-249

Nelson, Max; Public School Audiometry; 1961, *63,* 282-283; 305

Newhart, Horace; Efforts Toward Prevention of Deafness in School Children; 1926, *28,* 440-449

Nilson, Roy F.; Acoustic Education; 1927, *29,* 296-297

Nober, E. Harris; Pure Tone Air Conduction Thresholds of Deaf Children; 1963, *65,* 229-233; 241

Nober, E. Harris; The Role of an Audiologist at a School for the Deaf; 1962, *64,* 428-429

Numbers, Mary E.; Learning to Hear; 1942, *44,* 557-558; 600-601

Numbers, Mary E.; Using the Hearing of Children So Deaf that They Entered School Speechless; 1937, *39,* 133-137

O'Connor, Clarence D.; Acoustic Training in the Curriculum; 1936, *38,* 263-269; 308-309

O'Connor, Clarence D.; Speech Acoustic Training and Related Problems; 1937, *39,* 267-270

Palva, Tauno; Self-Recording Audiometry in Hearing Evaluation; 1958, *60,* 156-163; 190

——————; A Panel Discussion on Acoustics; 1944, *46,* 261-263; 318; 332-334; 380-382

Pauls, Miriam, and Hardy, William G.; Basic Audiologic Concepts; 1953, *55,* 407-408

Paxson, Ruth; Acoustic Work Done at Central Institute; 1925, *27,* 10-13

Pharis, Dorothy M.; Auricular Training; 1931, *33,* 163-164

Pollack, Doreen; Acoupedics: A Uni-Sensory Approach to Auditory Training; 1964, *66,* 400-409

Poulos, Thomas H.; Acuity and Perceptive Accuracy of Monaural and Binaural Hearing; 1950, *52*, 314-316; 326
Poulos, Thomas H.; A Short Term Aural Rehabilitation Program; 1960, *62*, 345-347
Probyn, June Y.; The Training of Residual Hearing; 1941, *43*, 5-8; 74; 90-92; 154-156
Proctor, Dorothy M.; Giving My Little Boy a Hearing Vocabulary; 1937, *39*, 494-496; 562-564; 595-598
Quigley, Stephen P.; The Vocal Effects of Delayed Auditory Feedback and Their Implications for the Teaching of Speech to the Deaf: 1958, *60*, 314-316
Rachlin, Carol; Auditory Training Remade My Life; 1949, *51*, 276-277
Resnick, Libby, and Walsh, Margaret; Auditory Training: Design for Growth, Sources for Auditory Experiences and Related Activities; 1959, *61*, 413-419
Richards, George L.; Hearing Tests From a Practical Standpoint; 1917, *19*, 590-594
Rierdon, Beatrice; Speech; 1933, *35*, 130; 139-140
Roach, Robert E.; Preparation of the Audiologist and His Responsibilities in the Residential School for the Deaf; 1958, *60*, 398-403
Rosen, Jack; The Place of GSR Audiometry in Work with Young Children; 1956, *58*, 387-391
Rotter, Paul; A Guide to Group Hearing Aids; 1956, *58*, 23-27
Rushford, Georgina; Glossary of Terms Relating to Children With Hearing Problems; 1964, *66*, 750-753
Scott, Elizabeth V.; Auditory Training; 1955, *57*, 297-299
Scott, Elizabeth; Auditory Training Cannot Begin Too Early; 1948, *50*, 423-425
Sensenig, Anne; Speech and Vocabulary Development Through Auricular Training; 1933, *35*, 212-213
Shepherd, David C., et al.; Audiologic Assessment of Children; 1963, *65*, 486-495
Simmons, Audrey A.; Some Hints for Auditory Training for the Young Child; 1955, *57*, 397-398
Sister Mary Fanchea; Auditory Training at St. Joseph's Institute; 1955, *57*, 260-262
Sister Marianna; Let's Help Them Listen; 1958, *60*, 413-416
Smalley, Lillian D.; Some Angles of the Acoustic Method; 1932, *34*, 248-251; 280-281
Smith, Gale M.; Telephone Service for the Totally Deaf; 1963, *65*, 579-583
Smith, Sherman K.; Auditory Training for the Deaf; 1938, *40*, 199-203; 252
Sortini, Adam J.; The Efficacy of Acoustic Programs; 1952, *54*, 201-203

AUDIOLOGY & AUDITORY TRAINING—*continued*

Volta Review

Stein, Shirley P.; Hearing Conservation in Rural Areas; 1951, *53*, 316; 324-326

Stein, Shirley P.; Mobile Clinics in the Field of Hearing; 1950, *52*, 17-20; 50-52

Stevenson, Elwood A.; Misconceptions and Misinterpretations of Auricular Work with the Deaf; 1926, *28*, 677-683

Stockdell, Kenneth G.; A Hearing Conservation Program; 1960, *62*, 376-377

Strizver, Gerald L.; Frequency Discrimination; 1958, *60*, 304-306

Szanton, Victor L., and Willette C.; Allergic Paracusis: New Allergic Syndrome; 1964, *66*, 248-252

Taber, Frank A.; The Audiometer and Our Hearing Aids; 1945, *47*, 453-454; 464

Taussig, E., and Stoner, M.; Phonograph Records for the Young Child; 1950, *52*, 355-358; 378

Timberlake, Josephine B.; The Re-Education of Residual Hearing; 1937, *39*, 349-351; 372-373

Titsworth, Elizabeth; Aims and Goals of an Auditory Program in a School for the Deaf; 1958, *60*, 408-411

Uden, A. v.; Sound Perception and Breath Control; 1955, *57*, 61-62

Upham, Louise; Experiments With Bone Conduction at Mount Airy; 1932, *34*, 252-253

Urbantschitsch, Victor; On the Value of Methodical Exercises in Hearing; 1904, *6*, 48-52

Van Der Veer, Gladys; Class for the Conservation of Hearing and Speech Correction; 1953, *55*, 355-356

Van Ingen, Elizabeth; Aural Work With Acousticons; 1920, *22*, 68-73

Van Ingen, Elizabeth; Eight Years of Auricular Work at Rochester; 1925, *27*, 13-16

Wallin, Margaret K.; Auditory Training: Design for Growth, Guiding Principles; 1959, *61*, 374-376

Watson, Norman A.; Selective Amplification; 1939, *41*, 338-340; 371

Watson, T. J.; The Use of Residual Hearing in the Education of Deaf Children; 1961, *63*, 328-334; 385-392; 435-440; 487-492; 1962, *64*, 31-38; 84-88

Whitehurst, Mary W.; Auricular Training at Hoff Hospital; 1946, *48*, 277-278; 300-308

Whitehurst, Mary W.; Integration of Auditory Training and Lipreading; 1964, *66*, 730-733

Whitehurst, Mary W.; Testing the Hearing of Preschool Children; 1961, *63*, 430-432; 463

Whitehurst, Mary W.; Training the Hearing of a Young Deaf Child; 1947, *49*, 215; 252-254

Wilcox, Rachel M.; Training Residual Hearing (The Clarke School); 1931, *33*, 341-344
Wright, John D.; Sound Perception in "Deaf-Mutes"; 1918, *20*, 290-292
Wright, John D.; Teaching a Deaf Child to Hear Language; 1918, *20*, 7-9; 1923, *25*, 171-173
Wright, John D.; Teaching a Hearing Vocabulary; 1920, *22*, 720-723
Wright, John D., and Winston, Matie E.; Training Little Deaf Children to Use Their Small Amounts of Hearing; 1932, *34*, 583-589
Wright, John D.; What Do You Mean By "Auricular Training?"; 1920, *22*, 6-8
Yearsley, Macleod; The Classification of Deaf Children; 1911, *13*, 345-349
Yenrick, D. E.; Audiology and the Deaf Child; 1955, *57*, 353-356
Yenrick, D. E.; The Use of Amplification in Schools for the Deaf; 1955, *57*, 158-160

Annals of the Deaf

Albright, Arline; Audiometric Testing Methods and Classification of Original Hearing Acuity Response Curves; 1948, *93*, 360-376
Anderson, Mrs. J. Scott; The Development of Hearing; 1910, *55*, 349-353
Bell, Alexander G.; The Process of Audition; 1906, *51*, 280-286
Boyd, John, and Jamroz, Anthony; A Comparison of Group Hearing Aid Systems; 1963, *108*, 245-251
Bunch, C. C.; Deafness and Residual Hearing; 1925, *70*, 104-122
Camp, Anna R.; Some Lessons in Auricular Training; 1903, *48*, 217-237
Elstad, Leonard M.; Auricular Training and Oral Instruction; 1929, *74*, 199-205
Forrester, T. C.; The Problems of Training the Remnants of Auditory Perception; 1928, *73*, 145-155
Forrester, T. C.; Residual Hearing and Its Bearing on Oral Training; 1929, *74*, 193-199
Frisina, D. Robert; Basic Considerations in Auditory Training; 1958, *103*, 459-466
Frueh, Frank; Audiological Services at a School for the Deaf; 1962, *107*, 229-231
Goetzinger, Cornelius; A Consideration of Audiometric Curves in Relation to Intelligibility for Speech; 1947, *92*, 238-250
Goldstein, Max A.; An Acoustic Method; 1920, *65*, 472-481
Goldstein, Max A.; The Acoustic Method; 1924, *69*, 160-187
Hedgecock, Leroy D.; Audiological Aspects of Rehabilitation of the Deaf; 1958, *103*, 210-214

AUDIOLOGY & AUDITORY TRAINING—*continued*

Annals of the Deaf

Henderson, Sara C., and Francis, Doris H. (editors); The Meaning of Deafness: The Report of a Workshop for Audiologists; 1962, *107*, 464-596

Jesseman, Victoria C.; The Use of Residual Hearing; 1942, *87*, 408-414

Johnson, Clyde W.; A Survey of Acoustic Training Programs and Accomplishments in the Public Residential Schools for the Deaf; 1943, *88*, 279-295

Johnson, Elizabeth H.; Testing Results of Acoustic Training; 1939, *84*, 223-233

La Crosse, Edwin L.; Auricular Training in the Wright Oral School; 1925, *70*, 302-310

Lloyd, Glenn T.; A Beginning Experimental Program in the Use of the Telephone for Deaf and Hard of Hearing Children; 1960, *105*, 427-429

Nelson, Boyd E.; The Essentials of Acoustic Programs; 1942, *87*, 274-287

Schick, Helen C., and Meyer, Max F.; The Use of the Lectometer; 1932, *77*, 292-304

Stevenson, Elwood A.; Are Our Deaf All Deaf?; 1919, *64*, 351-359

Voelker, Charles H.; Tested Auditory Behavior Rather than Hearing Acuity Is a Function of Age; 1941, *86*, 1-6.

Wright, John D.; The Partially Deaf Child—A School Program; 1917, *62*, 321-329

BELL FAMILY

Volta Review

Andrews, Harriet U.; The Melville Bell Symbols, Tried and True; 1916, *18*, 311-312

Bell, Alexander G.; Address of the President; 1899, *1*, 67-82

Bell, Alexander G.; A Census of the Able-bodied; 1910, *12*, 403-406

Bell, Alexander G.; Notes of Early Life; 1910, *12*, 155-160

Bell, Alexander G.; The Sanders Reader (reproduction of excerpts from the original written by Mr. Bell in 1872-73); 1964, *66*, 122-123

Bell, Alexander G.; Utility of Action and Gesture; 1915, *17*, 13-18

————; A Bell Bibliography; 1960, *62*, 111-112; 139

————; Dr. Bell, Pioneer of a New Era; 1958, *60*, 110-111; 141

Bell, Mrs. Alexander G.; What the Melville Bell Symbols Mean to Me; 1908, *10*, 308-311

Bentley, Keilor; Monument to a Genius—The Alexander Graham Bell Museum at Baddeck, Nova Scotia; 1965, *67*, 188-190

DeLand, Fred; Alexander Graham Bell's Benefactions to Aid the Hard of Hearing Adult; 1928, *30*, 440-442
DeLand, Fred; The Bell Telephone Memorial; 1918, *20*, 231-236
DeLand, Fred; An Early Use of the Melville Bell Symbols With the Deaf; 1915, *17*, 487-489
DeLand, Fred; An Ever-Continuing Memorial; 1922, *24*, 351-363; 413-422; 465-471; *25*, 1923, 34-39; 90-99; 145-152; 190-197
DeLand, Fred; The Telephone, the Radiophone, the Graphophone, the Music Record, and Modern Lip-Reading; 1924, *26*, 251-253
DeLand, Fred; World Benefactions of Alexander Graham Bell; 1905, *7*, 167-171
Fuller, Sarah; Alexander Melville Bell; 1907, *9*, 269-272
Grosvenor, Elsie B.; My Father, The Volta Bureau, and the Association; 1950, *52*, 112-114
Grosvenor, Elsie M.; My Father, Alexander Graham Bell; 1951, *53*, 349; 386-388
Grosvenor, Mrs. Gilbert; Mrs. Alexander Graham Bell—A Reminiscence; 1957, *59*, 299-305
Grosvenor, Melville B.; Memories of My Grandfather; 1940, *42*, 621-622
Hitz, John; Alexander Melville Bell; 1905, *7*, 421-439
Mayne, Richard E.; The Bell Family and English Speech; 1929, *31*, 453-456
——————; Melville Bell Symbols; 1918, *20*, 65; 71; 88; 498; 582
——————; The Melville Bell Symbols; Line-writing Form; 1914, *16*, 266-270; 477-485; 569-576; 723-730
——————; In Memoriam; Alexander Graham Bell; 1922, *24*, 307
Montague, Harriet; Mr. Bell's Private School; 1940, *42*, 325-326
Montague, Harriet; A Man Who Loved Deaf Children; 1938, *40*, 74-77; 116
——————; Monument Erected Honoring Alexander Graham Bell; 1954, *56*, 9-10
Murphy, Albert T.; Dr. Bell and Boston University; 1954, *56*, 249-250
Silverman, S. Richard; The Legacy of Mr. Bell; 1957, *59*, 103-104
Taylor, Harris, et al.; Alexander Graham Bell Memorial Session; 1925, *27*, 61-65
Taylor, Harris; Dr. Bell, The Great, The Good, The Lovable; 1922, *24*, 345-346
——————; Tributes to Dr. Bell; 1922, *24*, 346-349; 365-379
Yale, Caroline A.; Dr. Bell's Connection with Clarke School; 1922, *24*, 364-365
Yale, Caroline A.; Mabel Hubbard Bell—1859-1923; 1923, *25*, 105-110

DAY SCHOOLS

Volta Review

Adams, Mabel E.; Day-Schools and Institutional; 1910, *12*, 354-357
Adams, Mabel E.; Relative Advantages of Day-Schools; 1911, *13*, 292-297
Arnold, Mercer; Advantages of Oral Day Schools; 1914, *16*, 354-357
Anderson, Norman O.; Wyoming's Unique Program for the Hearing Impaired; 1964, *66*, 537-539
————; Course of Study in Public School No. 47, the Day School for the Deaf in New York City; 1917, *19*, 353-357
————; Day Schools for the Deaf; 1919, *21*, 593-595; 682-684
Drennen, Genevieve; Adjustment of the Hearing Handicapped Child in a Day Class; 1958, *60*, 482-484
Duff, Jessie; Advantages of an Oral Day School for the Deaf; 1915, *17*, 138-140
Neas, B. Jack; A Day Class Program; 1960, *62*, 347-350
Quill, Leonora; The Teenager in a Day Class; 1962, *64*, 442-443
Robinson, Anna E.; Day Schools in Large Cities; 1900, *2*, 150-158; 248-253
Spencer, Robert C.; The Day-Schools of Wisconsin; 1900, *2*, 254-256
Taylor, Harris; Public Day Schools for the Deaf in the U.S.; 1937, *39*, 328-329; 377; 389-390; 428; 555-557; 594-595; 618-619; 660; 690-693; 720-721; 1938, *40*, 15-21; 60; 83-87; 114-116; 133-139; 178-179; 215-217; 241-242; 279-281; 312-316
Wesselius, Sybrant; The Law and the Day School for the Deaf; 1901, *3*, 311-319
Wettstein, Frances; The Education of the Deaf in Day Schools; 1914, *16*, 559-564
Wettstein, Frances; The Efficiency of the Day School; 1906, *8*, 136-142
————; Why Parents of Deaf Children Move to Cities Having Oral Day Schools; 1917, *19*, 183-185

DEAF-BLIND

Volta Review

Alcorn, Sophia; Tad Chapman's Demonstration; 1930, *32*, 517-518
Blankenhorn, M. D.; Miracle for Angeliki; 1951, *53*, 157; 178
Bowman, Dorothy L.; Carol's First Three Years; 1945, *47*, 439-442; 472-478
Chapman, W. C.; Carrying Out My Plans; 1952, *54*, 382; 394
Cohen, Sonya S.; Helen Keller Visits Haifa, Israel; 1952, *54*, 377-378; 396-398

Czily, Prof. A.; Conversing with the Blind-Deaf; 1910, *12*, 77-85
DeLand, Fred; Helen Keller's Flag; 1914, *16*, 357-360
DeLand, Fred; Sarah Fuller as Helen Keller's Teacher of Speech; 1927, *29*, 353-355
Donald, Dora; Linnie Haguewood; 1901, *3*, 97-105
Farrar, A.; A Nineteenth Century Educator and His Interest in the Deaf Blind; 1937, *39*, 335-336
Fearon, J.; Charlie Crane: A Deaf-Blind Boy; 1917, *19*, 83-86
Ferreri, Giulio; The Development of Intelligence in the Case of One Deprived of Both Sight and Hearing; 1905, *7*, 440-448
Ferreri, Giulio; The Possibility of the Education of the Blind-Deaf; 1907, *9*, 363-369
Ferreri, Giulio; Principles for the Instruction of the Blind-Deaf as Given in the Work of the Abbé Deschamps; 1913, *15*, 35-37
Hall, Inis B.; Deaf-Blind Pupils at Perkins; 1940, *42*, 21-22; 52-53; 83-84; 116
Hall, Inis B.; The Education of the Blind-Deaf; 1940, *42*, 681-684
Hall, Inis B.; More About Leonard Dowdy; 1939, *41*, 202-203; 243
Hansen, Anders; The First Case in the World; 1930, *32*, 223-228
Harris, Lena; Meeting the Challenge, The Story of Jackie Coker—Deaf and Blind; 1941, *43*, 24-25; 74
Heider, Grace M.; Learning from the Blind; 1939, *41*, 11; 51-53
Heider, Grace M.; Leonard Dowdy's Vocabulary; 1935, *37*, 340-341; 388-389
Krohn, Emmylou; Out of the Quiet Shadows; 1956, *58*, 440-442
Lange, Paul; The Truth About Helen Keller; 1910, *12*, 750-754
Merry, Ralph V.; Applying Psychological Tests to the Deaf-Blind; 1932, *34*, 406-407
Montague, Harriet A.; Helen Keller's Personal History, A Review; 1938, *40*, 330-331; 376
Montague, Harriet A.; More About Helen Keller; 1930, *32*, 53-56
Montague, Harriet A.; Penetrating the Darkness; 1930, *32*, 421-423; 425-426
Montague, Harriet A.; Tad Chapman at Home; 1952; *54*, 58-59; 86-88
Newell, Nettie; The Doubly Handicapped Child; 1929, *31*, 257-258
Pitrois, Yvonne; The Heurtin Family; 1911, *12*, 733-749
Pitrois, Yvonne; The Sunbeam of the Deaf-Blind; 1930, *32*, 181-184
Riemann, G. (Trans. by Brill, T.); The Care of the Blind-Deaf Children; 1910, *12*, 766-771
Rocheleau, Corinne; The Deaf-Blind; 1930, *32*, 518-524
Shaw, Janet P.; Our Jess; 1927, *29*, 370-374
Wade, W.; The Deaf-Blind; 1901, *3*, 41-42

DEAF-BLIND—continued

Annals of the Deaf

Balis, Sylvia C.; They Who See Darkly; 1922, *67*, 99-111
Barrett, E. M.; The Importance of Early Training for the Deaf Blind; 1903, *48*, 149-155
Bolton, Thaddeus L.; The Psychology of the Deaf-Blind; 1915, *60*, 222-227
Burnet, John R.; The Case of Laura Bridgman; 1856, *8*, 195-172
Dinsmore, Annette B.; National Approach to the Education of Deaf-Blind Children; 1953, *98*, 418-430
Farrell, Gabriel; Extension of the Work of Perkins Institution; 1935, *80*, 157-159
Fay, E. A.; Blind and Deaf Persons; 1887, *32*, 233-236
Fish, Anna G.; Laura Bridgman; 1937, *82*, 402-405
Fox, Thomas F.; The Education of Deaf-Blind Children in the New York Institution for the Instruction of the Deaf and Dumb; 1904, *49*, 240-251
Fox, Thomas F.; Miss Helen Adams Keller's First Year of College Preparatory Work; 1897, *42*, 387-401
Frick, Kathryne M.; Shall the Deaf-Blind Be Educated in Residential Schools for the Deaf?; 1931, *76*, 496-497
Fuller, Sarah; How Helen Keller Learned to Speak; 1892, *37*, 23-30
Hall, G. Stanley; Laura Bridgman; 1879, *24*, 202-228
Howe, Samuel G.; Laura Bridgman and Oliver Caswell; 1875, *20*, 100-110
Jones, J. W.; The Education of the Deaf-Blind; 1906, *51*, 359-366
Keller, Helen; The Value of the Sense of Smell to the Blind-Deaf; 1910, *55*, 282-284
Morris, Minnie E.; The Training of a Congenitally Deaf-Blind Child; 1904, *49*, 167-171
Neuschutz, Louise I.; Proposed Measures for the Relief of the Deaf-Blind; 1933, *78*, 427-430
Nordin, Elizabeth A.; The Care and Instruction of the Blind-Deaf; 1905, *50*, 125-140
Porter, Samuel; Particulars Respecting James Mitchell, A Person Deaf, Dumb and Blind from Birth; 1847, *1*, 246-258
Robinson, Stanley; The Education of the Deaf-Blind at the New York Institution; 1900, *45*, 376-383
————; A study of the Proceedings of the Convention of the American Instructors of the Deaf, 1850-1849: Deaf-Blind; 1950, *95*, 303-306
Sullivan, Annie M.; How Helen Keller Acquired Language; 1892, *37*, 127-154
Wade, William; The Senses of the Blind-Deaf; 1909, *54*, 451-455
Williams, Job; Is Helen Keller a Fraud?; 1892, *37*, 156-159

EDUCATION

Volta Review

Adams, Bradford C.; The Independent Study Plan for the Deaf Student at College (with discussion by Jerry A. Pierce); 1933, *35*, 445-448; 474-475

———; Analysis of the Annals Statistics (pupils and teachers in American Schools for the Deaf, 1893 through 1910); 1911, *12*, 719-720

———; The Annals Statistics; 1904, *6*, 93-95

Arbaugh, Laura L.; Making Drill Work Pleasant; 1928, *30*, 284-290

Arbaugh, Laura L.; Training the Deaf Child; 1914, *16*, 687-689

Archer, T. V.; The Summer School at Northampton; 1906, *8*, 40-46

Barnes, F. G.; Talks to Young Teachers; 1917, *19*, 367-370

Barrows, Albert L.; Work of the National Research Council on Problems of the Deaf; 1928, *30*, 531-536

Bell, Alexander G.; The Association and its Purposes; 1940, *42*, 622-625

Bell, Alexander G.; Auto-Education Continued in the Primary School; 1916, *18*, 135-142

Bell, Alexander G.; The International Congress; 1900, *2*, 427-437

Bell, Alexander G.; Simple Experiments; 1912, *14*, 103-106

Bell, Alexander G.; Special Report Upon the Deaf, Based on the Returns of the Twelfth Census; 1906, *8*, 351-370; 442-469; 1907, *9*, 336-356; 427-444; 533-545; 1908, *10*, 36-47; 138-147; 240-255; 349-364; 455-464

Berry, Gordon; Deafness in the United States, A Statistical Review; 1938, *40*, 69-71; 120

Betterly, E. J.; Ye That Are Deaf; 1925, *27*, 447-449

Bickley, Celia; Inasmuch; 1918, *20*, 624-626

Bingham, Katherine T.; All Along the Line; 1900, *2*, 20-29

Blair, Mary; Projects in First and Second Grades; 1932, *34*, 59; 85

Blish, Stanford C.; Problems Involved in Sex Education in Residential Schools for the Deaf; 1940, *42*, 133-138; 208-213; 246; 268-272; 310; 501-505; 550

Bluett, Charles G.; Tests and Follow-up of Deaf Graduates; 1944, *46*, 617-622; 662; 686-689; 772; 1945, *47*, 12-16; 82-85; 106-108

Boatner, Edmund B.; A Half-Century of Progress in the New England Schools—I. The American School for the Deaf; 1939, *41*, 485-488

Bodycomb, Margaret, et al.; Can Children Who Enter School Without Speech and Apparently Without Hearing Ever Leave School "Hard of Hearing" Rather than "Deaf"?; 1938, *40*, 729-740

Booth, Frank W.; The Education of the Deaf; 1921, *23*, 25-29

Booth, Frank W.; A Roster of Former Pupils of Schools for the Deaf Now in Schools for the Hearing; 1905, *7*, 275-279

Breitwieser, J. V.; The Conservation of Energy in the Training of the Deaf; 1926, *28*, 642-648

EDUCATION—continued

Volta Review

Breunig, H. Latham; An Analysis of a Group of Deaf Students in Colleges with the Hearing; 1965, *67*, 17-27; 94

Brill, Richard G.; The California School for the Deaf; 1954, *56*, 14-16

Buell, Edith M.; Which Subjects Should Receive Special Emphasis?; 1928, *30*, 577-579

Chamberlain, Naomi H.; A Screening Outline for Determining Group Readiness; 1959, *61*, 455-457; 476

Chaplin, Joyce W.; Sex Education of Deaf Children; 1957, *59*, 201-203; 225

————; The Clarke School; 1912, *14*, 31-40

————; The Clarke School Alumni; 1952, *54*, 363-369; 402

————; An Historical Pageant Produced on the Fiftieth Anniversary of the Founding of Clarke School, Northampton, Mass.; 1918, *20*, 31-44.

————; Prepared by Research Dept. of Clarke School; Abstracts of Scientific Studies (Clarke); 1934, *36*, 408-411; 474-475; 506; 663-665; 1935, *37*, 25; 56-57; 289; 320-322; 412-413; 441; 529; 553

Clayton, Nellie C.; Seat Work as a Normalizing Agent for Deaf Children; 1929, *31*, 728-730

————; Compulsory Education of the Deaf; 1924, *26*, 77-80

Connor, Leo E.; Diagnostic Teaching—The Teacher's New Role; 1959, *61*, 311-315

Connor, Leo E.; Research in the Education of the Deaf in the United States; 1963, *65*, 523-534

Connor, Leo E.; Secondary Education of Deaf Children; 1965, *67*, 126-132; 165

Cooper, Helen M.; The Deafened at Play; 1923, *25*, 299-303; 378-381; 467-470; 530-532; 1924, *26*, 27-30

————; Council on Education of the Deaf, Indianapolis, Ind.; Minutes of the Annual Meeting; 1964, *66*, 213-216

Crouter, A. L.; Examinations, Promotions and Grading; 1905, *7*, 107-120

Crum, Carole; The Normality of Deaf Children; 1961, *63*, 231-232; 249

Dallet, Jean; Physical Education for the Deaf Child—Is it Worthwhile?; 1934, *36*, 331-335

Daly, Margaret A.; Physical Training for the Deaf Child; 1913, *15*, 131-136

Danger, O.; The Education of the Deaf for Life in Human Society; 1904, *6*, 101-108

Daniel, Elizabeth; Work and Play in Our Junior Classes; 1928, *30*, 802-806

Davidson, S. G.; Pessimism of Parents and Teachers; 1910, *12*, 363-366

————; The Deaf Before and After Attendance at School; 1906, *8*, 243-248

————; Deaf Graduates of Schools and Colleges for Hearing Students; 1930, *32*, 73-75; 1931, *33*, 71-73; 527-529; 1932, *34*, 631-633; 1933, *35*, 499-501; 1934, *36*, 715-720; 1935, *37*, 725-729; 1936,

38, 703-705; 1937, *39*, 687-689; 1938, *40*, 773-775; 1939, *41*, 690-691; 1940, *42*, 515-518; 1941, *43*, 716-720; 1943, *45*, 686-691; 1944, *46*, 691-694; 1945, *47*, 693-696; 1946, *48*, 770-773; 1947, *49*, 552-555; 1949, *51*, 10-16; 1950, *52*, 7-11; 1951, *53*, 58-61; 1952, *54*, 113-118; 1962, *64*, 299-313; 1963, *65*, 363-375; 1965, *67*, 30-81

DeHaven, Mabel; Our Mail: A Visit to the Post Office; 1962, *64*, 595-598
DeLand, Fred; The Able De L'Epée; 1917, *19*, 40-45
DeLand, Fred; Home Schools for Little Deaf Children; 1915, *17*, 440-442
DeLand, Fred; Pedro Ponce De Leon (Born, 1520); Juan Pablo Bonet (Author, 1620); 1920, *22*, 391-421
DeLand, Fred, and Spofford, Florence P.; Public School Pupils with Imperfect Hearing; 1925, *27*, 414-417
DeLand, Fred; The Real Romance of the Telephone, or Why Deaf Children Need No Longer Be Dumb; 1905, *7*, 306-326; 389-399; 1906, *8*, 1-27; 120-135; 205-222; 329-334; 406-427; 1907, *9*, 324-335; 401-419; 505-520; 1908, *10*, 1-35; 123-137; 233-239; 343-348; 449-454; 1909, *11*, 1-12
DeLand, Fred; The Volta Bureau; 1913, *14*, 605-621
DeLand, Fred; Working in Behalf of Deaf Children; (or How, When, and Why the American Association to Promote the Teaching of Speech to the Deaf Was Organized); 1919, *21*, 523-530; 581-585; 663-669; 701-702
DeVries, J. G.; The Fear of the Written Word; 1908, *10*, 174-185
Dewar, Dorothy G.; Educating Deaf Children for Democracy; 1949, *51*, 157-158
Driggs, Frank M.; Curriculum and Texts; 1913, *15*, 288-293
Dunlap, Mary M.; Activities with a Special Group; 1935, *37*, 461-462; 497
Dunlap, Mary M.; Two Helpful Projects; 1927, *29*, 98-100
Earhart, E. K., McCain, M., et al.; New Things We Have Undertaken; 1935, *37*, 519-520; 566-568; 586-587; 623; 655-656; 708-709
—————; The Education of the Deaf; 1910, *12*, 180-181
—————; Education of the Deaf in the United States; The Advisory Committee's Report; 1965, *67*, 345-351
Egan, Ann R.; We Learn By Doing; 1930, *32*, 409-411
Evans, Mildred; Common Sense in Modernization; 1935, *37*, 510-511; 558-559
Farrar, A.; The Deaf in Medieval Times; 1926, *28*, 389-393
Fay, Edward A.; Progress in the Education of the Deaf; 1916, *18*, 71-76
Fechheimer, A. Lincoln; University Experiences; 1899, *1*, 27-34
Ferreri, Giulio C.; The American Institutions for the Education of the Deaf; 1904, *6*, 211-221; 288-300; 395-401; 1905, *7*, 23-31; 145-152; 201-209; 297-305; 1906, *8*, 109-119; 318-328; 397-405; 1907, *9*, 297-323; 420-426

EDUCATION—continued

Volta Review

Ferreri, Giulio C.; The Oral Method: Its Fitness for the Deaf; 1902, *4*, 344-353
Ferreri, Giulio C.; Some Didactic Questions; 1903, *5*, 254-263
Ferreri, Giulio C.; Teachers and Physicians; 1903, *5*, 423-430
Flegel, Elynor; Services for the Hearing Handicapped in a Special School District; 1964, *66*, 253-257
Fornari, P.; American Institutions for the Deaf; 1904, *6*, 1-8
Foss, Bertha M.; Current Events in Rhode Island; 1933, *35*, 372-374
Fullington, Angeline B.; Some Principles of Teaching; 1911, *12*, 622-625
Fusfeld, Irving S.; The Academic Program of Schools for the Deaf; 1955, *57*, 63-70
Goldberg, Herman R.; Administering Curriculum Change; 1960, *62*, 378-383
Goldstein, M. A.; The Deaf Child; 1920, *22*, 347-354
Goldstein, M. A.; The Society of Progressive Oral Advocates: Its Origin and Purpose; 1917, *19*, 443-447
Green, Grace G.; The Importance of Physical Training for the Deaf; 1907, *9*, 180-188
Groht, Mildred; Hearing Children and Deaf Children: Helping the Two Groups to Understand Each Other; 1945, *47*, 204-205; 236
Gruver, Elbert A.; Stands and Trends in the Education of the Deaf; 1938, *40*, 621-626
Gruver, Elbert A.; Training of Backward Deaf Children; 1920, *22*, 687-699
Gruver, Margaret H.; Educating the Profoundly Deaf Child; 1955, *57*, 243-247
Guthrie, Virginia S.; Creative and Expressive Activities for Young Deaf Children; 1945, *47*, 679-682; 724-728; 1946, *48*, 14-17; 54-58
Hagens, E. W.; Some Facts Obtained in a Survey of the State Schools for the Deaf; 1930, *32*, 524-529
Hall, Percival; Retrospect and Prospect; 1920, *22*, 546-550
Hammer, Helen L.; A Project in Community Life, An Opportunity for the Teacher of the Deaf; 1930, *32*, 217-220
Hansen, Anders; A Visit to American Schools for the Deaf; 1908, *10*, 48-63
Hardy, William G.; Human Communication—Ordered and Disordered; 1962, *64*, 354-362
Harman, Augusta; A Vacation Pupil; 1917, *19*, 698-700
Harrell, Hattie; The Education of the Deaf in Oregon; 1963, *65*, 349-350
Haycock, George S.; The Early Education of Young Deaf Children; 1914, *16*, 33-43
Henderson, Jennie M.; A Half-Century of Progress in the New England Schools—III. The Horace Mann School for the Deaf; 1939, *41*, 627-630; 662

Heward, Mr. and Mrs. H.; Oral Education Brings Success in College; 1959, *61*, 284-287

Hill, A. C.; From the Notebook of An Inspector; 1918, *20*, 223-227; 315-316; 397-401

Hill, A. C.; The School Journal as a Factor in the Education of the Deaf; 1917, *19*, 190-192

Hillard, Ethel M.; Practical Demonstration with Pupils of Central Institute for the Deaf: St. Louis; 1915, *17*, 345-350

Hines, Edward J.; Physical Education; 1914, *16*, 248-250

Hoffmann, Hugo; The Division of Pupils in the Instruction of the Deaf According to Their Capacity; 1904, *6*, 35-40

Horowitz, Leola S., and Rees, Norma S.; Attitudes and Information About Deafness; 1962, *64*, 180-189

Hurd, Anna C.; Home Life in the School, An Important Factor in the Education of the Deaf Child; 1926, *28*, 243-246

Ingram, Christine P.; Trends in Special Education; 1944, *46*, 197-199; 252-254

Jenkins, Weston; Use and Abuse of Memory in Education; 1900, *2*, 6-15

Jennings, Gertrude J.; A Half-Century of Progress in the New England Schools—VI. The Rhode Island School for the Deaf; 1940, *42*, 73-76; 118-119

Johansen, Donald; "Should I Go to College in Spite of My Deafness?"; 1925, *27*, 505-507

Joiner, Enfield; Shall We or Shall We Not? (rewards); 1934, *36*, 73-74

Jolly, Faith; Educating the Deaf and Hard of Hearing in Our 50th State; 1960, *62*, 158-160

Jones, Christina C.; Curriculum Controls; 1964, *66*, 431-434

Jones, Kate H.; Communication Skills; 1961, *63*, 72-77; 94

Justman, Joseph, and Moskowitz, Sue; Graduates of P.S. #47—A Half Century Report; 1965, *67*, 275-280

Kearns, C. W., et al.; Statements by Experienced Teachers; 1917, *19*, 319-329

Keaster, Jacqueline; Educational Recommendations; 1965, *67*, 545-547; 589

Keaster, Jacqueline; How Shall the Deaf Child Be Educated?; 1954, *56*, 293-297

Kinsley, Grace; Beginning Study Periods; 1929, *31*, 250-251

Kopp, Harriet G.; Elementary School Subjects in the Curriculum for the Deaf; 1964, *66*, 474-480

Lane, Helen S.; Research and Its Application to the Classroom; 1964, *66*, 480-490

Lee, John J.; A New Challenge in Education; 1938, *40*, 261-263; 309-312

EDUCATION—continued

Volta Review

Leonard, Eleanor C.; The Fiftieth Anniversary of the Founding of the Clarke School, Northampton, Mass.; 1918, *20*, 45-65

Leonard, Eleanor C.; The Normal Course at Northampton; 1919, *21*, 72-75

Leonard, Eleanor C.; Preparing a Little Deaf Child for School; 1917, *19*, 253-280

Leonard, Eleanor C.; "When?" and "Where?" in the Education of the Deaf Child; 1913, *15*, 180-182

Leonard, Myrtle H.; The Deaf Child and Something of His Early Training; 1922, *24*, 150-152

Leshin, George J., and Stahlecker, Lotar V.; Academic Expectancies of Slow-Learning Deaf Children; 1962, *64*, 599-602

Love, J. K.; The Deaf Child from the View-Point of the Physician and of the Teacher; 1910, *12*, 143-154

Love, J. K.; Education of the Very Young Deaf Child; 1910, *12*, 602-603

McCowen, Mary; Dramatization As a Factor in Education; 1904, *6*, 109-115

McDaniel, Nettie; A Half-Century of Progress in the New England Schools —VII. The Beverly School for the Deaf; 1940, *42*, 139-143

McDowell, Evelyn; A Charming Southern School; 1919, *21*, 231-236

McFarlane, J. H.; The Alabama School for the Deaf; 1913, *15*, 212-218

McIntire, Wayne (panel chairman); A Discussion of Children with Severe Hearing Impairments in Schools with Hearing Children; 1957, *59*, 53-63; 84-85

McLaughlin, H. F.; The Advantage of the Oral Method; 1955, *57*, 209-210

McManaway, Howard M.; New Objectives in the Education of the Deaf; 1934, *36*, 5-6

Macloingsigh, Peadar; Teaching Deaf Children; 1917, *19*, 231-233

Madison, J. L.; The Iowa Convention; 1925, *27*, 483-492

Mangan, Kenneth R.; Six Weeks Is Not Enough; 1964, *66*, 452-455

Manning, Clarence A.; School Hours: Academical and Industrial; 1913, *15*, 245-250

Manz, Fred M., and Pruitt, Elberta E.; Social Independence: (A Secondary School Program for Its Development in the Acoustically Handicapped); 1950, *52*, 445-446; 474-476

————; Maxon Oral School; 1953, *55*, 387-388

Miller, Anne S.; Academic Preparation to Insure Adjustment Into Classes with Hearing Students; 1964, *66*, 414-425

Miller, Anne S.; Personal Hygiene for Teenagers; 1964, *66*, 179-183

Miller, June B.; Academic Achievement; 1958, *60*, 302-304

Miller, June B.; Educational Assessment; 1965, *67*, 676-680; 701

Miller, Reid C.; Adequate Programming on a Junior and Senior High School Level; 1964, *66*, 439-445

Montague, Harriet; The Education of the Deaf in the United States; 1933, *35*, 338-342
Motto, Joseph, and Wawrzaszek, Frank J.; Integration of the Hearing Handicapped: Evaluation of the Current Status; 1963, *65*, 124-129; 160
Murphy, Albert T.; The Educational Needs of the Acoustically Handicapped; 1955, *57*, 301-304
——————; The National Technical Institute for the Deaf; 1965, *67*, 484-492
Nelson, Boyd E.; The Classroom Tells About the Teacher; 1945, *47*, 557-558
Nelson, Boyd E.; Habits in Handwriting; 1947, *49*, 72; 106
Nevile, Miss B.; Our Greatest Need in the Schools; 1922, *24*, 105-108
Newlee, Clara E.; About Compulsory Education for Deaf Children; 1919, *21*, 1-3
Norris, Anne C.; With American Educators in Europe; 1929, *31*, 50-54
Numbers, F. C.; Objects of Study; 1916, *18*, 180-182
Numbers, Mary E.; Broader Horizons; 1936, *38*, 629-632; 684
Numbers, Mary E., and Hudgins, Clarence V.; Speech Perception in Present Day Education for Deaf Children; 1948, *50*, 449-456
O'Connor, Clarence D.; Benefits of an Oral Climate for All Deaf Children; 1957, *59*, 335-336
O'Connor, Clarence D.; Children with Impaired Hearing; 1954, *56*, 433-439
O'Connor, Clarence D.; How Our Schools Can Solve Some of Today's Problems; 1948, *50*, 399-402
O'Connor, Clarence D.; To Promote Oral Education for the Deaf; 1956, *58*, 287-288
O'Connor, Clarence D.; The Role of the Deaf Academic Classroom Teacher; 1964, *66*, 397-398
O'Connor, Clarence D.; Some Modern Trends in the Education of the Deaf; 1945, *47*, 197-200; 248-250
O'Connor, Clarence D.; What Is "Special" About the Education of the Deaf?; 1954, *56*, 291-292; 318
Owsley, Peter J.; Issues in the Education of the Deaf; 1964, *66*, 308-311
Palen, Imogen B.; The Grade Teacher and the Deafened Child; 1926, *28*, 437-440
Panconcelli-Calzia, G.; What Experimental Phonetics Has Accomplished for the Instruction of the Hard of Hearing and the Deaf; 1921, *23*, 417-422
Peck, B. J.; The Residential School Community; 1964, *66*, 425-429
Perry, Charles S.; Training Period of Our Deaf as Compared with Our Hearing Youth; 1899, *1*, 150-157

EDUCATION—continued

Volta Review

Peterson, Gordon E.; Technological Frontiers in Communication; 1962, *64*, 369-374

Pintner, Rudolf; Report of Clarke School Research; 1940, *42*, 767-768; 812

Pintner, Rudolf; Standardization of Schools for the Deaf; 1920, *22*, 662-669

Poitras, Bonnie; The Case for the Deaf Child in the Regular School; 1961, *63*, 16-17; 43

Pratt, George T.; Oral Education for Deaf Children: Why and How; 1961, *63*, 480-483

————; Proceedings of the First Annual Convention of the Society of Progressive Oral Advocates; 1919, *21*, 95-120; 157-183

————; Proceedings of the Second Annual Convention of Progressive Oral Advocates; 1919, *21*, 629-660; 716-746; 759-796

Pugh, Bessie; Teaching Children to Use the Dictionary; 1961, *63*, 178-185

Pugh, Bessie; Twentieth Century Trends in the Education of the Deaf; 1947, *49*, 261-262; 300-302

Quick, Marion A.; Development and Presentation of Classroom Observations; 1964, *66*, 449-452

Reed, Katherine F.; The Teacher's Relation with the Parents of Deaf Children; 1913, *14*, 634-636

Reed, Nell D.; They Are Prepared; 1955, *57*, 247-250

Reinhardt, Anna C.; The Home School for Little Deaf Children, Kensington, Maryland; 1913, *15*, 51-55

Reinhardt, Anna C.; Progressive Education for the Deaf; 1927, *29*, 204-206

Reinhardt, Anna C., et al.; Schools Where Deaf Children Talk and Talk, and Where No Use Is Made of the Sign-Language or the Finger Alphabet; 1918, *20*, 476-484

Reinhardt, Anna C.; What Has Been Done with One Deaf Child in his Own Home; 1906, *8*, 36-39

Reiter, Frank H.; A Half-Century of Progress in the New England Schools—II. The Clarke School for the Deaf; 1939, *41*, 562-565; 601

Remnitz, Annabel; Education in a Hearing High School; 1955, *57*, 117-119

Richardson, Paul C.; Developing Natural Time Expressions; 1962, *64*, 543-545; 574

Rittenhouse, Marion F.; Experimental Teaching; 1913, *15*, 361-365

Roberts, Emma; A Southern Oral School; 1914, *16*, 793-797

Roberts, Emma; Training the Deaf Child; 1915, *17*, 305-311

Roe, W. Carey; Dr. Forchhammer's Mouth-and-Hand System: A Discussion; 1918, *20*, 175-177

Roe, W. Carey; The Inquisitive Habit; 1916, *18*, 161-165

Rogers, Francis L.; Teachers and Night Schools for the Adult Deaf; 1924, *26*, 509-511

Sanders, K. D.; A Half-Century of Progress in the New England Schools—IX. The Austine School, Brattleboro, Vt.; 1940, *42*, 263-265
Schilling, B. W.; Another Key: Art; 1958, *60*, 437-438; 464
──────; Schools for the Deaf in New York State; 1918, *20*, 601-603
Schunhoff, Hugo F.; Comprehensive Programming to Meet Today's Needs for All Deaf Children; 1964, *66*, 410-414
Schwartz, Marcia G.; A Deaf Child in My Hearing Class; 1964, *66*, 627-630
Silverman, S. Richard (moderator); Education of the Deaf Today—An Assessment and a Look Into the Future; 1953, *55*, 187-207
Simon, Arthur B.; An Answer to a Teacher of the Deaf; 1950, *52*, 157-159; 196-198
Simon, Arthur B.; Helping Your Deaf Child Grow Up—Let Him Experiment and Explore; 1961, *63*, 35-39
Simon, Arthur B.; Wanted: A Program for the Adult Deaf; 1956, *58*, 256
Sister M. Henriella; The Slow-Learning Deaf Child; 1961, *63*, 380-384; 444-448
Sister Mary Oswald; A Half-Century of Progress in the New England Schools: The Boston School for the Deaf; 1940, *42*, 202-205; 252
Sister Anna Rose; Oralism at St. Joseph Institute for the Deaf; 1962, *64*, 496-499
Sister Mary Walter; Individual Instructional Seatwork; 1960, *62*, 162-165
──────; Slow Learning Deaf Children Can Learn; 1956, *58*, 101-102
Stahlem, Evelyn M.; Major Problems in the Instruction of the Deaf; 1958, *60*, 248-251; 279
Steed, Lyman; The Education of the Deaf; 1921, *23*, 18-20; 25-29
Stelle, Roy M. (moderator, panel discussion); Where Should the Deaf Child Be Educated?; 1954, *56*, 297-313
Stolp, Lauren E.; A Curriculum for the Slow-Learning Deaf Child; 1964, *66*, 494-498
Story, Arthur J.; Analysis and Synthesis in Teaching Methods; 1915, *17*, 95-96
Story, Arthur J.; The Approach to the Normal; 1913, *15*, 111-116
Streng, Alice; Curriculum in Schools for the Deaf; 1957, *59*, 291-296
Sturdivant, Elizabeth; The Deaf Child's Heritage; 1925, *27*, 385-387
──────; Summer Courses in Speech and Hearing; 1956, *58*, 107-116; 1957, *59*, 111-124; 1958, *60*, 112-119; 1959, *61*, 117-128; 1960, *62*, 117-136; 1961, *63*, 111-130; 1962, *64*, 133-148; 1963, *65*, 132-145; 1964, *66*, 134-148; 1965, *67*, 210-225
Sylvester, Elfrieda; Betty Thinks; 1918, *20*, 675-679
Taylor, Harris; The Male Teacher; 1900, *2*, 363-366
Thomas, Donald; Separate Programming for the Deaf and Hard of Hearing; 1964, *66*, 436-438

EDUCATION—*continued*

Volta Review

Thompson, Emma R.; The First Year of the Child's Life in the Institution; 1907, *9*, 90-98

Thorne, Bert; The Problem of the Marginally Deaf; 1961, *63*, 133-134; 146

Tillinghast, Edward S.; The Drift of Opinion as to Pure Oral Departments in Combined System Schools; 1917, *19*, 1-3

Tillinghast, Edward S.; The Oral Method of Education of the Deaf; 1917, *19*, 457-462

Tillinghast, Edward S.; School Home Ideals; 1928, *30*, 355, 360; 472-477; 1929, *31*, 12-15

Timberlake, Josephine B.; Deaf Graduates of Schools and Colleges for Hearing Students; 1929, *31*, 489-491

Timberlake, Josephine B., and Hunter, Mabel R.; Deaf Graduates of Hearing Schools and Colleges; 1928, *30*, 449-450

Tucker, Walter J.; A Half-Century of Progress at the New England Schools —IV. The Mystic Oral School; 1939, *41*, 682-684

VanWyk, Mary K.; Integration? Yes, if . . . ; 1959, *61*, 59-62

Waldron, Grace A., et al.; A Half-Century of Progress in the New England Schools—X. Three Massachusetts Day Schools; 1940, *42*, 334-338; 385-386

Wall, Alice P.; Projects for the Special Class; 1933, *35*, 418-420

Warner, Larae; Community Living as a Basis of a Curriculum; 1964, *66*, 499-503

Wasell, Irene T.; Discipline in the Classroom—a Positive Factor; 1964, *66*, 514-517

Welty, Harry L.; Teaching the Use of the Dictionary; 1936, *38*, 133-136; 178-179

Whildin, Olive A.; Modern Education of the Deaf; 1942, *44*, 618-620

Wilson, D. K.; The Hearing Team; 1962, *64*, 22-25

Winnie, A. J.; What A Study of the Deaf Child Will Do for the Hearing Child; 1905, *7*, 137-144

Withrow, Frank B.; A Special Education Program in a State Residential School for the Deaf; 1962, *64*, 431-433

Wright, John D.; Are the Taxpayers Getting What They Pay For?; 1915, *17*, 73-75

Wright, John D.; A Common Platform on Which All Can Stand; 1917, *19*, 452-455

Wright, John D.; The Disadvantages of Private Instruction in the Home; 1913, *15*, 352-356

Wright, John D.; The Dual System Eventually: Why Not Now?; 1915, *17*, 369-370; 387-388

Wright, John D.; Extracts from Report Submitted to the Board of Education of Massachusetts; 1913, *15*, 183-194

Wright, John D.; A Fair Chance for Every Deaf Child; 1917, *19*, 3-9

Wright, John D.; The Partially Deaf Child: A School Problem; 1917, *19*, 449-452
Wright, John D.; Proper Teaching of Deaf Children; 1918, *20*, 473-475
Wright, John D.; A Weak Spot in the Combined System; 1916, *18*, 3-5
—————; The Wright Oral School for the Deaf, New York City; 1914, *16*, 273-301
Yale, Caroline A.; Special Training for the Deaf Child: When Shall It Begin? When Shall It End?; 1926, *28*, 139-142
Young, Ellery; Oral Education in Louisiana; 1965, *67*, 208-209
Young, Louise T.; A Half-Century of Progress in the New England Schools —V. Maine School for the Deaf; 1940, *42*, 19-20

Annals of the Deaf

Anderson, Tom L.; Fair Consideration for the Profoundly Deaf Pupil; 1941, *86*, 159-165
Askew, Louise M.; Interesting Slow Pupils; 1930, *75*, 2-5
Aurell, Ernest; A New Era in the History of the Education of the Deaf; 1934, *79*, 223-230
Avery, Elizabeth B.; Calling Up Visual Memories to be Used in Educating the Deaf; 1916, *61*, 117-123
Ayres, J. A.; A Complete Education for the Deaf and Dumb; 1849, *2*, 24-32
Balis, Sylvia C.; The Deadness of Education; 1914, *59*, 253-259
Bell, Alexander G.; Fallacies Concerning the Deaf; 1884, *29*, 32-60
Bindon, D.; Personality Characteristics of Rubella Deaf Children: Implications for Teaching of the Deaf in General; 1957, *102*, 264-270
Binet, A., and Simon, Th.; An Investigation Concerning the Value of the Oral Method; 1910, *55*, 4-33
Blair, Francis X.; A Study of the Visual Memory of Deaf and Hearing Children; 1957, *102*, 254-263
Blattner, J. W.; The Natural Method; 1891, *36*, 1-11
Blattner, J. W.; Problems of the Deaf; 1925, *70*, 130-139
Boatner, Maxine T.; The Washington Life of Edward Miner Gallaudet; 1955, *100*, 313-318
Breckinridge, Mary S.; Useful Devices for a Primary Class; 1902, *47*, 143-146
Brill, Tobias; A Guide to the Literature on the Deaf—Particularly the Education of the Deaf; 1936, *81*, 100-112
Brill, Tobias; An Outline for Study for Intermediate and Advanced Grades; 1925, *70*, 140-163; 254-267; 1926, *71*, 227-248; 419-430; *72*, 437-445

EDUCATION—continued

Annals of the Deaf

Bull, J. C.; A Few Suggestions on the Higher Education of Deaf-Mutes; 1870, *15*, 224-231

Burns, Margaret A.; Are We So Very Different?; 1932, *77*, 315-321

Clarke, Francis D.; The First Year's Work; 1894, *39*, 209-225; 1895, *40*, 14-30; 137-148; The Second Year's Work; 1896, *41*, 129-146; 242-251; 274-278; The Third Year's Work; 1897, *42*, 1-16; 75-83; 143-152; The Fourth Year's Work; 1897, *42*, 224-237; 317-325; 371-386; The Fifth Year's Work; 1898, *43*, 309-315; 360-380; 1899, *44*, 7-23

Cobb, Jennie L.; Schoolroom Efficiency; 1913, *58*, 207-213

Connally, Eileen E.; Implications of Research for the Classroom Teacher; 1961, *106*, 397-404

Cox, Ian; Deafness in Young Children; 1948, *93*, 330-332

Crouter, A. L.; The Possibilities of Oral Methods; 1911, *56*, 390-407

Crouter, A. L.; The Vital Point in Our Work and Certain Ways to Reach It; 1914, *59*, 6-14

Dalgarno, Geo.; Dalgarno's Didascalocophus (Didascalocophus, or the Deaf and Dumb Man's Tutor, reprinted from the 1680 edition); 1857, *9*, 14-64

Davis, W. M.; Interest and Attention; 1916, *61*, 205-212

Day, Herbert A.; A Classification Test Given to the Students of Gallaudet College; 1921, *66*, 409-424

Dean, Louise E.; Experiments in the Academic Education of Adolescent Deaf Pupils; 1934, *79*, 292-305

Divine, L. R.; Revised Curriculum, As Compiled for the Southern Conference of Executives of Schools for the Deaf; 1938, *83*, 103-113; 235-242; 1939, *84*, 260-276; 432-444

Doctor, Powrie V., et al.; The American Annals of the Deaf, 1847-1947; 1947, *92*, 367-449

Doctor, Powrie V.; Deafness in the 20th Century; 1959, *104*, 330-334

Doctor, Powrie V.; A Guide to Literature in Journals, Proceedings, Indexes and Abstracts on the Education and Welfare of the Deaf; 1951, *96*, 432-446

Doctor, Powrie V.; A Liberal Education for the Deaf; 1964, *109*, 423-426

Dozier, J. D.; Problems Involved in the Placement of a Deaf Puerto Rican Child in an Educational Environment in the U.S.; 1953, *98*, 260-279

Driggs, Frank M.; Progress in the Education of the Deaf; 1929, *74*, 351-373

Drouot, E.; The Binet Investigation of the Oral Method; 1910, *55*, 307-324

Elliott, A. Edwina; Teaching Time Relations to Deaf Children; 1937, *82*, 168-175

Elliott, Ida D.; Educational Problems; 1933, *78*, 96-100

Elstad, Leonard M.; Higher Education; 1953, *98*, 374-378

Elstad, Leonard M.; Historical Background of Types of Schools and Methods of Communication; 1958, *103*, 300-308

Erd, Robert; The Place of Physical Education in a School for the Deaf; 1909, *54*, 393-401

Falberg, R.; An Adventure Into Adult Education of the Deaf; 1962, *107*, 329-338

Falconer, G. A.; A Mechanical Device for Teaching Sight Vocabulary to Young Deaf Children; 1961, *106*, 251-257

Fauth, Bette L., and Warren, W.; Methods of Instruction; 1951, *96*, 301-319

Fauth, La Verne, and Warren, W.; A Study of the Proceedings of the Convention of the American Instructors of the Deaf, 1850-1949: Auricular Training; 1950, *95*, 280-311

Fay, G. O.; The Methods of Deaf-Mute Education; 1873, *18*, 13-26

Fay, Helen; Classroom Suggestions; 1919, *64*, 421-428

Ferreri, Giulio; Mistaken Investigation Concerning the Value of the Oral Method; 1910, *55*, 34-38

Fox, Thomas F.; Character Building in Deaf Mutes; 1912, *57*, 453-461

Fusfeld, Irving S.; A Critique on the Question of College Enrollment for Deaf Persons in the U.S.; 1963, *108*, 220-236

Fusfeld, Irving S.; Dr. Goldstein's "Problems of the Deaf"; 1933, *78*, 352-358

Fusfeld, Irving S.; Higher Education for the Deaf; 1945, *90*, 142-153

Fusfeld, Irving S.; Is the Male Teacher Becoming an Extinct Species?; 1921, *66*, 21-32

Fusfeld, Irving S., et al.; The Survey of Schools for the Deaf; 1925, *70*, 391-421; 1926, *71*, 97-135; 284-348; 1927, *72*, 2-34; 355-359; 377-414; 1928, *73*, 1-36; 184-201; 1-36; 184-201; 273-300

Gallaudet, Edward M.; The American System, Its Defects and Their Remedies; 1861, *13*, 147-170

Gallaudet, Edward M.; The Combined System of Instruction; 1891, *36*, 255-266

Gallaudet, Edward M.; History of the Education of the Deaf in the United States; 1886, *31*, 130-147

Gallaudet, Edward M.; The Pre-Natal History of the College; 1914, *59*, 281-285

Gault, R. H.; The Use of the Sense of Touch; 1928, *73*, 134-146

Gemmill, W. H.; The State: Its Relation and Obligations to the Deaf Child (Iowa); 1919, *64*, 289-297

Gillespie, Frances E.; The Theory and Practice of Instruction for an Oral Class of Beginners; 1901, *46*, 492-507; 1902, *47*, 233-242

EDUCATION—*continued*

Annals of the Deaf

Goetzinger, C. P., and Rousey, C. L.; Educational Achievement of Deaf Children; 1959, *104*, 221-231

Goldstein, Hyman, and Schein, Jerome D.; First Steps Toward the Collection of Uniform Statistics of Severe Hearing Impairments and Deafness in the United States; 1964, *109*, 400-409

Goldstein, Robert; Differential Classification of Disorders of Communication in Children; 1958, *103*, 215-233

Gough, J. A.; Guidance for the Deaf Child in a Residential School; 1945, *90*, 206-220

Green, Samuel A.; The Earliest Advocate of the Education of the Deaf-Mutes; 1861, *13*, 1-8

Greenmun, Robert M.; Society's Attitudes and Popular Conceptions Concerning the Deaf; 1958, *103*, 372-377

Griffing, W. T.; The Slow Pupil; 1939, *84*, 383-386

Guedel, A. E.; Physical Training; 1914, *59*, 172-180

Hall, Percival; Educational Problems of the Deaf; 1928, *73*, 163-168

Hall, Percival; Our Debt to the American School for the Deaf; 1923, *68*, 217-225

Hanson, Olof; Comparative Statistics of Methods of Educating the Deaf in the United States; 1902, *47*, 349-357

Harris, Nathan P.; Some Aspects of School Placement of Young Deaf Children; 1954, *99*, 293-302

Henderson, S., and Francis, D. H.; The Meaning of Deafness: The Report of a Workshop for Audiologists; 1962, *107*, 464-596

Higgins, F. C.; The Education of the Deaf—The Book Mart; 1947, *92*, 151-168; 1950, *95*, 315-349

Hirsch, D.; Mr. Hirsch's Views of the "Combined Method" for the Deaf and Dumb; 1869, *14*, 48-53

Howard, Caroline M.; The Assigning of Lessons; 1916, *61*, 168-171

Howson, James W.; Motivation in Schools for the Deaf; 1922, *67*, 125-143

Hurd, Anna C.; Busy Work for Primary Classes; 1896, *41*, 88-97

————; The International Congress on the Education of the Deaf; 1961, *106*, 411-413

Johnson, Elizabeth H.; The Ability of Pupils in a School for the Deaf to Understand Various Methods of Communication; 1948, *93*, 194-213; 258-314

Jones, John W.; One Hundred Years of History in the Education of the Deaf in America and Its Present Status; 1918, *63*, 1-47

Kenner, Marcus L.; Preliminary Education of Deaf Children; 1920, *65*, 447-451

Kent, Margaret; Administrative Procedures Concerning Admission of New Students to Residential Schools for the Deaf; 1959, *104*, 271-276

Kerr, M. M.; Research in the Education of the Deaf; 1948, *93*, 185-193

Kiesel, Theodore A.; The Early Stages in the Education of the Deaf; 1891, *36,* 211-221
Kiesel, Theodore A.; How to Start the Deaf Child; 1887, *32,* 6-10
Kirkhuff, J. D.; The Nature Method; 1891, *36,* 120-128
Landis, Kate S.; Six Months With a Beginning Class; 1892, *37,* 189-198
LaRue, Mary S.; For Variety in Drill; 1938, *83,* 367-371
Latham, W. H.; Difficulties in Deaf-Mute Instruction; 1870, *15,* 104-111
Lewis, Bertha; Health Education for the Deaf at the Elementary Level; 1958, *103,* 564-571
Long, J. Schuyler; Our Aim in Teaching the Deaf; 1917, *62,* 413-425
McClure, George M.; The First State School for the Deaf; 1923, *68,* 97-120
McIntire, W. F.; Leadership Training in the Area of the Deaf; 1961, *106,* 488-490
Mackie, Romaine P.; The School Building and the Child with Impaired Hearing; 1951, *96,* 494-501
McManaway, Howard M.; Recent Educational Advancements and Our Reactions to Them; 1929, *74,* 180-192
Miller, June; Hearing and Speech Program at the University of Kansas Medical Center; 1951, *96,* 353-362
Moore, L. M., and Yale, Caroline A.—Pioneer and Builder; 1934, *79,* 189-196
Morris, M. E.; The Conservation of Material in the School; 1914, *59,* 118-131
Morsh, Joseph E.; A Comparative Study of Deaf and Hearing Students; 1937, *82,* 223-233
Mosley, C. C.; Education for Life: The Mississippi School for the Negro Deaf Rethinks Its Program; 1956, *101,* 251-253
Myklebust, Helmer R.; A Study of the Usefulness of Objective Measures of Mechanical Aptitude in Guidance Programs for the Hypacousic; 1946, *91,* 123-150; 205-225
Myklebust, Helmer R., and Brutten, Milton; A Survey of the Research Needs in the Education of the Deaf; 1951, *96,* 512-523
Noyes, J. L.; Compulsory Education as Applied to Deaf-Mutes; 1870, *15,* 216-223
O'Connor, Clarence D.; The Integration of the Deaf in Schools for the Normally Hearing; 1961, *106,* 229-232
Paterson, Donald G.; Problems in the Education of the Deaf; 1929, *74,* 373-385
Patterson, Robert; The Romance of the Education of the Deaf; 1926, *71,* 177-185
Peet, Edward; Biographical Sketch of Dr. Itard; 1853, *5,* 110-124
Peet, Elizabeth; Gallaudet College: Seventy-five Years of Higher Education for the Deaf; 1939, *84,* 198-217

EDUCATION—continued

Annals of the Deaf

Peet, Harvey P.; Memoir on the Origin & Early History of the Art of Instructing the Deaf and Dumb; 1851, *3*, 129-160

Peet, Isaac L.; A Practical View of Deaf-Mute Instruction; 1871, *16*, 69-97

Pettengill, B. D.; The Higher Education of Deaf-Mutes and Semi-Mutes; 1881, *26*, 17-22

Pintner, Rudolf; Ever-Widening Fields of Research; 1938, *83*, 225-234

Pintner, Rudolf; The Survey of Institutions for the Deaf; 1928, *73*, 155-163

Pittenger, Priscilla; New Approaches to Teaching the Young Deaf Children; 1956, *101*, 340-348

Porter, Sarah H.; The Individuality of Schools for the Deaf: The Institute for Improved Instruction, N.Y. (Lexington School); 1917, *62*, 426-439

Poulos, Thomas H.; Is Our Teaching Meaningful?; 1953, *98*, 251-256

Powers, Margaret H.; The Prevalence of Deafness in School-Age Children; 1964, *109*, 410-417

————; Project No. 6065, W.P.A.; A Special Report of Retardation of Children with Impaired Hearing in the N.Y.C. Schools; 1937, *82*, 234-243

————; Public Law 87-276, 87th Congress S. 336; 1961, *106*, 481-483

Quigley, Howard M., and Elstad, Leonard M.; Educational Problems of the Deaf; 1953, *98*, 431-476

Rankin, C. E.; The Education of a Child Handicapped by a Loss of Hearing; 1945, *90*, 276-283

Ray, Luzerne; Historical Sketch of the Instruction of the Deaf & Dumb Before the Time of De l'Epée; 1848, *1*, 197-208

Read, Utten; Spelling; 1926, *71*, 407-419

Schein, Jerome, and Bushnaq, Suleiman; Higher Education for the Deaf in the U.S.—A Retrospective Investigation; 1962, *107*, 416-420

Schunhoff, Hugo F.; Bases of a Comprehensive Program in the Education of Deaf Children; 1964, *109*, 240-247

Sheridan, Laura C.; Schoolroom Problems; 1914, *59*, 205-214

Silverman, S. Richard; Child-Accounting in the Administration of Pupil Personnel in Public Residential Schools for the Deaf; 1943, *88*, 220-240

Silverman, S. Richard; Report of the President, Council on Education of the Deaf; 1964, *109*, 420-422

Sister Mary A. Burke; Views on the Combined Method; 1880, *25*, 172-174

Smith, James L.; Making Education More Practical; 1914, *59*, 425-442

Smith, James L.; Physical Characteristics of Pupils; 1902, *47*, 301-323; 1903, *48*, 1-18

————; St. Joseph College for the Deaf; 1962, *107*, 343

Stone, Collins; The History and Methods of Deaf-Mute Instruction; 1869, *14*, 95-121

Storrs, Richard S.; Deaf-Mutes and the Combined Method; 1883, *28*, 77-94

Storrs, Richard S.; Deaf-Mutes and the Oral Method; 1883, *28*, 145-168

Storrs, Richard S.; Methods of Deaf-Mute Instruction; 1880, *25*, 105-119; 233-250; 1881, *26*, 141-160

Storrs, Richard S.; Semi-Deaf, Semi-Mute and the Combined Method; 1883, *28*, 21-36

Sutton, E. V.; Kindergarten Work In Its Relation to Primary Education; 1893, *38*, 25-32

Talbot, Benjamin; Responsibility of the Teacher of the Deaf and Dumb; 1856, *8*, 82-93

Taylor, Mrs. La Verne; Some Problems Confronting a Teacher During the First Few Years in a School for the Deaf, and How They May Be Met; 1914, *59*, 15-19

Taylor, Sam D.; A Plea for the Activity Method of Education; 1956, *101*, 254-257

Templin, Mildred C.; A Qualitative Analysis of Explanations of Physical Casualty; 1954, *99*, 252-269; 351-361

Thollon, B.; Let Us Make Haste; 1917, *62*, 199-208

Thollon, B.; The Organization of Schoolroom Work; 1916, *61*, 255-264; 434-443; 1917, *62*, 130-134

Tillinghast, E. S.; Correlation of Instruction and Environment; 1898, *43*, 22-32; 220-228

Tillinghast, Hilda; Progressive Education in Schools for the Deaf; 1934, *79*, 369-376

Turner, W. W.; Courses of Instruction; 1849, *2*, 97-105; 217-232

——————; The Twelfth Census of the Deaf of the United States, 1900; 1906, *51*, 288-296; 487-499; 1907, *52*, 13-27; 158-167; 245-254; 1908, *53*, 159-172

Vaisse, Leon; Practical Suggestions Relating to the Instruction of the Deaf and Dumb; 1874, *19*, 10-20

Walker, Isabelle, et al.; The Federal Survey of the Deaf and Hard of Hearing; 1935, *80*, 116-125; 126-142; 200-242; 342-366; 295-407

Westervelt, Z. F.; American Association To Promote the Teaching of Speech to the Deaf; 1891, *36*, 222-224

Westervelt, Z. F.; The Natural Method as Applied to the Instruction of Young Children; 1880, *25*, 212-216

Williams, Boyce R.; Making Those Leisure Time Hours Count; 1939, *84*, 377-382

Williams, Katharine; The Correlation of All School Work; 1914, *59*, 461-471

EDUCATION—continued

Annals of the Deaf

Wing, George; The Associative Feature in the Education of the Deaf; 1886, *31*, 22-35
Woodruff, Lucius H.; Primary Instruction of the Deaf and Dumb; 1848, *1*, 46-55
Worthington, Anna M.; Applying Communication Theory to Education of the Deaf; 1956, *101*, 280-287
Wright, John D.; The Fundamental Principles that Must Underlie the Successful Education of the Deaf; 1926, *71*, 142-146
Wright, John D.; Working Suggestions; 1918, *63*, 324-342
Yearsley, Macleod; The Education of the Deaf: Its Present State, with Suggestions as to its Future Modifications and Development; 1911, *56*, 284-323; 484-499; 1912, *57*, 23-31
Zeckel, Adolf; Research Possibilities with the Deaf; 1942, *87*, 173-191

FOREIGN

Volta Review

Adametz, Josef; The Schools for Hard of Hearing Children in Vienna, Austria; 1922, *24*, 331-334
Addison, W. H.; The Present State of the Education of the Deaf in Scotland; 1914, *16*, 165-173
Bodensiek, Gustav; The Present Status of the Education of the Backward Deaf in Prussia; 1909, *11*, 20-29; 91-102; 169-178
Buchli, M. J.; Home Education of Deaf Children in The Netherlands; 1963, *65*, 279-285; 316
Danger, O.; Education of the Deaf in Prussia; 1902, *4*, 122-128; 201-207
Danger, O.; The 'Mixed Method" and the "Pure Oral Method" in Germany; 1901, *3*, 411-417
————; The Education of the Deaf in Western Europe; 1962, *64*, 487-495
Ferreri, Giulio C.; The Munich School and Auricular Instruction; 1904, *6*, 411-417
Ferreri, Giulio C.; The Oral Method in the School of Frankfurt-on-the-Main; 1902, *4*, 1-6
Fetterly, H. B.; Social Education in the Ontario School; 1933, *35*, 122-123
Forchhammer, G.; A New Expedient for the Teaching of the Deaf; 1902, *4*, 413-423
Haycock, George S.; Training of Teachers of the Deaf in England; 1923, *25*, 345-351

Hansen, Anders; The Belgian Method; 1928, *30*, 8-13

Hoffmann, Hugo; The Education of Deaf Mutes in Germany at the End of the Nineteenth Century; 1901, *3*, 1-10

Hoffmann, Hugo; Language and Language Teaching in German Schools; 1908, *10*, 265-271

————; Hungarian Institutions for the Deaf; 1904, *6*, 191-197

Hunt, J. F.; Education of the Deaf in the U.S.S.R.; 1959, *61*, 356-363; 390

Jones, Lilian G.; Education of the Deaf Behind the Iron Curtain; 1958, *60*, 152-155; 203-205; 222-225; 260-266

Klopfer, Stephen; The Belgian Method; 1931, *33*, 245-247; 280-281

Magner, Marjorie E.; An American Teacher's Comments on Education of the Deaf in England; 1956, *58*, 11-14

Magner, Marjorie E.; Home and Parent Guidance in England; 1956, *58*, 341-345; 348

Morkovin, Boris V.; Experiment in Teaching Deaf Preschool Children in the Soviet Union; 1960, *62*, 260-268

Nall, Frances; History and Operation of Ewing House; 1955, *57*, 145-146

Nelson, William; A Brief Account of the Principles of Teaching in the Manchester School; 1914, *16*, 251-257

Pascoe, D.; A New School in Venezuela; 1958, *60*, 21-23

Perelló, Jorge; From Spain: A Method of Liminal Audiometry for Children; 1965, *67*, 588-589

Pitrois, Yvonne; The National Institution for the Deaf in Paris; 1913, *14*, 710-718

Prettyman, Eileen; The Education of the Deaf in Toronto; 1965, *67*, 420-421

Rau, E. F.; Methods of Educating Very Young Deaf Children (Translated from Russian by Helen G. Smith); 1935, *37*, 514-518; 579-583; 649-654; 700-701

Schmidt, A.; Principal Italian Institutions for the Deaf; 1902, *4*, 455-470

Scripture, E. W.; The Laboratory of Experimental Phonetics at Hamburg; 1921, *23*, 238-240

Stelling, H.; Schools for the Weak Minded in Denmark and Norway; 1903, *5*, 16-24

Stevens, J. E.; Schools for the Deaf in Europe; 1915, *17*, 221-225

Story, Arthur J.; The English Movement in Favor of the Earlier Education of the Deaf; 1913, *15*, 7-11

Story, Arthur J.; The Glasgow Conference of Teachers of the Deaf; 1913, *15*, 394-398

Story, Arthur J.; How London Educates the Deaf; 1912, *14*, 263-299

Story, Arthur J.; The Present Position of the Education of the Deaf in Great Britain; 1926, *28*, 39-46

Swainson, Miss; The Education of the Deaf in India; 1914, *16*, 173-177

FOREIGN—continued

Volta Review

Taylor, W. W., and I. W.; The Education of the Deaf in Western Europe; 1962, *64*, 487-495

Timberlake, Josephine B.; An Educator of the Deaf Who Has Revolutionized His Field; 1953, *55*, 148-149; 160

Uden, A. v.; Observations of Education of the Deaf in The Netherlands and the U.S.A.; 1960, *62*, 10-14

Walter, Jean; Supervision in Australian Schools for the Deaf; 1958, *60*, 361-365

————; War Deafnesses; 1917, *19*, 683-686

Watson, T. J.; Research in the Education of the Deaf Outside the United States; 1963, *65*, 535-541

Wettstein, Carl T.; Schools for the Deaf in North Europe; 1911, *12*, 605-612

Williams, Howard; Speech and Language for the Deaf in Russia; 1957, *59*, 387-390

Wolf, Edna L.; Impressions Gained Through Visits to Schools for the Deaf in Europe; 1932, *34*, 447-452

Wright, John D.; School for the Deaf, Colombo, Ceylon; 1926, *28*, 415-417

Wright, John D.; Schools for the Deaf in India; 1926, *28*, 348-355; 593-595; 769-770

Wright, John D.; Schools for the Deaf in Italy; 1925; *27*, 91-97; 221-222; 282-284; 330-334; 383-385

Wright, John D.; Schools for the Deaf in the Orient; 1926, *28*, 49-52

Wright, John D.; Speech Reading in Switzerland for the Adult Deaf; 1925, *27*, 289-291

Wright, John D.; Swiss Schools for the Deaf; 1925, *27*, 713-717

Yearsley, Macleod; The Co-operation of the Teacher and the Doctor; 1913, *15*, 374-377

Yearsley, Macleod; Hard of Hearing Classes in London; 1915, *17*, 41-48

Yunghans, Marian; Teaching Art to the Deaf in Nigeria; 1964, *66*, 275-279

Zebrowski, Alexander; The Institute for the Instruction of the Deaf in Warsaw (Poland); 1922, *24*, 174-176

Annals of the Deaf

DeCondillac, E'tienne B. (1715-1780); The Language of Action (a translation by Mrs. E. M. Gallaudet); 1886, *13*, 35-41

Ewing, Irene, and A. W. G.; Educating the Deaf in Britain; 1949, *94*, 318-324

Höxter, Richard; The Bárczi Method and Its Application in the School for the Deaf of the Alliance Israélite Universelle; 1938, *83*, 386-403

Taylor, Sam D.; Education for the Deaf in England; 1953, *98*, 240-248

HARD OF HEARING

Volta Review

Bellows, Howard P.; The Harsh Voice of the Hard of Hearing; 1929, *31*, 393-394

Berry, Gordon; Problems of the Hard of Hearing; 1928, *30*, 127-136

Brown, Ruth; Hard of Hearing Children Among the Deaf; 1953, *55*, 289-291; 324

Bruhn, Martha E.; The Hard of Hearing Adult; 1915, *17*, 381-385

Cloud, D. T.; Meeting the Problem of the Hard of Hearing Child; 1937, *39*, 487-489; 540

Craig, Sam B., et al.; What Should Be Done for the Hard of Hearing Child in a School for the Deaf?; 1937, *39*, 490-493; 536

De Lany, Elizabeth G.; The Problems of the Hard of Hearing and How We Meet Them; 1935, *37*, 545-546; 564

Drennen, Genevieve; Preparing Teachers for Hard of Hearing in Public Schools; 1959, *61*, 111-114

Durfee, Marion A.; Public School Teaching of Hard of Hearing Adults and Children; 1927, *29*, 565-572

Eubank, Earle E.; The Need of Educational Preparation for Social Work with the Hard-of-Hearing; 1923, *25*, 450-453

Evans, Florence L.; Voice Placing and Enunciation for the Hard of Hearing; 1923, *25*, 203-204

——————; Extracts from the Proceedings of the Second Annual Meeting of the American Association for the Hard of Hearing; 1921, *23*, 471-491; 525-531; 1922, *24*, 16-28; 54-64; 79-87

——————; Extracts from the Proceedings of the Third Annual Meeting of the American Federation of Organizations for the Hard of Hearing, Inc., Toledo, Ohio; 1922, *24*, 308-330; 397-407; 441-450

Ferreri, Giulio C.; Children Who Are Hard of Hearing; 1902, *4*, 232-239

Fruewald, E.; The Hard of Hearing Child in a School for the Deaf; 1939, *41*, 325-327; 375

Gildston, Phyllis; The Hard of Hearing Child in the Classroom—A Guide for the Classroom Teacher; 1962, *64*, 239-245

Goetzinger, Cornelius P.; Effects of Small Perceptive Losses on Language and on Speech Discrimination; 1962, *64*, 408-414

Goetzinger, Cornelius P., et al.; Small Perceptive Hearing Loss: Its Effect in School-Age Children; 1964, *66*, 124-131

——————; Hard of Hearing Child (Questions and Answers); 1953, *55*, 401-405

Howe, Alice G.; The Hard of Hearing Child in the Public Schools of Rochester, N.Y.; 1923, *25*, 40-43

Kelley, J. C.; The Older Hard of Hearing Child; 1954, *56*, 403-405

Leighton, Etta V.; The Hard of Hearing Child in the Public School; 1913, *14*, 672-679

HARD OF HEARING—*continued*

Volta Review

Macnutt, Ena G.; Program for the Hard of Hearing Child in the Public School; 1953, *55*, 385-386
Miller, June; Classroom Methods and Materials for Hard of Hearing Children; 1957, *59*, 343-345
Montague, Harriet; What Can a Hard of Hearing Person Do?; 1935, *37*, 743-746
Nelson, Boyd E.; Hard of Hearing Pupils in Schools for the Deaf; 1942, *44*, 325-328; 368
New, Mary C.; Speech for the Hard of Hearing; 1945, *47*, 282-284
Norris, Mrs. James F.; Committee on the Survey of Hard of Hearing Children; 1926, *28*, 451-461
Peck, Annetta W.; Organizations for the Hard-of-Hearing; Their History, Purpose and Promotion; 1923, *25*, 391-395
——————; Proceedings of the Fifth Annual Conference of the American Federation of Organizations for the Hard of Hearing, Inc.; 1924, *26*, 385-477
——————; Proceedings of the Sixth Annual Conference of the American Federation of Organizations for the Hard of Hearing, Inc.; 1925, *27*, 545-665
Reeve, Jesse W.; A Five-Day School for the Hard of Hearing; 1953, *55*, 208-209; 228; 248-249; 264-266; 298-299; 320-322; 349-350; 406
Samuelson, Estelle E.; The Hard of Hearing Child from the Social Worker's Viewpoint; 1923, *25*, 44-47
Trask, Alice N.; A Plea for the Hard of Hearing; 1914, *16*, 693-696
Troll, George D.; The Hard of Hearing Adolescent; 1926, *28*, 221-223
Walker, Jane B.; An Open Door for the Hard of Hearing; 1917, *19*, 439-441

HEARING AIDS

Volta Review

Barrett, Katherine; The Value of Individual Hearing Aids—A Comparative Study of Selective Achievements of Two Groups of School Children; 1944, *46*, 553-557; 608; 628-631; 668-670; 681-685; 728
Bender, Ruth E., and Wiig, Elisabeth; Binaural Hearing Aids for Young Children; 1960, *62*, 113-115
Bradford, Charles A.; Hearing Aids in Schools for the Deaf; 1946, *48*, 649-651
Braly, Kenneth; Fitting Hearing Aids; 1938, *40*, 777-779; 808

Burger, Richard; Interest in the Hearing Aid and Its User (The Hearing Aid Industry Conference); 1964, *66*, 775-778

Carter, Howard A.; Something New in Hearing Aids; 1953, *55*, 357-358

Cavaliere, R. A., and Cutler, S. James; Rehabilitating with Hearing Aids; 1943, *45*, 635-639

Corliss, Edith L.; How Are Hearing Aids Tested?; 1948, *50*, 567-568; 598-604; 613-615; 646-648

Crouter, Alan Y.; Exploring With a Hearing Aid; 1941, *43*, 93-94; 156-157

Crutchett, Ralph; Just How Should Hearing Aids Be Fitted, An Explanation; 1941, *43*, 546-548

De La Bat, G.; Individual Hearing Aids for Children; 1941, *43*, 125-127

Di Carlo, Louis M.; Hearing Aids: Factors in Adjustment; 1946, *48*, 647-649

Duncan, R. C.; The Hearing Aid Is Not Enough; 1952, *54*, 379-381; 394-396

Fellendorf, George W.; Interest in the Hearing Aid and Its User (The Alexander Graham Bell Association for the Deaf); 1964, *66*, 767-769

Fogel, Howard H.; The Role of the Modern Hearing Aid Dealer; 1965, *67*, 566-569

Galloway, James H.; The Value of Individual Hearing Aids; 1945, *47*, 617-618

Goldstein, Robert; Relation of Some Audiologic Findings to the Use of Hearing Aids; 1958, *60*, 404

Haller, G. L., and Lybarger, S. F.; Selection of Electrical Apparatus for Auricular Training; 1933, *35*, 295-298; 316

Hanson, Earl C.; The Vactuphone—an Electric Hearing Aid Employing the Vacuum-Tube Amplifier; 1921, *23*, 331-333

Hardy, William G.; Hearing Aids for Deaf Children; 1954, *56*, 355-358

Harrington, Donald A.; Interest in the Hearing Aid and Its User (The Children's Bureau); 1964, *66*, 774-775

Haskins, Harriet; Listening with the Help of a Hearing Aid; 1955, *57*, 408-410; 417

Haug, O., et al.; A Comparison of Hearing Aid Evaluation Test Instruments and Aids Purchased from Dealers; 1963, *65*, 26-29

—————; Hearing Aids for Children; 1955, *57*, 357-359

Hudgins, Clarence V.; Modern Hearing Aid Equipment in Schools for the Deaf; 1953, *55*, 185-186

Hudgins, Clarence V.; Testing the Performance of Hearing Aids; 1947, *49*, 5-6; 60-62

—————; Investigation of Hearing Devices for the Deafened; 1926, *28*, 84-86

HEARING AIDS—*continued*

Volta Review

Johnson, Elizabeth H.; Audiometric Testing of Hearing Aids; 1947, *49*, 7-12

Kenwood, John C.; Interest in the Hearing Aid and Its User (The Society of Hearing Aid Audiologists); 1964, *66*, 778-779

Knudsen, Vern O.; Artificial Aids to Hearing; 1934, *36*, 581-587; 630

Lassman, Grace, and Montague, Harriet; Hearing Aids and Young Deaf Children; 1949, *51*, 447-449; 478; 518-520; 524-526

Levine, Edna S., and Ness, Agnes D.; Personal Hearing Aids for Deaf Children; 1945, *47*, 619-620

Lewis, Dorothy N., and Green, Ruth R.; Value of Binaural Hearing Aids for Hearing Impaired Children in Elementary Schools; 1962, *64*, 537-542; 571

Ling, Daniel, Implications of Hearing Aid Amplification Below 300 CPS; 1964, *66*, 723-729

Montague, Harriet; Hearing Aids for Deaf Children; 1946, *48*, 9-13; 60

Moore, Charles E.; Selecting Hearing Aids for High School; 1947, *49*, 504; 536-538

O'Connor, Clarence D.; What Every Superintendent of a School for the Deaf Should Know About Hearing Aids and Their Use; 1938, *40*, 710-717

Olson, Florence, and Soissons, Margaret; Problems in the Selection of Hearing Aids for Children; 1948, *50*, 478-484

Pless, Marie A., et al.; Our Hearing Aid Consultation Service; 1937, *39*, 512-513; 529-530

Pollack, Doreen C., and Downs, Marion P.; Hearing Aids for Children; 1955, *57*, 357-359

Pollack, Doreen C., and Downs, Marion P.; A Parent's Guide to Hearing Aids for Young Children; 1964, *66*, 745-749

Prall, Josephine; Hearing Aid Selection and Use; 1955, *57*, 390-392

Reeves, J. K.; Some Parental and Social Attitudes Towards Children Using Hearing Aids; 1962, *64*, 314-316; 331

Righter, George J., and Winkler, Pauline K.; Observations on Grade School Children Wearing Hearing Aids; 1946, *48*, 568-570; 594

Sortini, Adam J.; Hearing Aids for Preschool Children; 1956, *58*, 103-106; 130

Timberlake, Josephine B.; Hearing Aids on Their Fiftieth Anniversary; 1951, *53*, 507-510; 534-538

Ventry, Ira M.; Interest in the Hearing Aid and Its User (The American Speech and Hearing Association); 1964, *66*, 771-773

Victoreen, J. A.; The Audiologist and the Hearing Instrument Dispenser; 1963, *65*, 76-78; 87

Walker, Crayton; Interest in the Hearing Aid and Its User (The American Hearing Society); 1964, *66*, 769-771

Watson, Ruth B., and Norman A.; Hearing Aids in Schools for the Deaf; 1937, *39*, 261-266; 314-315
Watson, T. J.; The Use of Hearing Aids by Hearing Impaired Pupils in Ordinary Schools; 1964, *66*, 741-744; 787
Whildin, Olive A.; Hearing Aid Service for Children; 1946, *48*, 23-26
Woodward, Helen; A Child and His Hearing Aid; 1952, *54*, 261-262; 288-289
Yenrick, D. E.; The Hearing Aid—Its Acceptance and Use; 1954, *56*, 171-172

Annals of the Deaf

Galloway, James H.; A Hearing-Aid-Testing Clinic; 1941, *86*, 429-440
Knudsen, Vern O.; Hearing Aids Today and Tomorrow; 1939, *84*, 316-321
Lorge, Irving; Gains in Hearing Capacity in a Two Year Period for Hearing Aid and Control Groups; 1946, *91*, 391-396
Myklebust, Helmer R.; The Use of Hearing Aids in a Residential School for the Deaf; 1943, *88*, 270-278
Myklebust, Helmer R.; The Use of Individual Hearing Aids in a Residential School for the Deaf with Implications for Acoustic Training; 1946, *91*, 255-261
Pope, Alvin E.; The Use of Hearing Tests and Hearing Aids in the Education of the Deaf; 1936, *81*, 323-332
Prall, Josephine; Group and Wearable Hearing Aids in a Residential School for the Deaf; 1957, *102*, 240-250
Reiter, F. H.; Hearing Aids Not a Substitute for Lack of Hearing; 1950, *95*, 249-253
Silverman, S. Richard; The Implications for Schools for the Deaf of Recent Research on Hearing Aids; 1949, *94*, 325-339
Silverman, S. Richard, and Harrison, C. E.; The National Research Council Group Hearing Aid Project, A Progress Report; 1951, *96*, 420-431
Stevenson, Elwood P.; Hearing Aids—The Deaf—The Hard of Hearing; 1939, *84*, 3-7

HEREDITY

Volta Review

Bell, Alexander G.; A Few Thoughts Concerning Eugenics; 1908, *10*, 166-173

Bell, Alexander G.; Graphical Studies of Marriages of the Deaf; 1913, *15*, 146-152; 196-203; 230-238; 280-287; 322-329; 366-373; 408-415

Bell, Alexander G.; Marriage—An Address to the Deaf; 1935, *37*, 457-460; 491

Brill, Richard G.; Hereditary Aspects of Deafness; 1961, *63*, 168-175

Brockman, Seymour J.; Recent Advances in Experimental Otologic Research; 1957, *59*, 105-110

Cramp, Arthur J.; Deafness—Cure Quackery and Pseudo-Medicine; 1926, *28*, 497-504

Danger, O.; The Heredity of Deafness; 1900, *2*, 343-348

DeLand, Fred; Keep the Nose Clean and Free from Obstructions; 1921, *23*, 3-4; 82-84; 159-161

DeLand, Fred; Marriages of the Deaf; 1912, *14*, 186-189

Driggs, Frank M.; The Causes of Deafness; 1913, *15*, 330-334

—————; Genealogy and Eugenics; 1915, *17*, 361-363

Goldstein, M. A.; The Physician and the Deaf Child; 1910, *12*, 279-287

—————; Graphical Studies of Marriages of the Deaf; 1913, *15*, 80-91

Hickernell, W. F.; Eugenics and the United States Census; 1911, *13*, 399-402

Holowach, Jean; The Pediatrician and the Deaf Child; 1955, *57*, 121-122

Love, James K.; The Medical Inspection of School Children; 1911, *13*, 332-343

Love, James K.; The Study of the Deaf Child: Being a Research on Deaf-Mutism; 1907, *9*, 449-462

McCabe, Brian F.; The Etiology of Deafness; 1963, *65*, 471-477

McGee, T. Manford; Otologic Research; 1963, *65*, 478-485

Miller, James R.; Pediatrics and Disorders in Communication: Some Genetic Counseling Problems in Families with Congenital Hearing Defect; 1965, *67*, 118-123; 165

Newhart, Horace; The Responsibility of the Physician in Otology; 1921, *23*, 170-173

—————; The Otologist and the Deaf Child; 1953, *55*, 15-16

Reinhardt, Anna C.; The Early Recognition of Deafness; 1920, *22*, 74-77

Roberts, Linnaeus; Heredity and Intermarriage: Factors in Deafmutism; 1912, *14*, 184-186

Rott, O. M.; The Prevention of Deafness in Children and the Teacher's Responsibility Thereto; 1924, *26*, 495-500

Sank, Diane, and Kallman, Franz J.; The Role of Heredity in Early Total Deafness; 1963, *65*, 461-470

Sataloff, Joseph; The Rh Factor in Congenital Deafness; 1950, *52*, 311; 332

Annals of the Deaf

Cobb, Jennie L.; The Influence of Heredity; 1911, *56*, 253-259
Fay, Edward A.; Illegitimate Unions; 1897, *42*, 141-143
Fay, Edward A.; Marriages of the Deaf in America; 1896, *41*, 22-31; 79-88; 171-183; 215-242; 299-331; 391-402; 1897, *42*, 29-33; 96-109
Fowler, Edmund P.; Prevention of Diseases and Disorders of the Ears between the Ages of Three and Twelve Years (Inclusive); 1938, *83*, 306-319
Taylor, Harris; Hereditary Deafness; 1892, *37*, 249-259

LANGUAGE

Volta Review

Adams, Mabel E.; The Reinforcement of Speech by Writing; 1899, *1*, 144-149
Adams, Mabel E.; A Symposium on "Live Language"; 1925, *27*, 30-40
Ashby, Madelyn T.; Language in the Fifth Grade; 1933, *35*, 422-423
Avery, Elizabeth B.; Teaching the Passive Voice; 1927, *29*, 473-477
Babcock, E. J., and Jessie T.; A Plea for the Play Coefficient in Teaching Conversation to Deaf Children; 1914, *16*, 613-616
Baltzer, Susanna; Language Problems in Speech Therapy Programs for Teenagers; 1963, *65*, 401-406
Banks, Marjorie S.; An Amplified Idea; 1927, *29*, 696-698
Barnes, F. G.; The Development of Language; 1914, *16*, 177-187
Barnes, F. G.; Talks to Young Teachers of Language; 1916, *18*, 501-505
Beatty, Mary M.; Developing the Power of Thought in Connection with Language Teaching; 1926, *28*, 203-204
Bell, Alexander G.; Teaching Language to a Young Deaf Child; 1939, *41*, 437-441
Benedict, A. L.; English Spelling; 1915, *17*, 477-481
Benedict, A. L.; The Extent of the Vocabulary; 1920, *22*, 494-500
Bennett, Josephine; "To Have" and "To Be" in the Primary Grades; 1933, *35*, 254-258
Bennett, Josephine; A Verb Device; 1944, *46*, 325-330
Berry, Helen; The Hayne Grocery Store (An Activity); 1933, *35*, 11-12; 41
Blair, Cora L.; Connected Language; 1912, *14*, 499-501
Blankenship, Ota C.; A Language Game—Primary Work; 1929, *31*, 113-114
Bliss, Susan E.; Language Work in Intermediate Grades; 1907, *9*, 143-153

LANGUAGE—continued

Volta Review

Bollback, Betty L.; Visual Language; 1958, *60*, 108-109
Boone, Daniel R.; Infant Speech and Language Development; 1965, *67*, 414-419
Booth, Frank W.; Language Learning by the Intuitive Method; 1905, *7*, 215-224
Bown, Jesse C., and Mecham, Merlin J.; The Assessment of Verbal Language Development in Deaf Children; 1961, *63*, 228-230
Brill, Tobias; Direct and Indirect Discourse; 1928, *30*, 49-51
Brill, Tobias; Language in Advanced Grades; 1946, *48*, 680-681
Brown, J.; The Improved Development and Use of Language by Our Deaf Pupils; 1921, *23*, 78-82
Bruce, M. Ethel; Application of Language in the Lower Grades; 1926, *28*, 198-200
Bruhn, Martha E.; Practical Exercises on Advanced Study of Homophenous Words; 1916, *18*, 215-224; 331-339; 361-368; 447-453
Buchman, Martha; The Role of Language in Speech Training for the Hearing Impaired Child; 1954, *56*, 205-208
Buell, Edith M.; Ask, Say and Tell; 1928, *30*, 597-601
Buell, Edith M.; A Comparison of the "Barry Five Slate System" and the "Fitzgerald Key;" 1931, *33*, 5-19
Buell, Edith M.; In the Classroom: Adjective Phrases (story suggested by pictures); 1931, *33*, 248-250; 348-349; 367; 371; 502-506
Buell, Edith M.; Lessons on Relative Clauses; 1934, *36*, 270-271; 312-313
Buell, Edith M.; Lessons on Relative Pronouns; 1934, *36*, 146-147; 184-185
Buell, Edith M.; Word Pictures; 1926, *28*, 289-295
Buell, Edith M.; Word-Pictures As A Means of Mental Development; 1912, *14*, 495-499
Caldwell, Elizabeth H.; The Hyphenated Subject; 1964, *66*, 557-561
Caldwell, Elizabeth H.; Some Adventures in Language Development; 1961, *63*, 60-64
Caldwell, William A.; Devices for Teaching English; 1926, *28*, 706-707
Cleary, E. P.; Teaching Language to the Deaf; 1930, *32*, 174-175
Cota, Agnes; What Can Basic English Offer Us?; 1944, *46*, 441-443; 480
Cox, Mary R.; Improving the Use of Language by the Deaf; 1920, *22*, 188-193
Crandell, Marian P.; Natural Language for the Deaf; 1944, *46*, 264-266; 304-306
Crawford, May T.; Three Plans for Teaching Language; 1935, *37*, 13-14; 51-52
Crouter, Alan Y.; Let's Teach Language; 1941, *43*, 297-300; 340-342; 376-378; 399-400

Davidson, S. G.; The Proper Treatment of the Verb; 1907, *9*, 221-230
Davidson, S. G.; The Relation of Language to Mental Development and of Speech to Language Teaching; 1899, *1*, 129-139
Davies, Rachel D.; My New Job; 1937, *39*, 138-139
Dawes, Rachel E.; Primary Language, 1926, *28*, 691-693
————; A Device for Teaching Months and Seasons; 1926, *28*, 101-112
Dibos, Lucille, et al.; Language; 1925, *27*, 24-30
Doctor, Powrie V.; Bibliography for the Teaching of Vocabulary to the Deaf; 1954, *56*, 217-218
Doctor, Powrie V.; On Teaching the Abstract to the Deaf; 1950, *52*, 547-549; 568-572
Donald, Ida M.; English in the Intermediate Grades; 1926, *28*, 702-705
Doneghy, Lucy; Some Helps in Language Teaching; 1931, *33*, 122-135
Driggs, Frank M.; The Use of English in Schools for the Deaf; 1920, *22*, 529-535
Dunlap, S. C.; Second Grade Language (Third Year); 1930, *32*, 411-413
Eiseman, Marie H.; Teaching the Comparison of Adjectives; 1933, *35*, 218-219; 234-235
Elliott, Shirley S.; Structural Language Blocks; 1964, *66*, 526-531
Ervin, Annie M.; Some Language Difficulties; 1922, *24*, 64-70
Evans, Mildred; Sugar Coated Drills; 1926, *28*, 201-203
Ewing, Alexander W.; Linguistic Development and Mental Growth in Hearing Impaired Children; 1963, *65*, 180-187
Fehr, Joann D.; Programing Language for Deaf Children; 1962, *64*, 14-21
Fitzgerald, Edith; Direct and Indirect Discourse; 1927, *29*, 700-703
Fitzgerald, Edith; Technical Language Work in the Primary Dept.; 1923, *25*, 205-214
Ford, Catherine; Language for the Slow Child; 1938, *40*, 681-684
Foy, Robert E.; Teaching Language Appreciation to the Deaf; 1964, *66*, 205-207
Gantenbein, Andrew, and Noller, Joanne; Descriptive Grammar, an Approach to Expressive Language for the Auditorially Impaired; 1965, *67*, 136-143
Gantenbein, Andrew; Expressive Inner Language for the Deaf Through a Descriptive Grammar Program; 1964, *66*, 521-525
Gare, Marion W.; Teaching the Present Perfect Tense; 1933, *35*, 73-77
Giangreco, Marianne, and C. Joseph; Teaching English to Teenagers; 1957, *59*, 437-439
Goetzinger, Cornelius P.; Effects of Small Perceptive Losses on Language and on Speech Discrimination; 1962, *64*, 408-414
Goodwin, Elizabeth; An Experiment in Teaching Languages on Individual Lines; 1921, *23*, 435-445

LANGUAGE—continued

Volta Review

Gordon, Mary L.; Thoughts on the Articles; 1928, *30*, 229-230
Grammatico, Leahea; Building a Language Foundation at the Preschool Level; 1964, *66*, 378-381
Groht, Mildred A.; Adjustment to Industry Through Language; 1940, *42*, 648-655
Groht, Mildred A.; Composition in the Grammar Grades; 1933, *35*, 251-254
Groht, Mildred A.; Individual Language Drill Stories; 1934, *36*, 528-530; 564-565
Groht, Mildred A.; The Language Arts in a School for the Deaf; 1957, *59*, 337-342
Groht, Mildred A.; Language for the Deaf; 1953, *55*, 243-246; 274-276
Groht, Mildred A.; Living Language for the Deaf; 1958, *60*, 347-350
Groht, Mildred A.; More Notes on the Teaching of Language; 1937, *39*, 197-200; 244
Groht, Mildred A., On Making Language Natural; 1932, *34*, 368-369
Groht, Mildred A.; Oral English; 1934, *36*, 650-654; 693
Groht, Mildred A.; Oral English; 1938, *40*, 631-632
Groht, Mildred A.; Suggestions for Teaching English; 1934, *36*, 199-204; 244
Groht, Mildred A.; The Teaching of Vocabulary—An Introduction; 1954, *56*, 57
Gruver, Elbert A.; The Teaching of Technical Grammar; 1913, *15*, 293-297
Guilmartin, Mary D.; A Year of Language Projects; 1927, *29*, 91-97
Guinness, S., Goodspeed, E., Atwood, M.; Language in Intermediate Grades; 1922, *24*, 1-9
Hamel, Clara A.; The Teaching of High School English; 1938, *40*, 685-688
Harkness, Margaret M.; Language in the Pre-School and Primary Classes; 1946, *48*, 676-677
Harrington, D. A.; Language and Perception; 1965, *67*, 191-196
Hart, Beatrice O., and Rosenstein, Joseph; Examining the Language Behavior of Deaf Children; 1964, *66*, 679-682
Hart, Beatrice O.; The Language Program at the Lexington School for the Deaf; 1964, *66*, 468-473
Heider, Fritz, and Grace M.; Comparison of Sentence Structure of Deaf and Hearing Children; 1941, *43*, 364-367; 406; 536-540; 564; 599-604; 628-630
Heider, Fritz; On the Construction of a Language Usage Test for the Deaf; 1946, *48*, 742-744
Higgins, Lydia F.; Language in the Home; 1915, *17*, 442-444
Hilliard, Ethel; Corrective Work in Language; 1909, *11*, 388-397

Hobart, Elsa L.; Devices for English Teaching; 1930, *32*, 136-138
Holley, Minnie C.; Developing a Consciousness of Language; 1941, *43*, 660; 685-686
Hurst, Fannie D.; Type-Errors in Language of the Deaf; 1930, *32*, 511-512
Ingle, Helen F.; Language for the Deaf Child; 1941, *43*, 645-648; 690; 726-728; 748
Ingvarsson, Ivar M.; Language Teaching in a School for the Deaf; 1933, *35*, 5-10; 346-350; 352
Jackson, Anne W.; Ladders to Vocabulary Building; 1930, *32*, 170-172
Joiner, Enfield; Original Language in the Primary Grades; 1926, *28*, 693-695
Jones, J. W.; The Development of Language in the Deaf Child; 1910, *12*, 299-306
Jones, J. W.; Language for Advanced Grades of Deaf Pupils; 1920, *22*, 655-662
Jones, Kate-Helen; Communication Skills; 1961, *63*, 72-77; 94
Jones, Mabel K.; Language Development for Primary Grades; 1920, *22*, 597-603; 680-684; 790-792
Kawamoto, Unosuke; The Psychological Basis of Teaching Language to the Deaf; 1934, *36*, 12-16
Keefer, M. B.; Original Language in the Primary Classes; 1930, *32*, 619-622
Keller, Lillian, et al.; Language for the Deaf; 1948, *50*, 432-442
Kirk, Louise; Teaching Language to the Deaf Through Poetry; 1929, *31*, 33-35
Knox, Addie C.; The Teaching of Common Things; 1941, *43*, 362-363
Lacy, Mabel V.; Language Work in the Honolulu School for the Deaf; 1938, *40*, 692-695
Leonard, Eleanor C.; Which Tense?; 1912, *14*, 261-262
Lewis, Sarah E.; The Wing Symbols; 1931, *33*, 491; 507
Lindstrom, Thure A.; Learning Language Through Reading; 1932, *34*, 269-271
McAloney, Thomas S.; The Barry (Five) Slate System; 1931, *33*, 530-542
McGrady, Harold J.; The Influence of a Program of Instruction Upon the Conceptual Thinking of the Deaf; 1964, *66*, 531-536
MacMillan, Betty; The Value of Diagrams in Teaching Grammar; 1932, *34*, 377-378
Mannen, Grace; Conversational Language (Parts I-V); 1959, *61*, 11-16; 66-70; 89; 137-141; 170-177; 225-227
Mannen, Grace; Everyday Expressions Through Speech: Their Understanding and Use; 1956, *58*, 57-60
Maxson, Kathryn P.; Calendar Work; 1933, *35*, 258-259; 272

LANGUAGE—continued

Volta Review

Miller, Marjorie; First Steps in Language Development; 1934, *36*, 665; 697
Miller, Marjorie; The Present Tense Is Alive; 1943, *45*, 331; 370
Mirrielees, Ruchiel; The Beginnings of Language and Reading; 1909, *11*, 385-388
Mitchell, Dorothy; Conjugations in the First Grade; 1931, *33*, 490-491
Moore, Helen T.; Corrective Work on the Passive Voice; 1931, *33*, 351-352; 367; 371
Moore, Helen T.; Teaching News Condensing; 1926, *28*, 589-590
Morris, M. Esther; Intermediate Language in a Special Class; 1926, *28*, 699-702
Mulholland, Ann M.; The Columbia University Institute in Language; 1965, *67*, 623-626
Murphy, Margaret; A Third Grade Lesson in Questions; 1934, *36*, 526-528
New, Mary C.; The Deaf Child's Speech Vocabulary; 1954 *56*, 105-108
Numbers, Mary E.; Language in the Middle Grades; 1946, *48*, 677-679
Numbers, Mary E.; A Word Is a Word Is a Word; 1954, *56*, 66-71
Orr, Marie P.; An Exercise in Connected Language; 1927, *29*, 102-103
Orr, Marie P.; Incentives to Better English; 1934, *36*, 592; 630
Pauls, Miriam D.; Language Development Through Reading; 1958, *60*, 105-107; 142
Peterson, Edwin G.; Itinerant Teachers of Language; 1934, *36*, 197-198; 243
Pintner, Rudolf; The Measurement of Language Ability and Language Progress of Deaf Children; 1918, *20*, 755-766
Pittinger, Priscilla; The Development of Language; 1958, *60*, 12-20
Pittinger, Priscilla; Preparation for the Teaching of Vocabulary; 1954, *56*, 71-74
Pittinger, Priscilla; What Is a Basic Vocabulary; 1958, *60*, 528-529; 531
Pugh, Bessie; Teaching Children to Use the Dictionary; 1961, *63*, 178-185
Quinn, Josephine; First Year's Work; 1937, *39*, 284-285; 316
Quinn, Josephine; Fundamental Language; 1939, *41*, 104-105; 243
Quinn, Josephine; The Use of Symbols in Language Teaching; 1930, *32*, 611-612
Richards, Edith; A Device for First Year Language Work; 1941, *43*, 174; 218
Richardson, Paul C.; Developing Natural Time Expressions; 1962, *64*, 543-545
Richardson, Paul C.; Expressive Writing for the Deaf; 1956, *58*, 161-163
Roberts, M.; Some Special Phases of Language Work in Our Primary and Lower Intermediate Grades; 1928, *30*, 222-223
Robinson, Warren; Every-Day Language; 1906, *8*, 223, 227

Robinson, Warren; The Vocabulary of the Deaf; 1910, *12*, 553-560
Roe, W. Carey; Language and the Deaf Child; 1919, *21*, 49-52
Roe, W. Carey; Language Development; 1926, *28*, 419-421
Roe, W. Carey; Reading and Language Development; 1920, *22*, 80-84
Rose, Lillian; Duration of Time; 1933, *35*, 214-216
Rupley, Stella; Language Games as a Help in Teaching Language; 1931, *33*, 394-395
Scott, Elizabeth V.; Language and Reading; 1962, *64*, 128-132
Shellgrain, Evelyn M.; Realizing, Enriching, and Anticipating Vocabulary for Primary Deaf Classes; 1954, *56*, 62-65
Simmons, Audrey A.; A Comparison of the Type-Token Ratio of Spoken and Written Language of Deaf and Hearing Children; 1962, *64*, 417-421
Sister Anne Bernadine; Let's Increase Their Vocabulary; 1960, *62*, 218-219
Sister James Lorene; Developing Language through Vertical Learning and Horizontal Association; 1965, *67*, 201-207
Sister James Lorene; Pronouns Puzzle Primary Pupils; 1960, *62*, 17-19; 46
Sister Jeanne d'Arc; The Development of Connected Language Skills; 1958, *60*, 58-65
Sister M. Therese; Illustrated Verbs; 1964, *66*, 272-274
Sister Mary Walter; The Calendar Dynamic; 1958, *60*, 439; 464
Smith, Gladys E.; Drill and Non-Drill Verbs; 1936, *38*, 270-273
Smith, James L.; Teaching Idiomatic English to the Deaf; 1904, *6*, 18-34
Smith, James L.; Teaching Idiomatic Language; 1930, *32*, 578-579
Smith, Margaret C.; Developing "Have" and "Be" by the Barry Method; 1929, *31*, 309-312
Strauch, Genevieve B.; Some Phases of Composition; 1932, *34*, 613-617
Streeter, Helen M.; Language in the Primary Dormitory; 1945, *47*, 549-553; 596
Streng, Alice; Action Verbs and Their Meanings; 1956, *58*, 305-309
Streng, Alice; Language Disability in Children with Hearing Impairments; 1958, *60*, 350-357
Strickland, Ruth G.; The Interrelationship between Language and Reading; 1958, *60*, 334-336
Strong, Arch; Action Work in the Fourth Grade; 1930, *32*, 580-581
Stuckless, E. Ross, and Birch, Jack W.; A Programed Approach to Written Language Development in Deaf Children; 1962, *64*, 415-417
Swayze, Rachel H.; How We Can Improve the Language in the Primary Department of Our School; 1927, *29*, 356-358
Taussig, Eleanor; Language Development as a Factor in School Placement; 1959, *61*, 168-169; 193

LANGUAGE—continued

Volta Review

Templin, Mildred C.; Relation of Speech and Language Development to Intelligence and Socio-economic Status; 1958, *60*, 331-334

Tervoort, Bernard Th.; Acoustic and Visual Language Communicating Systems; 1958, *60*, 374-380

Thompson, Etta M.; The Use of Diaries in Language Work; 1926, *28*, 205-206

Thornton, E.; Classification and Analysis of Language Errors; 1928, *30*, 224-226

Tiberio, C. S.; Teaching Vocabulary in the School Shop; 1954, *56*, 75-77

Upham, Louise; Language Lessons for Second Year Classes; 1926, *28*, 193-195

Van Nest, Mary R.; A Language Project (personal description); 1936, *38*, 509; 544-545

Vinson, Marietta R.; English for the Deaf; 1939, *41*, 271-273

Walker, Jane B.; Winged Words; 1918, *20*, 631-633

Ward, R. H.; Drill Exercises in Punctuation; 1931, *33*, 388-389

Watrous, Helen D.; Primary Language and Reading; 1932, *34*, 215-216

Weaver, James A.; Teaching Language in a School for the Deaf; 1941, *43*, 169-171; 210; 246-248; 280-282

Welsh, Eugenia T.; Teaching Practical Language; 1926, *28*, 247-249

Wetherill, Stella J.; Intermediate Language; 1927, *29*, 250-253

Wetherill, Stella J.; Technical Language in an Intermediate Class; 1923, *25*, 5-6

Whildin, Olive A.; Language for the Young Deaf Child in the School, in the Home; 1940, *42*, 641-648

Willoughby, J. Evelyn; Suggestions for Action Work; 1925, *27*, 273-276; 1926, *28*, 145-147

Winston, Matie E.; Classification of Words; 1928, *30*, 274-276

Withrow, Frank B.; Paired-Associate Learning of Moving Sequences by Deaf Children; 1964, *66*, 555-557

Withrow, Margaret S.; Reinforcing Speech and Language in the Family; 1962, *64*, 422-424

Wood, Nancy; Language in Personality Development; 1960, *62*, 321-322

Woodward, Helen; Language and the Elementary School Curriculum; 1959, *61*, 63-65; 89

Worcester, Eleanor B.; Simple Language for Young Children; 1917, *19*, 673-679

Annals of the Deaf

———; The Acquisition of Language; 1910, *55*, 486-493

Adams, Ida H.; Primary Conversation Lessons; 1893, *38*, 112-118

Adams, Mabel E.; The Language Sense; 1896, *41*, 278-292

Adams, Mabel E.; Natural Language Plus Drill; 1897, *42*, 160-179; 210-223

Adams, Mabel E.; Three Years of Language; 1904, *49*, 209-229; 301-318

Adams, Mabel E.; A Way of Imparting Notions of Tense to Young Deaf Children; 1909, *54*, 160-166

Archer, Tunis V.; The Natural Method of Teaching Language; 1893, *38*, 254-256

Ashley, J. B.; Language for the Deaf; 1890, *35*, 250-255

Avery, Elizabeth B.; The Habitual Present; 1944, *89*, 147-159

Baldrian, Karl; Differences in the Natural and Artificial Acquisition of Language; 1908, *53*, 7-15

Barnard, F. A.; The Difficulties of the Deaf and Dumb in the Acquisition of Language; 1870, *15*, 161-165

Barnes, F. G.; The Elementary Language Lesson; 1918, *63*, 446-450

Barnes, F. G.; The First Steps in Original Composition; 1917, *62*, 145-150

Bartlett, D. E.; The Acquisition of Language; 1851, *3*, 83-92

Bell, Alexander G.; Upon a Method of Teaching Language to a Very Young Congenitally Deaf Child; 1883, *28*, 124, 139

Birch, Jack W., and Stuckless, E. Ross; Programming Instruction in Written Language for Deaf Children; 1963, *108*, 317-336

Booth, Frank W.; The Lesson to be Learned by the General Teacher From Teaching Language to the Deaf; 1902, *47*, 323-330

Brandon, Wallace R.; Foreign Language Study and the Deaf Student's Vocabulary; 1957, *102*, 312-318

Buell, Edith M.; Word Pictures as a Means of Mental Development; 1912, *57*, 512-518

Burnet, John R.; Is It Easier for Deaf-Mutes to Spell Words Mentally, or to Regard Them as Units?; 1859, *11*, 17-32

Burnet, John R., and Porter, Samuel; Under What Forms Do Deaf-Mutes Apprehend Words?; 1858, *10*, 228-241

Caldwell, William A.; Expedients for Teaching Language; 1886, *31*, 169-180

Coburn, Alice T.; Language in the Primary Grades; 1908, *53*, 466-473

Cox, Mary R.; The Use of Language (How It May Be Improved); 1920, *65*, 301-311

Craig, William N., et al.; Comparison of Two Methods of Teaching Written Language to Deaf Students; 1964, *109*, 248-256

Croker, Gertrude W.; Intermediate Language Work; 1923, *68*, 384-392

LANGUAGE—continued

Annals of the Deaf

Crosby, Laura L.; Suggestions for Composition Work in Advanced Classes; 1942, *87*, 123-130

Crouter, Alan Y.; "A" and "The"; 1938, *83*, 323-329

Crouter, Alan Y.; The Infinitive of Purpose; 1936, *81*, 204-208

Davidson, Samuel G.; Mental Development Through Language Study; 1914, *59*, 113-117

Davidson, Samuel G.; The Principles of Language Teaching; 1911, *56*, 422-430

Davidson, Samuel G.; Some Observations on Language Methods; 1917, *62*, 308-320

Day, Herbert E.; Bridging Our Educational Gap by Broader Use of English; 1929, *74*, 288-291

Day, Herbert E.; Outline of Language for Deaf Children; 1930, *75*, 291-292

DeMotte, Amelia; Language; 1922, *67*, 386-392

Dietrich, Rose I.; Goals in Language Development for the Deaf and the Hard of Hearing; 1945, *90*, 121-127

Dodds, P.; The Natural Development of Language: Its Effect on Oral Teaching; 1891, *36*, 178-181

Dodds, P.; The Teaching of Language During the First, Second, and Third Year of a Deaf Child's School Life; 1900, *45*, 275-296

Fay, Edward A.; The Acquisition of Language by Deaf-Mutes; 1869, *14*, 193-204

Fitzgerald, Edith; Language Building in the Primary Grades; 1918, *63*, 342-353

Fitzgerald, Margaret H.; Vocabulary Development for Acoustically Handicapped Children; 1949, *94*, 409-449

Fletcher, Katharine; Concerning Aim and Method in Language Teaching; 1896, *41*, 1-12

Fonner, Mary D.; Primary Language; 1908, *53*, 473-478

Fox, Thomas F.; The Use of the Dictionary in Teaching Language; 1888, *33*, 259-262

Fusfeld, Irving S.; How the Deaf Communicate—Written Language; 1958, *103*, 255-263

Gale, Edward P.; More English As It Is Spoken; 1915, *60*, 329-333

Giangreco, Joseph; Developing Language Through A Daily News Period; 1954, *99*, 380-390

Gillespie, John A.; The Presentation of Language; 1892, *37*, 245-249

Gillet, H. S.; Language; 1870, *15*, 232-244

Göpfert, E.; The Place of Writing in the Language Instruction of the True Deaf Mutes, Especially the Less Intelligent; 1899, *44*, 92-110

Greenberger, D.; Language-Teaching; 1892, *37*, 267-279

Groff, Marné L.; An Analysis of First-Year Vocabularies of the Public Residential Schools for the Deaf in the U.S.; 1932, *77*, 304-314; 1933, *78*, 120-131; 219-228; 418-427; 1934, *79*, 147-160

Groff, Marné L.; The Psychology of Language with Special Reference to the Deaf; 1936, *81*, 113-125

Hall, Percival; A Method of Teaching the English Language to the Congenitally Deaf; 1893, *38*, 249-253

Henderson, Myrtle W.; Intermediate Language; 1925, *70*, 311-319

Hodgson, E. A.; The Division of Words into Syllables; 1882, *27*, 142-146

Howson, James W.; Teaching Language to the Deaf; 1914, *59*, 214-223

Hull, Susanna E.; The Psychological Method of Teaching Language; 1898, *43*, 190-196

Humason, Thomas A.; Words and Language; 1894, *39*, 249-258

Hurd, Anna C.; Asked, Said, Told; 1892, *37*, 94-103

Hurd, Anna C.; An Outline of Primary Language Work; 1895, *40*, 97-121; 187-206; 274-285

Hurd, Anna C.; Primary Language; 1906, *51*, 312-314

Hurst, Fannie D.; Composition—A Live Issue; 1933, *78*, 229-248

Hurst, Fannie D.; Drill Type-Errors Out by Drilling Smooth Phrasing In; 1928, *73*, 221-230

Hurst, Fannie D.; Some Methods of Teaching Grammar; 1928, *73*, 344-355; 442-458

Hurst, Fannie D.; Some Work in Grammar; 1930, *75*, 104-115

Hurst, Fannie D.; Vocabulary Building; 1938, *83*, 209-217

Ingle, Helen F.; Outline for Pronoun Work; 1927, *72*, 427-432

Ingvarsson, Ivar M.; Language Teaching in Schools for the Deaf: Psychological Aspects; 1952, *97*, 267-280

Irion, Theo. W.; The Place of Language in Mental Development; 1941, *86*, 364-373

Jenkins, Weston; The Teaching of English; 1901, *46*, 488-492

Jenkins, William G.; Language and Thought; 1895, *40*, 1-14

Jenkins, William G.; Teaching the Relative Pronouns; 1888, *33*, 229-234

Jones, John W.; The Development of Language in the Deaf Child; 1910, *55*, 353-363

Jones, John W.; Language for Advanced Grades of Deaf Pupils; 1920, *65*, 378-394

Keep, J. R.; How Should Deaf-Mute Children Learn Verbal Language?; 1870, *15*, 28-41

Kelly, Emma; The Difficulties of Language Teaching; 1916, *61*, 124-127

Kent, Margaret S.; Language for Young Deaf Children; 1960, *105*, 435-436

—————; Language Outline (C.I.D.); 1950, *95*, 353-378

LANGUAGE—continued

Annals of the Deaf

Lauritsen, Wesley; Language Teaching—The Greatest Thing; 1943, *88*, 296-299

Letzter, Margaret C.; Enriching the Vocabulary; 1935, *80*, 264-271

Lloyd, Glenn T.; Teaching Language to the Individual Deaf Child; 1964, *109*, 359-363

Long, J. Schuyler; The Story in Language Teaching; 1902, *47*, 331-339

McClure, George M.; The Correction of Errors in Language Work; 1901, *46*, 21-23

Marbut, Musa; A Fundamental Vocabulary Suggested for Deaf Children for the First Five Years in School; 1941, *86*, 137-158

Meyer, Max F.; Can Teaching the Deaf Profit From Philology?; 1934, *79*, 95-108

Moffat, L.; Voice, Alphabetics, and Language; 1885, *30*, 111-121; 251-258; 1886, *31*, 111-119; 180-191

Morris, Minnie E.; The Correction and Prevention of Mistakes in Language; 1901, *46*, 242-249

Mosely, T. F.; Learn Idioms by Using Them; 1890, *35*, 14-19

Mossel, Max N.; Words, Words Everywhere But—; 1943, *88*, 258-269

Nelson, Myrthel S.; The Evolutionary Process of Methods of Teaching Language to Deaf with a Survey of the Methods Now Employed; 1949, *94*, 230-294; 354-396; 491-511

Orman, James N.; The Language Sense; 1930, *75*, 124-131

Orman, James N.; A Verb-Type Method of Language Instruction; 1938, *83*, 330-337

Paddleford, Lillian; Punctuation as a Means, Not an End; 1926, *71*, 208-213

Patton, Livingston; Question Forms; 1960, *105*, 240-248

Peet, Elizabeth; More and Better English; 1925, *70*, 328-338

Peet, Elizabeth; Straight Language for the Deaf; 1926, *71*, 348-351

Perry, Charles S.; The Acquisition of Language; 1877, *22*, 72-73

Peterson, Peter N.; A Plea for More Technical Language in the Classroom; 1902, *47*, 23-30

Pettengill, B. D.; The Acquisition of Written Language by Deaf-Mutes; 1874, *19*, 230-237

Pettengill, B. D.; Methods of Teaching Language; 1882, *27*, 203, 208

Pettengill, B. D.; The Natural Method of Teaching Language; 1876, *21*, 1-10

Pettingell, J. H.; Language: Its Nature and Functions; 1875, *20*, 1-26

Pintner, Rudolf, and Paterson, Donald; A Measurement of the Language Ability of Deaf Children; 1917, *62*, 211-239

Pollard, Nannie A.; An Outline of First-Year Language Work at the Minnesota School; 1926, *71*, 399-407

Porter, Samuel; The Instruction of the Deaf and Dumb in Grammar; 1869, *14*, 30-48
Porter, Samuel; A Method of Teaching Complex and Compound Sentences; 1877, *22*, 232-233
Porter, Sarah H.; Language; 1892, *37*, 219-227
Putnam, George H.; Lessons in Language; 1900, *45*, 7-16
Quinn, Josephine; First Year's Language Work; 1946, *91*, 177-189
Rawlings, Charles G.; Review of "Logical System of Language-Teaching and an Analysis of the English Language"; 1938, *83*, 6-7
Reay, Edward W.; A Comparison Between Deaf and Hearing Children in Regard to the Use of Verbs and Nouns in Compositions Describing a Short Motion Picture Story; 1946, *91*, 453-491
Reed, Katherine F.; Language Through the Grades; 1904, *49*, 252-260
Reed, Katherine F.; Material for Language Work; 1910, *55*, 172-177
Robinson, Mary W.; Outline of Composition Work in the Intermediate Grades of the California School; 1939, *84*, 445-448
Robinson, Warren; The Bracket Device for Teaching Language; 1913, *58*, 249-271
Robinson, Warren; A New Device in Language Teaching; 1898, *43*, 78-87; 170-183
Rose, M. Lillian; Tell-Ask-Say; 1927, *72*, 415-426
Rush, Mary Lou; Programmed Instruction for "The Language of Direction"; 1964, *109*, 356-358
Scott, Wirt A.; Language Teaching in Connection With Other Studies; 1900, *45*, 265-271
Scouten, Edward L.; Meeting the Problem of Literalness in Deaf Students (College Prep Classes); 1960, *105*, 425-426
Sensenig, Barton; A Thousand Words Our Deaf Pupils Should Know When They Leave School; 1928, *73*, 216-221
Sheridan, Laura C.; Teaching the Article and Related Things; 1917, *62*, 440-447
Shiflet, Cleta; Drill Verbs; 1928, *73*, 251-253
Sister Mary Walter; The Fitzgerald Key on Wheels; 1959, *104*, 366-371
Stewart, Helen L.; A Vocabulary Project; 1945, *90*, 154-163
Stewart, W. J.; Language Teaching; 1919, *64*, 191-196
Stewart, W. J.; Lessons in English; 1929, *74*, 486-496; 1930, *75*, 115-124; 222-231; 375-389; 1932, *77*, 335-342; 1937, *82*, 272-279
Story, Arthur J.; Why the Deaf Do Not Use Language; 1907, *52*, 183-201
Streeter, Helen M.; A Study of the Dependent Clause in Primary Reading of the Deaf; 1956, *101*, 288-297
Streng, Alice; On Improving the Teaching of Language; 1958, *103*, 553-563

LANGUAGE—*continued*

Annals of the Deaf

Struck, A. N.; The Deaf and the Dictionary; 1915, *60*, 233-238

————; A Study of the Proceedings of the Convention of American Instructors of the Deaf, 1850-1949: Language; 1950, *95*, 501-518

Taylor, Harris; Certain Accepted Elements of a Course of Study: The Five-Slate System of Language Teaching; 1916, *61*, 393-404

Taylor, Nellie M.; How I Interested My Class in Calendar Work; 1918, *63*, 475-478

Tervoort, Bernard T.; Esoteric Symbolism in the Communication Behavior of Young Deaf Children; 1961, *106*, 436-480

Thollon, B.; Classification of the Determinatives of the Noun; 1921, *66*, 261-265

Thollon, B.; The Meaning of Words and Their Value; 1918, *63*, 435-440

Thomas, Elizabeth S.; A System of Sentence Structure for the Development of Language for the Deaf; 1958, *103*, 510-523

Thompson, William H.; An Analysis of Errors in Written Composition by Deaf Children; 1936, *81*, 95-99

Tillinghast, Edward S.; Memory Training and the Teaching of Language; 1900, *45*, 184-193

Tillinghast, Edward S.; Notes on Language Teaching; 1902, *47*, 137-143; 1903, *48*, 33-44

Tomb, John W.; On the Intuitive Capacity of Children to Understand Spoken Language; 1926, *71*, 270-273

Voelker, Charles H.; The Vocabulary to Teach Deaf Children; 1942, *87*, 266-273

Walker, H. D.; Idioms; 1889, *34*, 21-29

Walker, H. D.; Sentence Forms and Analysis as Set Forth by Symbols and Diagrams; 1887, *32*, 217-224

Walter, Jean; Some Further Observations on the Written Sentence Construction of Profoundly Deaf Children; 1959, *104*, 282-285

Walter, Jean; A Study of the Written Sentence Construction of a Group of Profoundly Deaf Children; 1955, *100*, 235-252

Weaver, James A.; Simplifying the Simple; 1921, *66*, 147-164

Weaver, James A.; Some Remarks on the Teaching of Language; 1918, *63*, 407-415

Whittlesey, Addie; News; 1928, *73*, 257-262

Wing, George; The Acquisition of Language by Deaf-Mutes; 1895, *40*, 231-235

Wing, George; The Theory and Practice of Grammatical Methods; 1887, *32*, 84-92

Yelton, D. C.; Language and the Deaf; 1938, *83*, 114-119

MANUAL COMMUNICATION

Volta Review

Hanson, Olof; The Sign-Language in American Schools; 1901, *3*, 223-226; 1902, *4*, 129-131; 1903, *5*, 195-196; 1904, *6*, 150-151; 1905, *7*, 327-328; 1906, *8*, 162-163; 1907, *9*, 384; 1908, *10*, 282
Sutermeister, Eugene; Is the Sign-Language a Necessity Called Forth by Nature and Circumstances?; 1908, *10*, 365-380
Williams, Mary E.; The Betterment of a Speech Environment in a Combined-System School; 1915, *17*, 182-184
Wright, John D.; The "Combined System" Diagnoses Its Own Case With Remarkable Truth and Frankness; 1914, *16*, 699-701

Annals of the Deaf

Abernathy, Edward B.; An Historical Sketch of the Manual Alphabets; 1959, *104*, 232-239
Adler, Edna P.; Reading Out Loud in the Language of Signs; 1964, *109*, 364-366
Anderson, Tom L.; What of the Sign Language?; 1938, *83*, 120-130
Coats, G. Dewey; Manual English; 1948, *93*, 174-177
Cochrane, W. A.; Methodical Signs Instead of Colloquial; 1871, *16*, 11-17
DeHearne, D.; The Natural Language of Signs; 1875, *20*, 73-86; 137-153; 216-277; 1876, *21*, 11-16
Draper, Amos G.; How to Teach and Use the Manual Alphabet; 1897, *42*, 370-371
Dudley, D. C.; Signs in Oral Schools; 1894, *39*, 37-40
Fant, Louie, and Roy, Howard; Programmed Lessons for the Language of Signs; 1961, *106*, 484-486
Fay, O. Gilbert; The Sign-Language the Basis of Instruction for Deaf-Mutes; 1882, *27*, 208-211
Fitzgerald, Edith; Manual Spelling and English; 1912, *57*, 197-203
Fusfeld, Irving S.; How the Deaf Communicate—Manual Language; 1958, *103*, 264-282
Gallaudet, Edward M.; Is the Sign-Language Used to Excess in Teaching Deaf-Mutes?; 1871, *16*, 26-33
Gallaudet, Edward M.; Must the Sign-Language Go?; 1899, *44*, 221-229
Gallaudet, Edward M.; The Value of the Sign-Language to the Deaf; 1887, *32*, 141-147
George, D. W.; Signs and Finger Spelling; 1890, *35*, 115-117
Haskins, C. N.; The Sufficiency or Insufficiency of Signs—Which?; 1890, *35*, 27-30
Hollister, H. H.; The Manual Alphabet; 1870, *15*, 88-93
Hutton, George; The Practicability and Advantage of Writing and Printing Natural Signs; 1869, *14*, 157-182

MANUAL COMMUNICATION—*continued*

Annals of the Deaf

Jacobs, J. A.; The Relation of Written Words to Signs, the Same as Their Relation to Spoken Words; 1859, *11*, 65-78

Jenkins, Weston; The Sign Language: What Is It?; 1911, *56*, 461-468

Keep, John R., and Hubbard, Gardiner G.; The Language of Signs; 1869, *14*, 89-95

Keep, John R.; Natural Signs—Shall They Be Abandoned?; 1871, *16*, 17-25

Keep, John R.; The Sign Language; 1871, *16*, 221-234

Long, J. Schuyler; The Sign Language: A Manual of Signs; 1908, *53*, 230-249; 438-448; 1909, *54*, 23-37; 140-160; 263-281; 339-347; 420-438; 1910, *55*, 142-155

Peet, Harvey P.; Words Not "Representatives" of Signs, But of Ideas; 1859, *11*, 1-8

Peet, Isaac L.; Initial Signs; 1861, *13*, 171-184

Pettengill, B. D.; The Instruction of the Deaf and Dumb; 1872, *17*, 21-33

Pettengill, B. D.; The Sign Language; 1873, *18*, 1-2

Rowe, Frederick, et al.; Communication Through Gestures; 1960, *105*, 232-237

Scouten, Edward L.; Helping Your Child to Master English Through Finger-Spelling; 1960, *105*, 226-229

Smith, James L.; The Abuse of the Sign-Language; 1902, *47*, 157-182

Steppuhn; Our Present Attitude with Respect to the Sign Language; 1911, *56*, 127-142

Thomas, Margaret L.; An Appeal for Manual Spelling in Manual Classes; 1926, *71*, 213-218

Tilden, Douglas; Signs and Words; 1887, *32*, 176-179

Tylor, Edward B.; The Gesture-Language; 1878, *23*, 162-178; 251-260; 1879, *24*, 39-45

White, Harry; The Influence of Signs Upon the Study of Language; 1884, *29*, 174-178

White, Henry C.; Spelling Versus Signs; 1890, *35*, 111-114

Wilkinson, Warring; The Development of Speech and of the Sign Language; 1881, *26*, 167-178

MISCELLANEOUS

Volta Review

Barnes, F. G.; Seaside School and Camp for the Deaf; 1915, *17*, 229-235
Dombro, Robert H.; Meeting Recreational and Social Needs; 1960, *62*, 328-331
Herrick, Helen; The Need and Actual Functioning of Organized Activities Outside the Classroom; 1932, *34*, 492-496
Lane, Helen S.; Extracurricular Activities for Deaf Children; 1960, *62*, 169-173
Olanoff, Rose S.; Our House, an Activity Program; 1932, *34*, 618-622
Rotter, Paul; Camping for Deaf Children; 1959, *61*, 209-211; 227
——————; Scouting and the Deaf Boy; 1953, *55*, 343-348
Swain, N. G.; Teaching Red Cross First Aid to Deaf Students; 1955, *57*, 265-267

Annals of the Deaf

Ulmer, Thomas A.; Scouting in the Schools for the Deaf; 1947, *92*, 187-214

MULTIPLY HANDICAPPED

Volta Review

Anderson, Robert M.; Hearing Impairment and Mental Retardation: A Selected Bibliography; 1965, *67*, 425-432
Bangs, Jack L.; Preschool Language Education for the Brain-Damaged Child; 1957, *59*, 17-19; 39
Booth, Frank W.; Feeble-Minded and Backward Children; 1900, *2*, 197-202
Breckinridge, Mary S.; James: An Unusual Pupil; 1903, *5*, 228-230
Clark, Alice E.; Deaf Children With Multiple Handicaps; 1946, *48*, 393-395; 428-430
Costello, Patrice; Where Does Mike Belong?; 1960, *62*, 66-67; 91
DuBard, Etoile; A "Deaf" Child Who Did Not Learn; 1962, *64*, 589-592
Foley, Julia A.; Backward Children; 1900, *2*, 137-145; 231-237; 367-380
LaCrosse, Edward L., and Bidlake, Harry; A Method To Test the Hearing of Mentally Retarded Children; 1964, *66*, 27-30
Langdon, Marcia A.; The Multiply Handicapped in a Working World; 1964, *66*, 504-507

MULTIPLY HANDICAPPED—*continued*

Volta Review

Leshin, George J., and Stahlecker, Lotar V.; Academic Expectancies of Slow-Learning Deaf Children; 1962, *64*, 599-602

Monaghan, Alice; Educational Placement for the Multiply Handicapped Hearing Impaired Child; 1964, *66*, 383-387

Nelson, M., and Sibilio, J. P.; Audiologic Aspects of a Deaf-Retarded Population; 1962, *64*, 426-427

Pence, Helen W.; The Retarded Child—His Education; 1927, *29*, 190-192

Sellin, Donald F.; The Mentally Retarded, Hearing-Handicapped Learner: Implications for Teacher Education; 1964, *66*, 258-261

Shere, Marie O.; The Cerebral Palsied Child with a Hearing Loss; 1960, *62*, 438-441

Sister M. Pauline; The Multiply-Handicapped Deaf Child; 1960, *62*, 350-354

Sortini, Adam J.; Hearing Evaluation of Brain-Damaged Children; 1960, *62*, 536-540

Sortini, Adam; Rehabilitation of Brain-Damaged Children; 1961, *63*, 20-23; 42

Warren, Sue A., and Kraus, Matthew J., Jr.; Deaf Children, Mental Retardation and Academic Expectancies; 1963, *65*, 351-352; 383

Weir, Robert C.; Impact of the Multiple Handicapped Deaf on Special Education; 1963, *65*, 287-289; 325

Yale, Caroline A.; A Plea for the Instruction and After-School Care of the Feeble-Minded Deaf; 1917, *19*, 578-581

Annals of the Deaf

Cobb, Jennie L.; Teaching the Abnormal Deaf Child; 1914, *59*, 233-238

Doctor, Powrie V.; Multiple Handicaps in the Field of Rehabilitation; 1958, *103*, 409-413

Gruver, E. A.; The Subnormal Deaf; 1919, *64*, 298-305

LaRue, Mary S.; A Plan for Retarded Deaf Children; 1937, *82*, 445-449

MacPherson, James R.; The Status of the Deaf and/or Hard of Hearing Mentally Deficient in the United States; 1952, *97*, 375-386

Myklebust, Helmer R.; The Deaf Child with Other Handicaps; 1958, *103*, 496-509

Porter, Van C.; Cerebral-Palsied Deaf Pupil; 1957, *102*, 359-363

Vernon, McCay; The Brain Injured (Neurologically Impaired) Deaf Child: A Discussion of the Significance of the Problem, Its Symptoms and Causes in Deaf Children; 1961, *106*, 239-250

MUSIC, RHYTHM & ART

Volta Review

Berryman, Florence S.; Art as Compensation for the Deafened; 1927, *29*, 58-59
Birkenshaw, Lois; Teaching Music to Deaf Children; 1965, *67*, 352-358; 387
Brady, Wilma S.; The Development of Tone and Rhythm; 1926, *28*, 323-332
Cavanagh, Anita, and Winters, Loretta M.; We've Got Rhythm; 1949, *51*, 111; 146-148
Cornell, Louise E.; Rhythm in the Kindergarten and Junior Primary Departments; 1929, *31*, 782-784
Costello, Patrice; Music for the Deaf; 1964, *66*, 92-93
Doctor, Powrie V.; A Lesson Plan for Teaching Poetry in an Advanced Class; 1950, *52*, 205-208
Dyer, Helen L.; Harmonic Gymnastics; 1914, *16*, 5-12
Fagan, E.; Choral Speaking by Deaf Children; 1954, *56*, 17-18
Favors, A., and Krohn, E.; Amahl and the Night Visitors; 1961, *63*, 484-486; 509
Flanders, Gwendolyn A.; Rhythm for Deaf Children of Ungraded Schools; 1928, *30*, 477-481
Garbett, Arthur S.; Music for the Hard of Hearing; 1943, *45*, 571-575; 598-600
Garbett, Arthur S.; Music and Our Hearing Aids; 1944, *46*, 639-643; 662; 702-705; 732; 1945, *47*, 27-30; 50-52
Geddes, Kathleen R.; Music for the Hard of Hearing; 1920, *22*, 73-74
Hammer, Helen; A Project in Rhythm; 1928, *30*, 30-32
Henderson, Jennie M.; The Awakening of Latent Hearing by Means of Musical Tones and Vibrations; 1930, *32*, 185-187; 197-202
Jayne, Gladys G.; Rhythm—Our Kindergarten Bands; 1931, *33*, 387-388
Jordan, Sarah A.; Rhythm as an Aid to Voice Training; 1900, *2*, 16-19
Kawakami, Marcia; We Can Still Hear Music; 1937, *39*, 584-585
Kent, Margaret S.; Primary and Intermediate Rhythm; 1929, *31*, 512-513
Ketcham, Margaret B.; Rhythm; 1931, *33*, 80-82
Kharasch, Ethel N.; Fun for the Deaf Child; 1965, *67*, 376-378
Knight, Augustus C.; Why Give Up Your Music?; 1924, *26*, 297-299
McAlister, Grace W.; Rhythm and Personality Growth; 1938, *40*, 212-214
McCowen, Mary; Dramatization as a Factor in Education; 1904, *6*, 109-115
McKinney, Lettie W.; Music Appreciation; 1930, *32*, 189-190
Markell, Alan; Teaching Deaf Children to Dance; 1961, *63*, 176-177
May, Elizabeth; Music for Deaf Children; 1961, *63*, 220-223; 247
————; A Military School for the Deaf, and Its Band of Deaf Musicians; 1911, *13*, 201-207

MUSIC, RHYTHM & ART—*continued*

Volta Review

Miller, Bertha; Poetry in the Lives of the Deaf; 1950, *52*, 493; 532-534
Monro, Sarah J.; A Plea for the Use of the Piano in Speech and Voice Work; 1918, *20*, 93
Monro, Sarah J.; The Priceless Value of Rhythm to Deaf Children; 1915, *17*, 437-439
Monro, Sarah J.; A Résumé of the Rhythmic Work in the Horace Mann School, Boston; 1915, *17*, 133-138
Monro, Sarah J.; Rhythm; 1918, *20*, 781-783
Monro, Sarah J.; Rhythmic Exercises; 1916, *18*, 233-237
Monro, Sarah J.; Rhythmic Movements of the Body; 1917, *19*, 532-534
New, Mary C.; Rhythm-Work in the Alabama School for the Deaf; 1921, *23*, 148-149
Nielsen, Dorothy V.; Gay, Profitable Rhythm Classes; 1948, *50*, 17-18
Radcliffe, Edith; Advanced Rhythm; 1929, *31*, 514-515
————; Percussion Orchestra for Deaf Children; 1926, *28*, 93-94
————; Rhythm; 1925, *27*, 47-49
Richardson, Beatrice E.; Teaching Rhythm Visually; 1934, *36*, 405-407; 443
Sandberg, Irene L.; Rhythm; 1926, *28*, 310-323
Sandberg, Mabel W.; Rhythms and Music for the Deaf and Hard of Hearing; 1954, *56*, 255-256
Silver, Rawley; Art for the Deaf Child—Its Potentialities; 1963, *65*, 408-413; 417
Smith, Meredith J.; Songs for the Primary Grades; 1956, *58*, 253-255
Stevens, Kelly H.; Finger Painting for Little Deaf Children; 1946, *48*, 445-447; 484-486
Sunstrom, Florence; Our Rhythm Band; 1931, *33*, 488-489
Uden, A. v.; An Electrical Wind-Instrument for Severely or Totally Deaf Children; 1953, *55*, 241-242
Uden, A. v.; Music and Dancing for the Deaf; 1949, *51*, 386-388
Unholtz, Louise, and Negley, Katherine; Our Children's Heritage; 1953, *55*, 131; 170-172
Van Nest, Mary R.; Eurythmics; 1937, *39*, 337, 373
Wojan, Kathleen; Eurythmics; 1955, *57*, 253-254

Annals of the Deaf

Beattie, Mary B.; Drawing and Painting As Aids to Expression and Development of the Child; 1912, *57*, 167-177
Carter, Maud; Rhythm Outline; 1931, *76*, 397-402
Clarke, Francis D.; Mechanical Drawing for the Deaf; 1887, *32*, 1-6

Fiske, Stella A.; The Place That Hand Training Plays in the Education of the Deaf; 1922, *67*, 175-182
Fuller, Millicent B.; Rhythm; 1917, *62*, 257-261
Gay, Ruth C.; Some Values of the Rhythm Orchestra in Schools for the Deaf; 1940, *85*, 351-354
Jayne, Gladys G.; Rhythm and Its Relation to the Training of the Deaf; 1939, *84*, 137-150
Lampard, Marie T.; The Art Work of Deaf Children; 1960, *105*, 419-423
Ludlow, Fitz H.; The Music Essence; 1872, *17*, 94-126
Mills, Mary M.; Voice and Rhythm in the Primary Grades of the New Jersey School for the Deaf; 1942, *87*, 311-341
Monro, Sarah A.; The Piano as an Aid to Speech; 1901, *46*, 166-169
Pintner, Rudolf; Artistic Appreciation Among Deaf Children; 1941, *86*, 218-224
Porter, Sarah H.; Musical Vibrations for the Deaf; 1912, *57*, 137-158
Rosenstein, Joseph; Tactile Perception of Rhythmic Patterns by Normal, Blind, Deaf, and Aphasic Children; 1957, *102*, 399-403
Stevenson, Elwood A.; Musical Rhythm; 1919, *64*, 196-204
Thornton, Marjorie; An Outline of Rhythm Work and Its Application to Schoolroom Work; 1926, *71*, 361-386
Turner, W. W., and Bartlett, D. E.; Music Among the Deaf; 1849, *2*, 1-6
Wecker, Karl; Music for Deaf Children; 1939, *84*, 151-155

PARENTS

Volta Review

Anderson, Mrs. J. Scott; What Home Training Is to the Deaf Baby; 1910, *12*, 436-442
Anderson, William A.; That the Deaf May Speak; 1962, *64*, 456-458
Andrews, Harriet U.; The Diary of a Deaf Child's Mother; 1918, *20*, 614-619; 687-691; 739-743; 1919, *21*, 54-59; 78-82; 184-187; 1921, *23*, 112-137
Andrews, Harriet U.; A Deaf Boy Who Is Being Rightly Trained; 1915, *17*, 165-171
Andrews, Harriet U.; Home Training for Deaf Children; 1917, *19*, 145-174
Avery, Charlotte B.; A Suggested Reading List for Parents; 1948, *50*, 355-356; 376-378

PARENTS—continued

Volta Review

Bartlett, Bertha L.; How a Mother Taught Herself to Train Her Deaf Child; 1918, *20*, 609-614; 671-674; 733-738; 1919, *21*, 41-48; 1921, *23*, 193-210

Bell, Alexander G.; Suggestions Concerning the Formation of a Local Association of Parents of Deaf Children; 1914, *16*, 750-751

Bickler, Mary H.; How a Deaf Child Was Taught Speech-Reading and Speech; 1917, *19*, 305-313; 373-379; 426-431; 497-500; 605-610

Breunig, H. Latham; Parents and the Specialists; 1958, *60*, 372-373

Cayley, Stephanie; A Mother to Other Mothers; 1915, *17*, 341-344

Cole, Robert H., et al.; The Parents Speak in Open Forum; 1956, *58*, 351-361

Crum, Carole; The Normality of Deaf Children; 1961, *63*, 231-232; 249

Curry, Lorre; Home-School Relationships; 1954, *56*, 24-27

English, Sandra; What Parents Can Do About It: An Open Letter to Mothers of Hard of Hearing Children; 1938, *40*, 351-352; 374

Evans, Mildred; Self-Help for Your Deaf Child in Vacation Days; 1932, *34*, 342-351; 375-376

Evans, Mildred; What You Can Teach Your Deaf Child at Home This Summer; 1932, *34*, 293-299

Fay, Helen; How the Parents Can Help; 1922, *24*, 246-249

Fellendorf, George W.; Factors Affecting Parents' Decisions; 1960, *62*, 341-345

Fellendorf, Mr. and Mrs. George W.; What Parents Can Do For Their Deaf Child; 1957, *59*, 149-156

Field, Lois G.; Johnny Is a "Window of the Home"; 1964, *66*, 508-510

Fuller, Sarah; Home Training in the Development of Speech; 1912, *14*, 701-709

Funk, Stanton C.; The Parents' Role in Educational Planning; 1964, *66*, 517-520

Giangreco, C. Joseph; Parent Counseling—A Must; 1960, *62*, 543-545

Goda, Sidney; Parents as Teachers: How to Help Your School-age Hard of Hearing Child Communicate Better; 1941, *53*, 350-352; 382

Gusow, F.; The Family as Co-Worker in the Education of Deaf Children; 1900, *2*, 242-247

Hall, Grace D.; A Teacher of Deaf Children Speaks to Parents of Deaf Children; 1939, *41*, 495-498; 533-534

Haney, Mary R.; Teach Your Child the Language of Games; 1959, *61*, 212-213

Hansen, M. R.; A Letter to My Daughter; 1956, *58*, 69-72

Harman, Augusta; Helpful Suggestions for Mothers of Deaf Children; 1917, *19*, 650-653

Harris, Grace M.; For Parents of Very Young Deaf Children; 1964, *66*, 19-26; 70-77

Harris, Norma; A Pilot Study of Parental Attitudes; 1960, *62*, 355-361
———; Helpful Suggestions to Parents of Deaf Children; 1914, *16*, 777-779
Henderson, Myrtle L.; Problems of the Mother of the Young Deaf Child; 1918, *20*, 619-624; 777-781; 1919, *21*, 20-23; 133-140; 365-378; 417-422; 496-501
Hooper, Mrs. J. C.; A Mother Teaches Her Deaf Child; 1929, *31*, 345-346
Jacoby, Beatrice; The Relationship of the Speech and Hearing Center to the Parent of the Deaf Child; 1958, *60*, 373-374
Jelks, Mrs. F. W.; Teach Your Deaf Baby to Talk; 1914, *16*, 773-775
Johnson, Jeanette N.; Association Services; 1962, *64*, 458-460
Klienfeld, L.; What Are the Chances of Having Another Deaf Child?; 1952, *54*, 107; 136-137
Lane, Helen S.; Parent-Teacher Cooperation in the Communication of the Deaf Child; 1963, *65*, 595-598
Lane, Helen S.; Two Years of Progress; 1962, *64*, 446-448
Lassman, Grace, and Montague, Harriet; The Deaf Baby; 1949, *51*, 325-328; 372-374
Lehmann, Mrs. Floyd, and Buchan, Mrs. John; How the Teacher of a Deaf Child Can Help the Parents; 1959, *61*, 283; 289
Levine, Edna S.; Psychological Sidelights; 1947, *49*, 123-124; 154-156; 175-176; 200; 219; 246-248
MacAuley, Dorothy; What I Wish My Doctor Had Told Me; 1956, *58*, 310-311; 316
McClellan, Grace A.; A Talk with Parents of Deaf Children; 1933, *35*, 299-300; 316
Mannen, Grace; Enriching the Language of the Older Deaf Child: The Parent's Part; 1961, *63*, 224-227
Miller, June; Institute for Parents and Their Deaf Children; 1964, *66*, 185-197
Moore, Mrs. Sidney M.; Suggestions to Mothers of Little Deaf Children; 1912, *14*, 1-6
———; A Mother of Two: Training Deaf Children; 1918, *20*, 85-87
Nicholas, Georgia C.; Sincerely Yours, a Housemother; 1950, *52*, 494-495
Northcott, Winifred N.; To and for Parents; 1962, *64*, 603-605
O'Connor, Clarence D.; Sources of Help for Parents; 1950, *52*, 397-398; 438
O'Donnell, Elizabeth K.; Parent Co-operation; 1932, *34*, 152-153
Ostern, Beatrice; Home Help with Reading; 1960, *62*, 494-496
———; The Over-Specialization of Parents; 1914, *16*, 711-716
Pagenstecher, Adelyn; What Parents Can Do; 1958, *60*, 201-202
Pollack, Doreen C., and Downs, Marion P.; A Parent's Guide to Hearing Aids for Young Children; 1964, *66*, 745-749

PARENTS—*continued*

Volta Review

Quick, Marian; Parents' Responsibility in Their Deaf Child's Social Adjustment; 1965, *67*, 152-154

Ralston, Patricia and Frances; A Mother and Her Deaf Daughter Compare Notes; 1964, *66*, 209-212

Reed, Katharine F.; How to Approach the Parents of the Deaf; 1917, *19*, 586-590

Reineke, Mary E.; You Are Blessed Among Mothers; 1963, *65*, 190-192

Reiss, Mrs. K.; The Deaf Child's Place in the Hearing Family; 1955, *57*, 148

Roberts, Emma; Helpful Suggestions for the Mother of a Deaf Child; 1915, *17*, 445-450

Rooney, Alice G.; Parent Education: Emphasis on the Preschool; 1946, *48*, 759-761; 802-803

Rooney, Alice G.; Parents Go to School; 1948, *50*, 517-518; 552-554

Roorda, P.; The Deaf Child in the Family; 1912, *13*, 586-590

Rotter, Paul; A Guide for Educating Parents of Deaf Children; 1958, *60*, 28-32

Rotter, Paul; Human Relations in Parent Education; 1957, *59*, 20-24

Rotter, Paul; The Parents' Role in Encouraging Speech Growth; 1961, *63*, 12-15; 46

Rotter, Paul; Relationship Between the Educator and Parents of Deaf Children; 1958, *60*, 370-371

Sanders, Mrs. George T.; Instructors of Parents of Deaf Children; 1914, *16*, 812-814

Sawyer, Mrs. S. E.; What an Heroic Mother Accomplished; 1912, *14*, 193-198

Scheeline, Mrs. Isaiah; Planning for the Deaf Child's First School Days Away from Home; 1955, *57*, 211-212

Shippy, Ardell; How an Active Parent Group Can Strengthen a School Program; 1961, *63*, 297-298

Simon, Adele; Responsibility for the Speech of Our Children; 1932, *34*, 470-473

Simon, Arthur B.; Helping Your Deaf Child Grow Up—Let Him Experiment and Explore; 1961, *63*, 35-39

Simon, Mrs. Richard; A Parent Speaks; 1964, *66*, 570-573

Smith, Alathena J.; Guidance at the John Tracy Clinic; 1956, *58*, 301-304

Smith, Muriel A.; The Stammering Child in His Home; 1913, *15*, 69-72

Sortini, Adam J.; To the Parent of a Hearing Handicapped Child; 1960, *62*, 26-28; 46

Steffey, Mary E.; Proxy Ears for Mother; 1925, *27*, 682-686

Stoner, Marguerite (panel moderator); Parent Participation; 1953, *55*, 78-90

Tatman, Mrs. Donald; Let's Talk About Talk; 1962, *64*, 449-452
Thompson, Richard; Ups and Downs in the Hearing World; 1949, *51*, 5-6; 54
—————; To the Parents of Little Deaf Children: Suggestions Offered by the Lexington School for the Deaf; 1944, *46*, 69-71; 110-112
Van Wyk, Mary K.; Home Help with Speech; 1957, *59*, 207-208; 227
Vorce, Eleanor; Your Child Is Deaf—Advice for Parents; 1954, *56*, 201-204
Walcher, Helen; Parents Are Our Greatest Helpers; 1959, *61*, 325-326
Watts, Jo D.; A Preschool Program for Parents; 1942, *44*, 329-330; 368
Whildin, Olive A.; The Parent, the School, and the Community; 1950, *52*, 503-504; 522-524
White, Stella K.; The Home Instruction of a Little Deaf Child; 1901, *3*, 418-427
Williams, Boyce R.; Your Deaf Child's Job Prospects; 1962, *64*, 246-248; 273
Winston, Matie E.; What the Parent Can Do for the Preschool Child; 1933, *35*, 411-413
Woodward, Helen; Read with Your Children; 1960, *62*, 517-519
Worcester, Eleanor B.; To Mothers of Little Deaf Children; 1914, *16*, 335-338; 499-502; 1915, *17*, 207-212; 1925, *27*, 156-165; 217-220; 276-281
Work, Robert; Working With Your Young Deaf Child; 1954, *56*, 114-117
Wright, John D.; What Parents Can Do for Their Deaf Children in and out of School; 1932, *34*, 467-470
Yorty, Jeane B.; Parents, Let's Relax!; 1961, *63*, 30-33; 39
Zander, Alvin; How We Can Work Together; 1962, *64*, 30-33

Annals of the Deaf

Adams, Mabel E., et al.; What Parents Want for Their Deaf Children; 1931, *76*, 264-275
Anderson, Tom L.; Parental Co-operation; 1937, *82*, 244-248
Fuller, Carl W.; Your Child, Maturity, and You: A Talk with Parents; 1962, *107*, 320-328
Fuller, Sarah; To the Mothers of Very Young Deaf Children; 1930, *75*, 363-375
Gough, John A.; Use of Pictures in Teaching Young Deaf Children at Home; 1960, *105*, 442-445
Hedgecock, LeRoy D.; Counselling the Parents of Acoustically Handicapped Children; 1952, *97*, 329-339

PARENTS—continued

Annals of the Deaf

Hirsch, D.; Advice to Parents, Guardians, and Teachers Concerning the Education of Deaf-Mutes; 1877, *22*, 93-103
Jesseman, V. C.; Ways in Which the Home Should Cooperate With the School; 1943, *88*, 1-7
Magner, Marjorie E.; Parents Can Help Deaf Children to Acquire Ability in Speechreading; 1960, *105*, 431-433
Montague, Harriet; Parents of Deaf Children; 1953, *98*, 358-361
Pettengill, B. D.; Home Education for Deaf-Mutes; 1874, *19*, 1-10
Stern, Rose G.; The Problem of the Training of a Deaf Child as Viewed by a Mother; 1918, *63*, 151-189; 250-278
Vorce, Eleanor R.; You, Your Child and the Language; 1960, *105*, 437-441
Wright, John D.; Suggestions from a Correspondence Course for Parent-Teachers of Deaf Children; 1921, *66*, 462-475; 1922, *67*, 144-154; 241-252

PRESCHOOL

Volta Review

Adelson, L., Colepaugh, G., et al.; A New Approach to the Education of Two and Three Year Old Deaf Children; 1949, *51*, 205-208; 256-258; 273-275; 308-310
Anderson, Mrs. J. S.; The Montessori Method of Teaching Hearing Children; 1912, *14*, 95-102; 154-168
Anderson, Mrs. J. S.; Proving the Worth of the Montessori Method; 1913, *15*, 38-42
Appel, Catherine R.; Objectives of a Preschool Program; 1942, *44*, 621-622; 662
Avery, Charlotte B.; The Social Competence of Preschool Acoustically Handicapped Children; 1948, *50*, 256-257; 286-288
Beard, Richard O.; Deafening in the Pre-School Child; 1929, *31*, 457-460
Bodycomb, Margaret; Sense Training and Hand Work; 1928, *30*, 579-581
Burnett, Alice; Montessori Education Today and Yesterday; 1963, *65*, 235-239; 244
Cambon, K. G.; Otological Considerations in a Preschool Hearing Program; 1964, *66*, 603-609; 651
Chamberlain, Naomi H.; A Screening Outline for Determining Group Readiness; 1959, *61*, 455-457; 476

Cory, Patricia B.; A Child's First Books Should Be Fun; 1959, *61*, 411-412
Crouter, John Y.; The Nursery School in the Education of the Deaf; 1937, *39*, 613-614
Davidson, Helena M.; Residential Nursery Schools? No!; 1946, *48*, 494-495
Ewing, Irene B.; Training Deaf Babies; 1945, *47*, 208-209; 254
Fay, Edward A.; Montessori Training: Oral Teaching; 1914, *16*, 387-388
Forsythe, Kathrin B.; The Kindergarten Circle; 1929, *31*, 786-787
Gardner, Warren H.; A Pre-School Demonstration Class for Deaf Children; 1947, *49*, 169-171; 200-201
Gesell, Arnold; Normal and Deaf Child in the Preschool Years; 1946, *48*, 633-636
Gesell, Arnold; The Psychological Development of Normal and Deaf Children in Their Preschool Years; 1956, *58*, 117-120
Greenaway, E. S.; The Properly Organized Nursery is the Better Home for the Deaf Child; 1947, *49*, 121; 156-158
Griffiths, Ciwa; The Auditory Approach for Preschool Deaf Children; 1964, *66*, 387-397
Guthrie, Virginia S.; A History of Preschool Education for the Deaf; 1945, *47*, 5-9; 56-58; 72-76; 116-118; 142-146; 186-188
Heider, Grace, and Fritz; Studies of Preschool Deaf Children; 1943, *45*, 261-267
Heinrichs, Eunice L.; The Nursery in a Day School; 1954, *56*, 390-392
Hoffman, Virginia; Preschool Classes at the Lexington School; 1940, *42*, 69-72; 118; 144-146; 182
Howard, Evelyn S.; Nursery Schools: Their Development and Their Function; 1943, *45*, 437-441; 466
Howard, Evelyn S.; The Preschool Department at the Rochester School; 1940, *42*, 405-408; 440
Howes, Esther C.; What the Teacher Can Do for the Pre-School Child; 1933, *35*, 413-414
Hurd, Anna C.; The Montessori Method Applied to Deaf Children; 1915, *17*, 239-242
Iandoli, Edward A., et al.; The Albany Hospital Conservation of Hearing Center Preschool Testing Program; 1959, *61*, 452-454; 1960, *62*, 63-65; 271-273; 286
Lane, Helen S.; Influence of Nursery School Education on School Achievement; 1942, *44*, 677-680
Lassman, Grace H.; Lip Reading in Nursery School; 1948, *50*, 445-449
Levine, Edna S., and Groht, Mildred A.; Nursery School and the Deaf Child; 1955, *57*, 199-209
Longwill, Mrs. J. B.; The Training of Children of Tender Years; 1913, *15*, 398-402

PRESCHOOL—continued

Volta Review

Love, J. K.; Education of the Very Young Deaf Child; 1910, *12*, 602-603; 621

McArdle, S. M.; Kindergarten Methods; 1914, *16*, 517-521

McNeill, Naomi; Why Wait Until They Are Five?; 1936, *38*, 501-504; 542-543

MacDonald, Nellie V.; Home-Made Sense Training Material; 1951, *53*, 8-9; 42; 44

MacDonald, Nellie; A New Nursery School; 1948, *50*, 63; 84-86

Margulies, Mrs. A. R.; The Montessori Method and the Deaf Child; 1912, *14*, 74-85; 146-147; 1913, *15*, 334-338

Mendelson, N., and Cannon, Mary; Experiment in Language Development for Kindergarten Deaf Children; 1950, *52*, 65-66; 98-100

Miller, June (moderator); Nursery and Preschool (Panel Discussion); 1952, *54*, 421-434; 464-466

Miller, June; Speech and the Preschool Child; 1960, *62*, 315-317

Miller, June; Vocabulary Needs of Preschool Deaf Children; 1954, *56*, 58-62

Montague, Harriet; The Nursery School and the Deaf Child; 1935, *37*, 207; 249-250

Moore, Grace; The Nursery School Movement; 1928, *30*, 583-588

New, Mary C.; The Nursery School; 1946, *48*, 631-632

——————; Nursery and Preschool (Panel Discussion); 1948, *50*, 403-414

——————; Nursery Schools for Deaf Children: An Association Committee Report; 1942, *44*, 681-683; 718

O'Halloran, Dorothy M.; A Sense Training Program; 1953, *55*, 491-492

Poore, Mrs. H. T.; The Report on Nursery Schools for Deaf Children; 1943, *45*, 620-621; 660

Rankin, C. E.; Preschool Unit; 1953, *55*, 495-496

——————; Residential Nursery Schools—A Discussion; 1946, *48*, 496-513; 542

Richardson, Paul C.; Developing Fundamental Speech Patterns; 1959, *61*, 276-282

Rider, Edward C.; Kindergarten Work in Schools for the Deaf; 1899, *1*, 34-41

Roach, Robert E.; Severe Deafness in the Pre-Speech Years; 1954, *56*, 153-157

Robinson, Geoffrey C.; Hearing Loss in Infants and Young Preschool Children with Particular Reference to Medical Participation; 1964, *66*, 314-318

Rotter, Paul; The Development of Speech in Young Children; 1955, *57*, 53-57

——————; Schools and Classes for Deaf Children Under Six; 1957, *59*, 157-164; 1959, *61*, 264-275; 1961, *63*, 272-281; 1965, *67*, 512-524

Scyster, Margaret; Johnny Is Boss; 1939, *41*, 14-15; 55
Shanahan, Minette; Teaching Concepts to Preschool Deaf and Hard of Hearing Children; 1956, *58*, 121-122
Sister Rose Gertrude; The Preschool at St. Mary's; 1937, *39*, 325-327; 376
Stoner, Marguerite; The Development of Early Speech with Emphasis on the Synthetic Method; 1955, *57*, 15-17
Taylor, Ellen E.; Kindergartens for the Deaf; 1903, *5*, 1-11
Taylor, Helen; The Importance of a Right Beginning; 1899, *1*, 158-161
Thoma, Florence B.; The Nursery School; 1933, *35*, 369-371
Varwig, Renate; Pediatrics and Disorders in Communication: Social Considerations in the Care of the Preschool Hearing Handicapped Child; 1965, *67*, 434-438
Vorce, Eleanor R.; Speech in the Preschool for the Deaf; 1958, *60*, 478-481; 504
Wallin, Margaret; A New Program of Education; 1951, *53*, 420-424
Warren, Nell; Deaf Children with Hearing Children: A Nursery School Experiment; 1951, *53*, 199; 232-234
Wells, Anita; Keeping Beginners Happy and Interested; 1929, *31*, 248-250
Welsh, Eugenia T.; Sense Training; 1922, *24*, 111-113
Whitehurst, Mary W.; Testing the Hearing of Preschool Children; 1961, *63*, 430-432; 463
Winters, Loretta M.; Departmentalizing a Nursery School; 1944, *46*, 623-627; 660-662
Yearsley, Macleod; The Deaf Child's Proper School-Age; 1910, *12*, 695-699
Young, Irene B.; A Nursery School Experiment; 1935, *37*, 208; 252-253

Annals of the Deaf

Adams, Mabel E.; A Pre-School Experiment; 1928, *73*, 169-171
Bates, Laura M.; Montessori Models; 1913, *58*, 16-25
Benning, Doris B.; Nursery Schools for the Deaf; 1938, *83*, 417-424
Bingham, Cornelia D.; Flaws in Kindergarten Work; 1908, *53*, 381-384
Cloud, D. T.; The Illinois Preschool Experiment and Present Plan; 1940, *85*, 234-241
Craig, William N.; Effects of Preschool Training on the Development of Reading and Lipreading Skills of Deaf Children; 1964, *109*, 280-296
Hector, Elizabeth R.; The Deaf Child of Preschool Age; 1932, *77*, 290-291
Henderson, J. M.; Preschool Deaf Children; 1944, *89*, 297-302
Hudson, Alice F.; Kindergartens for the Deaf; 1894, *39*, 25-27

PRESCHOOL—continued

Annals of the Deaf

Johnson, Richard O.; Kindergarten Work; 1908, *53*, 378-380
Kiesel, Theodore A.; First Steps in Teaching Language to Our Little Ones; 1906, *51*, 208-225; 439-460; 1907, *52*, 134-158
Kilpatrick, W. M.; Preschool Needs of Handicapped Children—The Deaf Particularly; 1932, *77*, 321-327
Lamprecht, Emil; What Games are Suitable for Little Deaf Children before the School Age?; 1911, *56*, 472-478
Long, J. Schuyler; The Montessori Method: A Comparison; 1913, *58*, 117-125
McAloney, Thomas S.; Kindergarten for the Deaf; 1898, *43*, 184-190
Miller, Malinda K.; The Status of the Preschool Deaf Child; 1934, *79*, 414-427
Pattan, H. T.; Preschool Conservation of Hearing Program; 1955, *100*, 319-320
Pettengill, B. D.; The Primary Education of Deaf-Mutes and Semi-Mutes; 1879, *24*, 197-202
Poyntz, Leonidas; The Paramount Importance of Primary Education; 1880, *25*, 209-211
Scyster, M.; Summary of Four Years' Experiment with Preschool Deaf Children at the Illinois School for the Deaf; 1936, *81*, 212-230
Sutton, Estella V.; The Desirability of Kindergartens for the Deaf; 1894, *39*, 81-92
Sutton, Estella V.; Kindergarten Work in Its Relation to Primary Education; 1893, *38*, 25-32
Taylor, Harris; A Proper Adjustment of the Course of Study to Meet the Requirements of Very Young Children; 1927, *72*, 221-230
Wagner, Mary A.; The Experimental Preschool Group of Clarke School; 1935, *80*, 391-394
Waldo, Mary S.; Early Home Instruction of Deaf-Mutes; 1859, *11*, 146-150
Wright, John D.; Sense Training; 1921, *66*, 473

PSYCHOLOGICAL

Volta Review

Adrain, E. D., and Yealland, L. R.; The Treatment of Some Common War Neuroses; 1917, *19*, 680-682
Andrews, Harriet U.; Building a Bridge to the Child; 1913, *15*, 357-360
Andrews, Harriet U.; Misdirected Energies; 1914, *16*, 240-244

Allison, Margaret G.; Mental Hygiene as Applied to Work with the Deafened from the Psychiatric Social Worker's Point of View; 1929, *31*, 646-649

Andrews, Harriet U.; Thought Test Exercise; 1927, *29*, 452-454

Armstrong, Lola M.; You Can Learn to Live Without Them; 1954, *56*, 29-30

Arnold, Allie; Personality and Discipline; 1936, *38*, 582-583; 611

Balis, Sylvia C.; The Deaf and Their Social Relations with the Hearing; 1901, *3*, 141-144

Ballenger, Lula, and Zimmer, Louise; Socializing the Deaf and the Hearing Child; 1935, *37*, 397-400; 440-441

Bender, James F.; Seven Simple Tests of Motor Coordination; 1944, *46*, 267; 310

Berryman, Florence S.; Social Technique for the Submerged Tenth; 1944, *46*, 401-404; 426

Bilger, Robert; Limitations on the Use of Intelligence Scales to Estimate the Mental Ages of Children; 1958, *60*, 321-325

Bishop, Helen M.; Performance Scale Tests Applied to Deaf and Hard of Hearing Children; 1936, *38*, 447; 484-485

Blish, Stanford C.; An Educational and Vocational Counseling Program for Deaf Students; 1955, *57*, 385-389

Bopst, E. G.; Face It!; 1955, *57*, 343-346; 371

Boshler, Irene E.; Mental Tests; 1918, *20*, 193-195

Boyd, Hypatia; The Deaf and Their Social Relations with the Hearing; 1901, *3*, 227-235

Boyd, Hypatia; University Experiences; 1900, *2*, 127-136

Brown, Ruth; Adjusting to the Normally Hearing; 1954, *56*, 11-13

Calkins, Ernest E.; The Lives of the Deafened; 1926, *28*, 7-11; 114-117

Carr, Josephine; The Teacher's Role in Promoting Mental Health; 1961, *63*, 65-69; 89

Charles, Edna N.; Social Adjustment of a Deaf Child; 1937, *39*, 271-274

Cogswell, Elaine Ward; The Psychic Side of Deafness; 1939, *41*, 285-287

Collins, Virginia E.; The Important Thing Is Attitude; 1949, *51*, 121-122

Crawford, N. T., and Nace, J. C.; A Program of Social Guidance; 1939, *41*, 156-157

Crum, Carole; The Normality of Deaf Children; 1961, *63*, 231-232; 249

Danger, O.; The Education of the Deaf for Life in Human Society; 1904, *6*, 101-108

DeLany, Elizabeth G.; Cheer: A Symposium; 1917, *19*, 621-622

DeMotte, Amelia; Mental Hygiene of the Deaf Child; 1935, *37*, 224-225; 260-261

Dickinson, Myrle E.; Hearing Is Believing; 1949, *51*, 562-563; 586-588

PSYCHOLOGICAL—*continued*

Volta Review

————; Do Deaf Children Grasp Abstractions Readily?; 1931, *33*, 75-78
DuBard, Etoile; A "Deaf" Child Who Did Not Learn; 1962, *64*, 589-592
Edgar, Lucille S.; Determination in the Face of Prejudice; 1964, *66*, 31-34
Effler, Louis R.; Lost and Found; 1930, *32*, 115-118
Ewing, Ethel C.; Some Psychological Variables in the Training of Young Deaf Children; 1963, *65*, 68-73
————; The Feathering of the Ugly Duckling; 1925, *27*, 508-512
Ferrall, John A.; A Bottle of Tonic; 1919, *21*, 503-505
Ferrall, John A.; If I Were Deaf ————; 1918, *20*, 647-650
Ferrall, John A.; Please Pass the Butter!; 1922, *24*, 297-300
Ferrall, John A.; Smiling the Clouds Away; 1918, *20*, 149-152
Ferrall, John A.; Sound . . . And Nothing Else; 1925, *27*, 145-148
Ferreri, Giulio; Notes on Pedagogy and Psychology in Regard to the Deaf; 1914, *16*, 233-239; 365-368; 467-471; 523-527; 719-721
Finney, Mariette E., and Way, Daisy M.; The Deaf and Their Social Relations; 1901, *3*, 11-23
Flaxman, Mrs. G. D.; Socialization and the Deaf Teenager; 1962, *64*, 443-445
Franz, Shepherd I.; Psychological Problems of the Deaf; 1932, *34*, 545-546
Frohn, W.; Experiments on the Thinking of the Deaf; 1931, *33*, 313-315; 324-325
Gay, Ruth; Mental Hygiene Clinics in Schools for the Deaf; 1935, *37*, 741; 781-782
Gesell, Arnold; The Psychological Development of Normal and Deaf Children in Their Preschool Years; 1956, *58*, 117-120
Gibian, Rose; Social Work in a School for Deaf Children; 1933, *35*, 285-287
Goldberg, Rose E.; Laugh at Your Ears; 1950, *52*, 458-459; 472-474
Gratz, Leola A.; The Deaf Child's Contact with Hearing Children; 1934, *36*, 326-327; 379
Gruver, Elbert A.; The Adjustment of the Deaf to Their Hearing Contemporaries; 1945, *47*, 69-71; 112-116
Hansen, Anders; The Basis of the Binet-Simon Inquiry; 1910, *12*, 190-193
Hardy, William G.; Problems of Audition, Perception and Understanding; 1956, *58*, 289-300; 309
Harkness, Margaret; Deaf Children Do Have Imagination; 1936, *38*, 567-569
Hays, Harold; How Can We Meet the Problem of the Deaf; 1916, *18*, 506-510
Hedley, Arthur; The Futility of Fear; 1937, *39*, 167; 184-185

Heider, Grace M., and Fritz; The Adjustment of the Adult Deaf: After-School Problems as the Psychologist Sees Them; 1943, *45*, 389-391; 430

Heider, Grace M., and Fritz; The Adjustment of the Adult Deaf: Comments from the Deaf About After-School Problems; 1943, *45*, 325-328; 380-382

Heider, Grace M., and Fritz; Phonetic Symbolism of Deaf Children; 1941, *43*, 165-168; 233-236

Heider, Grace M.; A Psychological Study of the Effects of Deafness; 1933, *35*, 117-119

Heider, Grace M., and Fritz; The Thinking of the Young Deaf Child As Shown in Sorting Experiments; 1941, *43*, 111-113; 146

Hiskey, M. S.; Determining Mental Competence Levels of Children with Impaired Hearing; 1950, *52*, 349-351; 388-390; 406-408; 430-432

Hurst, et al.; Hysterical Deafness in Soldiers; 1917, *19*, 686-691

————; Hysterical Deafness in Soldiers; 1918, *20*, 173-175

Jenkins, Weston; Training for Practical Life; 1901, *3*, 199-203

Kennedy, Mildred; How to Bear and Forbear Deafness; 1917, *19*, 692-695; 1918, *20*, 19-22; 107-110

Kimber, W. J.; Some Psychology for the Deafened; 1946, *48*, 522-523

Kitson, H. D.; Psychological Tests for Lip-Reading Ability; 1915, *17*, 471-476

Knight, Maude H.; Emotions of the Young Deaf Child; 1942, *44*, 69-72; 122-124

Lane, Helen S.; Personality Adjustments of Adolescents; 1937, *39*, 166; 186

Larr, Alfred L., and Cain, Earl R.; Measurement of Native Learning Abilities of Deaf Children; 1959, *61*, 160-162

Lavos, George; W.I.S.C. Psychometric Patterns Among Deaf Children; 1962, *64*, 547-552

Leigh, Jean W.; Emotional Stability for the Deaf Child; 1942, *44*, 685-688; 724

Levine, Edna S.; Adolescence—What Is It?; 1954, *56*, 257-259

Levine, Edna S.; Can We Speed Up the Slow Child?; 1949, *51*, 269-270; 316-318

Levine, Edna S.; Psychological Sidelights; 1948, *50*, 5-6; 40-44; 152-154; 194-196; 309-310; 330-334

Levine, Edna S.; Studies in Psychological Evaluation of the Deaf; 1963, *65*, 496-512

Levine, Edna S.; The Work of the School Psychologist; 1946, *48*, 728-734

Liebman, Jeffrey; Reflections of a Presidential Scholar; 1964, *66*, 683-686

Lowry, C. D.; Physiology and Psychology of the Deaf Child; 1911, *13*, 386-391

PSYCHOLOGICAL—continued

Volta Review

Martineau, Harriet; Letter to the Deaf; 1913, *15*, 219-227
Mayer, Jonas H.; My Deafness; 1954, *56*, 440-442
Menninger, K. A.; The Mental Effects of Deafness; 1923, *25*, 439-445
Miller, E. O.; Studying the Psychology of the Deaf; 1935, *37*, 738; 780-781
Moore, Lucile M.; A Comparison of Deaf and Hearing Children; 1934, *36*, 325; 372-373
Morgenstern, Louise I.; The Philosophy of Self-culture; 1915, *17*, 171-174
Morkovin, Boris V.; Thought Patterns of Deaf Children: What Does This Imply for the Classroom Teacher?; 1964, *66*, 491-494
Murphy, A. T., et al.; Acceptance, Rejection and the Hearing Handicapped; 1960, *62*, 208-211
Myklebust, Helmer R.; Clinical Diagnosis and Classification of Children With Impaired Hearing; 1946, *48*, 738-742
Myklebust, Helmer R.; Clinical Psychology and Children with Impaired Hearing; 1948, *50*, 55-56; 90-91
Myklebust, Helmer R.; Diagnosis, Learning and Guidance; 1962, *64*, 363-369
Nevinson, Elizabeth; "Beg Pardon?"; 1925, *27*, 84-88
Newlee, Clara E.; Report of Learning Tests With Deaf Children; 1919, *21*, 216-223
Neyhus, Arthur I.; The Social and Emotional Adjustment of Deaf Adults; 1964, *66*, 319-325
Nitchie, Edward B.; The Association of Deaf and Hearing; 1911, *13*, 149-152
Nitchie, Edward B.; Some Assets of Deafness; 1913, *15*, 204-206
Nitchie, Edward B.; To Be or Not to Be; 1914, *16*, 53-55
Osler, Sonia F.; The Nature of Intelligence; 1965, *67*, 285-291; 319
Owsley, P. J.; A Study of Intelligence and Achievement Among Children Exhibiting Symptoms of the Waardenburg Syndrome; 1962, *64*, 429-431
Pierce, Jerry A.; Human Tragedies; 1915, *17*, 483-485
Pierce, Jerry A.; The Privilege of Being Deaf; 1914, *16*, 351-354
Pintner, Rudolf; Deductions from Tests of Mentality in Schools for the Deaf in Comparison with Schools for the Hearing; 1920, *22*, 197-207
Pintner, Rudolf, and Paterson, Donald; Psychological Tests of Deaf Children; 1917, *19*, 661-667
Pintner, Rudolf, and Paterson, Donald; Some Conclusions from Psychological Tests of the Deaf; 1918, *20*, 10-14
Pratt, George T.; Community Relations; 1958, *60*, 75-76
Pugh, Bessie; Developing the Deaf Child's Power of Reasoning; 1960, *62*, 334-340

Quick, Marian; Role of the Administrator in the Guidance Program; 1960, *62*, 418-420
Quinn, Josephine; A Comparison of Deaf and Hearing Children; 1934, *36*, 381; 311-312; 325; 372-373
Raubicheck, Letitia; Psychology of Multilingualism; 1934, *36*, 17-20; 57
Roe, W. Carey; Some Observations on the Psychology of the Deaf Child; 1921, *23*, 52-59
Ross, Ellen B.; Beating a Handicap; 1925, *27*, 181-184
Saunders, Nida; Personality Problems; 1934, *36*, 9-11
Schick, H. F.; A Performance Test for Children of School Age; 1934, *36*, 657-658; 694-695
Shontz, Franklin C.; Reactions to Crisis; 1965, *67*, 364-370
Sievers, A. D.; The Function of the Psychiatrist in the School; 1928, *30*, 561-566
Sigurdson, H. K.; Changing Attitudes; 1954, *56*, 118-119
Slankard, Harriet; Teaching the Deaf Child to Think; 1958, *60*, 523-527
Smith, Rena A.; The Veil of Silence; 1914, *16*, 198-207
Steffey, Mary E.; The Hollow Cross of Deafness; 1925, *27*, 138-142
Stevenson, Margaret J.; Discipline; 1904, *6*, 222-224
Stewart, P.; I Am One of the Lucky Ones; 1953, *55*, 41-42; 50
Stillson, S. V.; The Teacher and the Problem Child; 1930, *32*, 501-505
Stix, E. F.; Life in a Hearing World; 1955, *57*, 438-440
Stoner, Marguerite (moderator); Parent Participation; 1953, *55*, 78-90
Storey, John D.; The Psychology of Deafened People from a Layman's Point of View; 1920, *22*, 268-271
Story, Arthur J.; The Intelligence of the Deaf Child; 1911, *13*, 349-352
Sylvester, Elfrieda M.; Fourteen; 1919, *21*, 517-522
Tatman, Mrs. Donald; Let's Talk About Talk; 1962, *64*, 449-452
Templin, Mildred C.; Relation of Speech and Language Development to Intelligence and Socio-economic Status; 1958, *60*, 331-334
Timberlake, Josephine B.; A Plea for the Abolition of Prejudice; 1931, *33*, 200-202
Tompkins, Ernest; Is Stammering Emotional?; 1920, *22*, 752-754
Thompson, Richard; Adjustment in High School With Normal Hearing Contemporaries; 1960, *62*, 414-417
Thompson, Richard; Counseling and the Deaf Student; 1964, *66*, 511-513
Thompson, Richard; What Speech and Lipreading Mean to Me; 1950, *52*, 115-118
Tonley, Lucia S.; Ten Strangers; 1929, *31*, 207-208
Valentine, Cristina; How to be Happy in a Hearing World; 1943, *45*, 76-80; 120-122

PSYCHOLOGICAL—continued

Volta Review

Van Wyk, Mary K.; Integration—A Look at the Total Picture; 1960, *62*, 69-70; 82

Vinson, M. R.; Retardation Problems; 1934, *36*, 206; 246

Washburne, C.; Educational Significance of Individual Differences; 1930, *32*, 459-469

Watson, Charles W.; Subnormality or Late Enrollment?; 1936, *38*, 448-449; 480

Weil, Clara S.; Society Versus Solitude; 1929, *31*, 205-206

Weisbord, Marvin R.; Do You Understand the Language of Behavior?; 1964, *66*, 610-614

Whildin, Olive; By-Products of the Lip-Reading Class; 1934, *36*, 159-161; 181

Wilson, D. K.; The Hearing Team; 1962, *64*, 22-25

Woods, Elizabeth L.; Standard Tests in the Los Angeles School for the Deaf; 1926, *28*, 600-604

Annals of the Deaf

Abernathy, E. R.; Some Social Aspects of Deafness; 1940, *85*, 433-445

Altshuler, K. Z., and Rainer, J. D.; Institute on Personal, Social and Vocational Adjustment to Total Deafness: Psychiatric Aspects; 1958, *103*, 317-323

Birch, Jane R., and Jack W., and Stuckless, E. Ross; An Eleven Year Study of Predicting School Achievement in Young Deaf Children; 1963, *108*, 236-241

Birch, Jane R., and Jack W.; The Leiter International Performance Scale as an Aid in the Psychological Study of Deaf Children; 1951, *96*, 502-511

Birch, Jane R., and Jack W.; Predicting School Achievement in Young Deaf Children; 1956, *101*, 348-352

Bradway, Katherine P.; The Social Competence of Deaf Children; 1937, *82*, 122-140

Bridgman, Olga; The Estimation of Mental Ability in Deaf Children; 1939, *84*, 337-349

Brill, Tobias; Mental Hygiene and the Deaf; 1934, *79*, 279-285

Burchard, Edward M., and Myklebust, Helmer R.; A Comparison of Congenital and Adventitious Deafness with Respect to Its Effect on Intelligence, Personality, and Social Maturity; 1942, *87*, 140-154; 241-251; 342-360

Butler, Stahl; Formative Influences on the Deaf Child and Young Adult; 1958, *103*, 312-316

Cardwell, W. A.; Understanding Versus Expression; 1902, *47*, 11-19

Cobb, Jennie L.; Psychology in the Schoolroom; 1921, *66*, 186-190

Coleman, G. D.; The Efficiency of Touch and Smell; 1922, *67*, 301-325

Cutler, Elizabeth M.; Summary of Psychological Experiments with the Deaf; 1941, *86*, 181-192

Drennan, George L.; The Psychology of Deafness in Children; 1941, *86*, 393-404

DuToit, J. M.; Measuring the Intelligence of Deaf Children; 1954, *99*, 237-249

Eddy, L.; The Relations of Deaf-Mutes to the Hearing World; 1878, *23*, 226-231

Ely, Grace D.; Do We Think in Language; 1926, *71*, 205-207

Farrant, Roland H.; The Intellective Abilities of Deaf and Hearing Children Compared by Factor Analyses; 1964, *109*, 306-325

Florence, Geneva; Institution Life—Its Influence on Personality; 1932, *77*, 284-288

Frackelton, Berneda P.; Adjustments of the Deaf; 1944, *89*, 173-181

Gallaudet, Edward M.; The Mental Development of the Deaf Child; 1910, *55*, 342-349

Gardner, I. B.; Psychology of Intermediate Grades; 1927, *72*, 181-185

Gay, Ruth C.; A Case Study of Word Deafness; 1938, *83*, 169-176

Glowatsky, Edward; Verbal Element in the Intelligence Scores of Congenitally Deaf and Hard of Hearing Children; 1953, *98*, 328-335

Goetzinger, C. P., and Huber, T. G.; A Study of Immediate and Delayed Visual Retention with Deaf and Hearing Adolescents; 1964, *109*, 297-305

Goetzinger, C. P., and Rousey, C. L.; A Study of the Wechsler Performance Scale (Form) II and the Knox Cube Test with Deaf Adolescents; 1957, *102*, 388-398

Hickey, Marshall S.; A Study of the Intelligence of Deaf and Hearing Children; 1956, *101*, 329-339

Hofmarksrichter, R.; Do the Deaf See More than Those with All Their Senses?; 1933, *78*, 113-116

Hogsteater, H. T.; The "Institution Mind"—And Possible Means of Its Correction; 1934, *79*, 231-237

Hunt, J. F.; Abstracts of Articles Concerned with the Educational Psychology of the Deaf; 1937, *82*, 176-188

Jacobs, J. A.; Importance of Teaching Deaf-Mutes Self-reliance; 1858, *10*, 161-163

James, William; Thought before Language: Deaf-Mutes' Recollections; 1893, *38*, 135-145

Jenkins, William G.; Memory in the Education of the Deaf; 1892, *37*, 85-93

PSYCHOLOGICAL—continued

Annals of the Deaf

Johnson, E. H.; The Effect of Academic Level on Scores from the Chicago Non-Verbal Examination for Primary Pupils; 1947, *92*, 227-233

King, Gordon; A Case of Hysterical Deaf-Mutism; 1903, *48*, 44-55

Kirk, Samuel A.; Behavior Problem Tendencies in Deaf and Hard-of-Hearing Children; 1938, *83*, 131-137

Kirk, Samuel A., and Perry, June; A Comparative Study of the Ontario and Nebraska Tests for the Deaf; 1948, *93*, 315-323

Kline, Thomas K.; A Study of the Free Association Test with Deaf Children; 1945, *90*, 237-257

Lavos, George; The Chicago Non-Verbal Examination; 1950, *95*, 379-386

Lavos, George; Interrelationships Among Three Tests of Non-Language Intelligence Administered to the Deaf; 1954, *99*, 303-313

Lavos, George; The Reliability of an Educational Achievement Test Administered to the Deaf; 1944, *89*, 226-231

Levine, Edna S.; Psychiatric-Preventive and Sociogenetic Study of the Adjustive Capacities, Optimum Work Potentials and Total Family Problems of Literate Deaf Adolescents and Adults; 1960, *105*, 272-274

Levine, Edna S.; Psychological Aspects and Problems of Early Profound Deafness; 1958, *103*, 324-347

Levine, Edna S., and Safian, M. Z.; Psychological Evaluation in Vocational Adjustment; 1958, *103*, 348-364

Levine, Edna S.; The Psychological Service Program of the Lexington School for the Deaf; 1948, *93*, 149-164

Long, J. Schuyler; The Exceptional Child; 1917, *62*, 154-164

Long, J. Schuyler; Laggards; 1919, *64*, 208-213

Lowry, Charles D.; The Physiology & Psychology of the Deaf Child; 1912, *57*, 241-253

Lyon, V. W.; Personality Tests with the Deaf; 1934, *79*, 1-4

McPherson, Jane G., and Lane, Helen S.; A Comparison of Deaf and Hearing on the Hiskey Test and on Performance Scales; 1948, *93*, 178-184

Miller, Linda K.; Some Differences Between the Psychology of a Young Deaf Child and that of a Hearing Child; 1930, *75*, 212-215

Mira, Mary P.; The Use of the Arthur Adaptation of the Leiter Int'l Performance Scale and The Nebraska Test of Learning Aptitude with Preschool Deaf Children; 1962, *107*, 224-228

Moore, H. T.; Teaching Pupils How to Study; 1932, *77*, 248-253

Myklebust, Helmer R., Neyhus, Arthur, and Mulholland, A. M.; Guidance and Counseling for the Deaf; 1962, *107*, 370-415

Myklebust, Helmer R.; Psychological Effects of Deafness; 1960, *105*, 372-385

Myklebust, Helmer R.; Towards a New Understanding of the Deaf Child; 1953, *98*, 345-357

O'Connor, Clarence D., and Simon, E.; A Preliminary Survey Into the Problems of Adjustment Among Pupils of the Lexington School for the Deaf; 1942, *87*, 224-240
Oléron, Pierre; Conceptual Thinking of the Deaf; 1953, *98*, 304-310
Oléron, Pierre; A Study of the Intelligence of the Deaf; 1950, *95*, 179-192
Orman, James N., and Brill, Richard G.; An Experiment in the Training of Deaf Children in Memory for Sentences; 1953, *98*, 270-279
Peters, E. F.; Guidance for Exceptional Children; 1942, *87*, 1-7
Peterson, Edwin G.; Intelligence of Deaf Children as Measured by Drawings; 1930, *75*, 273-290
Phillips, Richard M.; Experiences in the Community; 1958, *103*, 382-388
Pintner, Rudolf, and Paterson, Donald G.; The Ability of Deaf and Hearing Children to Follow Printed Directions; 1917, *62*, 448-472
Pintner, Rudolf, and Brunschwig, L.; An Adjustment Inventory for Use in Schools for the Deaf; 1937, *82*, 152-167
Pintner, Rudolf, and Paterson, Donald; The Binet Scale and the Deaf Child; 1915, *60*, 301-311
Pintner, Rudolf, and Paterson, Donald; A Class Test with Deaf Children; 1916, *61*, 264-275
Pintner, Rudolf; Deductions from Tests of Mentality in Schools for the Deaf; 1920, *65*, 278-300
Pintner, Rudolf, and Paterson, Donald; The Form-Board Ability of Young Deaf and Hearing Children; 1916, *61*, 184-189
Pintner, Rudolf, and Reamer, Jeannette; Individual Differences Measured by Psychological Tests; 1921, *66*, 168-181
Pintner, Rudolf; Latest Phases of Psychological Testing with the Deaf; 1937, *82*, 327-337
Pintner, Rudolf, and Reamer, Jeannette; A Mental and Educational Survey of Schools for the Deaf; 1920, *65*, 451-472
Pintner, Rudolf, and Paterson, Donald; Mental Tests; 1915, *60*, 297-300
Pintner, Rudolf, and Osborn, Dorothy; The Mentality of Families of the Congenitally Deaf; 1919, *64*, 96-134
Pintner, Rudolf, and Reamer, Jeannette; Problems Raised by the Survey of Schools for the Deaf; 1921, *66*, 8-28
Pintner, Rudolf; The Survey of Schools for the Deaf: Psychological Survey; 1927, *72*, 377-414
Pintner, Rudolf; The Value of Mental Tests in the Classification of Pupils; 1918, *63*, 196-204
Putnam, G. H.; The Use of the Imagination in the Instruction of the Deaf; 1912, *57*, 229-241
Ray, Luzerne; Thoughts of the Deaf and Dumb Before Instruction; 1847, *1*, 149-157
Read, Elmer D.; Mental Reactions of Deafness; 1925, *70*, 246-253

PSYCHOLOGICAL—continued

Annals of the Deaf

Schick, Helen, et al.; A Performance Test for School-Age Deaf Children; 1941, *86*, 441-447

Shinpaugh, Joe R.; Follow-up and Adjustment Problems of the Acoustically Handicapped and Techniques of Solution; 1956, *101*, 298, 307

Schneider, Matthias; The Thought and Language of the Deaf-Mute: An Inquiry Concerning the True Foundation of Deaf-Mute Instruction; 1908, *53*, 483-492; 1909, *54*, 173-190; 254-281; 327-338; 402-412; 1910, *55*, 164-172; 474-486; 1911, *56*, 1-17

Schunhoff, Hugo F.; Conference on the Moral, Social and Religious Welfare of the Deaf; 1951, *96*, 414-419

Sheridan, Laura C.; The Art of Living Smoothly With One's Fellows; 1919, *64*, 174-181

Shirley, Mary, and Goodenough, F. L.; A Survey of Intelligence of Deaf Children in Minnesota Schools; 1932, *77*, 238-247

Skyberg, Victor O.; Deafness as a Social Problem—the Physical Side; 1929, *74*, 106-113

Smaltz, Warren M.; The Probability that Deafness Can Affect Personality; 1945, *90*, 330-339

Smith, James L.; Attention; 1917, *62*, 188-198

Smith, James L.; Training in Reasoning and Judgment and in the Formation and Expression of Correct Opinions; 1919, *64*, 166-174

Springer, N. Norton; A Comparative Study of the Behavior Traits of Deaf and Hearing Children of N.Y.C.; 1938, *83*, 255-273

Springer, N. Norton; A Comparative Study of the Intelligence of a Group of Deaf and Hearing Children; 1938, *83*, 138-152

Steinke, Elsie M.; How Best to Fit the Deaf for a Useful and Active Life; 1905, *50*, 300-304

Stevens, H. C.; The Encouragement of Individual Ideas; 1918, *63*, 279-285

Stewart, Helen L.; The Social Adjustment of the Deaf; 1943, *88*, 127-130

Stone, Elizabeth A.; Hints on Discipline; 1910, *55*, 177-182

Streng, Alice, and Kirk, Samuel A.; The Social Competence of Deaf and Hard-of-Hearing Children in a Public Day-School; 1938, *83*, 244-254

Stunkel, E.; The Performance of Deaf and Hearing College Students on Verbal and Non-Verbal Intelligence Tests; 1957, *102*, 342-355

Templin, Mildred C.; Personal References and Illustrations Used in Explaining Physical Casualty; 1951, *96*, 482-493

Vetidz, G. W.; The Relative Value of Sight and Hearing; 1937, *82*, 141-151

Walker, E. W.; The Possibilities and Limitations of the Deaf Mind; 1912, *57*, 474-483

Warfield, Ethel B.; Problems of Deafness; 1939, *83*, 300-305

Williams, T. J.; Extraordinary Development of the Tactile and Olfactory Senses; 1922, *67*, 418-432
Worthington, Anna M.; Psychological Implications of Integration of Deaf Children with Hearing Children; 1958, *103*, 467-472
Zeckel, Adolf; A Comparative Intelligence Test of Groups of Children Born Deaf and of Good Hearing, by Means of the Porteus Test; 1939, *84*, 114-123
Zeckel, Adolf; Research Possibilities with the Deaf; 1942, *87*, 173-191

READING

Volta Review

Anderson, Effie W.; Reading in the Advanced Department; 1930, *32*, 403-409
Avondino, Josephine; Silent Reading; 1930, *32*, 623-624
Beckmeyer, Theodore; Application of Programed Instruction to Remedial Reading for the Deaf; 1963, *65*, 415-417
Bell, Alexander G.; On Reading As a Means of Teaching Language to the Deaf; 1929, *31*, 191-195
Bennett, Josephine; Reading in the Primary Grades; 1934, *36*, 337-339; 378; 1938, *40*, 5-9
Bruce, Lula M.; Creating an Interest in Reading; 1934, *36*, 588-591
Casey, Sally L.; Teaching Reading to the Hearing Handicapped Child; 1954, *56*, 251-254
Church, Lilian L.; Reading for the Deaf Adolescent; 1931, *33*, 251-252; 279
Cory, Patricia; A Child's First Books Should Be Fun; 1959, *61*, 411-412
Cory, Patricia B.; Leisure Reading for Deaf Children; 1955, *57*, 449-451; 1956, *58*, 33-34; 123-125; 169-171; 213-214; 267-269; 409-411; 447-448; 1957, *59*, 27; 38; 72; 85; 217-219; 314-315; 365-366; 409-410; 1958, *60*, 35-36; 178-179; 447-449; 503; 506; 547; 1959, *61*, 35-36; 181-183; 187; 228-230; 239; 429; 1960, *62*, 36-38; 521; 1961, *63*, 244-245; 453; 464; 1962, *64*, 45-46; 153; 570-571; 1963, *65*, 245-246; 430-431
Cory, Patricia B.; Library Work with the Deaf; 1957, *59*, 169-173
Cory, Patricia B.; Recreational Reading and Library Program; 1958, *60*, 343-347
Cory, Patricia; Special Library Reading Project for Teenagers; 1964, *66*, 63-66

READING—continued

Volta Review

Crandell, Marian P.; Reading in the Primary Grades; 1946, *48*, 669-671
Davies, Rachel D.; Silent Reading But Oral English; 1948, *50*, 437-442
Davis, M. V.; A Silent Reading Experiment in Grade One; 1929, *31*, 66-72
Dean, Katherine S.; Our First Experience with Reading; 1929, *31*, 787-788
Doctor, Powrie V. (moderator, panel); Reading for the Deaf; 1953, *55*, 132-143
Edge, Lillie K.; Book Week at Western Pennsylvania School for the Deaf; 1957, *59*, 402-406
Eickhoff, Arlington J.; The Library Period; 1931, *33*, 445-446
Ervin, Annie M.; Reading—The Open Sesame to Language; 1926, *28*, 695-699
Ervin, Annie M.; Training Children to Read; 1926, *28*, 583-585
Farquhar, Grover C.; Reading for Intermediate Pupils; 1927, *29*, 194-196
Fitzgerald, Margaret H.; Improving the Reading Ability of Deaf Children; 1958, *60*, 341-343
Flint, Richard W., et al.; 1965 NDEA Institutes in Linguistics and Reading: The University of Kansas Institute in Reading; 1965, *67*, 618-623
Fordyce, Charles; Testing the Efficiency in Reading; 1917, *19*, 518-520
Fosmark, Laura B.; Reading for Pleasure; 1931, *33*, 214; 233
Fritz, Katherine; First Lessons in Reading; 1912, *14*, 602-604
Gates, A. I.; An Experimental Study of Teaching the Deaf to Read; 1926, *28*, 295-298
Gawith, Frances W.; Reading in Intermediate Grades; 1909, *11*, 397-403
Gesner, Elizabeth T.; Some Points on Reading Comprehension and Vocabulary Building; 1930, *32*, 24-36
Goda, Sidney; Early Reading for the Hard of Hearing Child; 1953, *55*, 97-98; 106-108
————; Good Books for Children's Reading; 1946, *48*, 199-200; 252-254
Griffin, Barbara; Reading Evaluation: A Continuing Study; 1958, *60*, 476-477; 506
Griffith, Mary J.; Comparing Results in Speech-Reading and in Silent Reading; 1931, *33*, 270-272
Groht, Mildred; Some Thoughts on Reading; 1955, *57*, 294-296
Gulick, Mabel; A Reading Program for First-Year Deaf School Children; 1954, *56*, 447-448
Hammer, Helen; A Nature Study Unit in Reading; 1931, *33*, 101-102
Hammer, Helen; The Second Step in a Silent Reading Experiment; 1929, *31*, 196-198
Hill, Miss W.; Reading and Language Development; 1920, *22*, 298-301

Howes, Esther C.; Teaching Young Deaf Children to Read; 1928, *30*, 19-20
Joiner, Enfield; The Personal Experience Story; 1926, *28*, 581-582
Kaufman, Maurice; A Reading Consultant in a School for the Deaf; 1965, *67*, 197-200
Kennard, Marie S.; Exercises in Reading Readiness; 1947, *49*, 213-214
Kent, Alice; To Each His Own in Reading; 1962, *64*, 387-389
Kidder, K. B.; One Approach to the Enjoyment of Reading—Dramatization; 1926, *28*, 300-302
MacDonald, Nellie V.; Books Suitable for Small Deaf Children; 1950, *52*, 256; 292
McLaughlin, Harriet F., et al.; A Reading Program; 1946, *48*, 666-675
McNeil, Marie T.; Group Reading; 1946, *48*, 671-673
Magner, Marjorie E.; Reading: Goals and Achievements at Clarke School for the Deaf; 1964, *66*, 464-468
Mangan, Kenneth R.; An Optimistic Outlook Toward Teaching Reading to Deaf Children; 1962, *64*, 392-393
Morrow, Elizabeth; An Introduction to Interpretative Reading; 1930, *32*, 277-281; 294
Moss, Margery; Reading; 1931, *33*, 446-447
Naiman, Doris; A Different Emphasis in Reading for Deaf Children; 1965, *67*, 632-634; 651
Newlee, Clara E.; A Study in Silent Reading with Deaf Children of Kindergarten Age; 1928, *30*, 523-526
Newton, Mary G.; Books for the Hard of Hearing Child; 1943, *45*, 455-458; 470-476
Newton, Mary G.; Readers, Not Leaf-Turners; 1964, *66*, 67-69
Nicoll, Mildred G.; Reading; 1932, *34*, 623-624; 649
Ostern, Beatrice; Home Help with Reading; 1960, *62*, 494-496
Pugh, Bessie; Teaching Children to Use the Dictionary; 1961, *63*, 178-185
Pugh, Bessie; Utilizing Research in Teaching Reading; 1962, *64*, 379-387
Pugh, Gladys S.; Appraisal of the Silent Reading Abilities of Acoustically Handicapped Children; 1946, *48*, 197-198; 254
Pugh, Gladys S., et al.; Reading for Deaf Children; 1948, *50*, 426-431
Pugh, Gladys S.; Recreational and Study-Type Reading; 1947, *49*, 547-548; 582-584
Pugh, Gladys S.; Recreational Reading for Deaf Children; 1949, *51*, 437-440; 484-486
Pugh, Gladys S.; Study-Type Reading; 1948, *50*, 205-207; 242-244
Read, Elizabeth; Cultivating the Reading Habit; 1931, *33*, 125-126
Reiss, Madeline; Can the Comics Help?; 1952, *54*, 155-157; 186

READING—*continued*

Volta Review

Richardson, Paul C.; A Reading Lesson Using the Fitzgerald Key Headings; 1957, *59*, 255-256
Roberts, Linnaeus; Cultivation of the Reading Habit; 1914, *16*, 82-85
Ruthven, Henrietta; Early Steps in Reading; 1933, *35*, 216-217
Schowe, Ben M., Jr.; Projecting Books as an Aid to Teaching Reading; 1962, *64*, 421-422
Serumgard, Inez M.; Teaching the Love of Reading; 1928, *30*, 333-334
Sinclair, Margaret; Interesting the Disinterested Reader; 1960, *62*, 488-492
Sister Anne Bernadine; A Developmental Curriculum; 1958, *60*, 337-340
Sister M. de LaSalle; Supervised Reading in the High School; 1932, *34*, 111-113
Sister M. Renée; Reading for Deaf Children; 1951, *53*, 104-107; 134
Sister Anna Rose; They Can't Help But Read; 1956, *58*, 381-385
Sterne, Lillian C.; Using Context Clues in a Reading Program for the Deaf; 1965, *67*, 371-375
Strickland, Ruth G.; The Interrelationship Between Language and Reading; 1958, *60*, 334-336
Thomas, Alyce, et al.; Reading for Deaf Children (panel discussion); 1956, *58*, 429-451
Vermillion, F. F.; Children's Experiences in Written Form (Chart Stories); 1947, *49*, 374; 382-384
————; Visual Reading; 1916, *18*, 430-434
Whitman, Mabel P.; Reading Made Interesting; 1929, *31*, 199-200
Wilman, M. Catherine; Reading in the Upper School; 1946, *48*, 673-675
Winters, L.; Reading Readiness and Beginning Reading in the Pre-School; 1946, *48*, 667-669
Withrow, Margaret S.; The Augmented Roman Alphabet—Can It Be Used for Teaching the Deaf?; 1964, *66*, 540-543
Woodward, Helen; Books for the Deaf Child; 1953, *55*, 391-399
Woodward, Helen; Read With Your Children; 1960, *62*, 517-519
Wright, Bruce, et al.; The Deaf Child and the Newspaper; 1940, *42*, 5-8
Yale, Caroline A.; Chart Stories for Class-Room Work with Young Children; 1920, *22*, 579-580

Annals of the Deaf

Allabough, B. R.; Reading As An Aid to Language-Teaching; 1893, *38*, 118-124
Bell, Alexander G.; Reading before Writing; 1891, *36*, 141-142
Benning, Doris B.; An Outline of Reading for the First Year; 1934, *79*, 109-119

Benning, Doris B.; A Unit of Reading for Deaf Children; 1937, *82*, 440-444

Berg, Lloyd E.; Some Oral Reading Problems in the Education of the Deaf; 1932, *77*, 257-260

Brill, Richard G.; Measurement of Progress in Reading; 1942, *87*, 135-139

Brill, Richard G.; The Prognosis of Reading Achievement of the Deaf; 1941, *86*, 227-241

Buell, Edith M.; Reading for the Deaf; 1915, *60*, 1-5

Caroll, David H.; Teaching Deaf-Mutes to Read; 1875, *20*, 228-229

Crosby, Laura L.; Books of High Interest and Low Vocabulary Level to Meet the Needs of Deaf Students in Grades Seven Through Twelve; 1948, *93*, 339-359

Denison, James; Reading for the Higher Classes; 1888, *33*, 89-96

Farquhar, Grover C., and Gough, John; An Experiment in Controlled Reading; 1940, *85*, 355-361

Farquhar, Grover C.; A Study of a Reading Test; 1928, *73*, 264-272

Fessant, John M.; Application of Programmed Learning for Deaf Children to Industrial Arts; 1963, *108*, 241-245

Fitzgerald, Margaret H.; Reading—The Key to Progress for Deaf Children; 1957, *102*, 404-415

Fitzgerald, Margaret H.; Silent Reading; 1924, *69*, 448-454

Hasenstab, Philip J.; An Instructor in Reading; 1892, *37*, 183-188

Heinl, S. S., et al.; Books for Recreational Reading of Primary Grades in the Illinois School for the Deaf, Jacksonville, Illinois, A Library Project to Determine Suitability of; 1951, *96*, 447-466; 524-543

Hurst, Fannie D.; Chart Work in Reading; 1932, *77*, 202-205

Hurst, Fannie D.; A Reading Project; 1938, *83*, 338-342

Hurst, Fannie D.; On Teaching Reading; 1932, *77*, 161-180

Jones, John W.; Reading the Road to Language; 1918, *63*, 237-249

Kendall, Elsie P.; A Reading and Language Unit—The Three Bears; 1934, *79*, 214-222

Kennedy, Eloise; Teaching the Deaf Child to Read; 1959, *104*, 372-382

Kirkley, James R.; What Should Be Done About Reading in Our Schools for the Deaf; 1938, *83*, 197-208

Kraft, Dorothy G.; Reading for the Deaf; 1945, *90*, 164-173

Lucas, Frances; Articulation and Lip-Reading in the Advanced Dept.; 1916, *61*, 330-332

Newlee, C. E.; Reading as a Means of Teaching Language to the Deaf; 1930, *75*, 345-361

Northrop, Helen; Reading for the Deaf; 1924, *69*, 401-425

Parks, Roy G.; Objectives and Skills in Teaching Reading in Schools for the Deaf; 1937, *82*, 425-432

READING—continued

Annals of the Deaf

Patten, Helen T.; Reading (Incidental Uses of Reading Seat Work Activities); 1930, *75*, 196-200
Pugh, Gladys S.; Summaries from "Appraisal of the Silent Reading Abilities of Acoustically Handicapped Children"; 1946, *91*, 331-349
Pugh, Gladys S.; Teaching Reading to the Deaf; 1945, *90*, 180-187
Richards, Edith; Flash Cards for Silent Reading; 1930, *75*, 201-203
Roberts, Linnaeus; A Reading Experiment; 1889, *34*, 117-120
Rogers, William B.; Reading and the Education of the Deaf; 1945, *90*, 221-236
Smith, James L.; Reading for the Little Ones; 1891, *36*, 190-193
Smith, James M.; Reading in the Schoolroom; 1915, *60*, 242-253
Stone, Elizabeth A.; Reading for the Deaf; 1914, *59*, 131-134
Streeter, Helen M.; A Study of the Dependent Clause in Primary Reading of the Deaf; 1956, *101*, 288-297
Taylor, Nellie M.; Teaching the Deaf to Read; 1919, *64*, 374-379
White, Henry; Reading as a Means of Acquiring a Good Command of Language; 1879, *24*, 100-104
Wood, M. W.; A Comparison of Techniques for Increasing the Rate of Comprehension in Reading by Deaf Children; 1944, *89*, 111-131; 182-213
Wrightstone, J. W., et al.; Developing Reading Test Norms for Deaf Children; 1963, *108*, 311-316

RELIGION

Volta Review

Anderson, Marian J.; An Appeal to the Ministers of Los Angeles; 1921, *23*, 232-234
Crowther, A. E.; Religious Training for the Deaf Child; 1948, *50*, 212; 232-236
————; The Deaf Child and His Faith; 1965, *67*, 627-631; 651
Fitzgerald, E.; The Daily Devotional Period in Schools for the Deaf; 1927, *29*, 245-248
Glasser, Mrs. Mac; A Deaf Boy's Bar Mitzvah; 1963, *65*, 602-605
Glenn, Frances L.; Chapel Exercises for the Primary Department; 1929, *31*, 245-247
Hanna, Elizabeth; Religious Education for the Deaf; 1932, *34*, 393-394; 625; 649
Hunter, Annie R.; The Church and the Hard of Hearing; 1936, *38*, 470; 490

Mays, Lenable; A Sunday School Suggestion; 1931, *33*, 392-393
Moore, Lucile M.; A Deaf Child's Religion; 1927, *29*, 88-90
Moseley, Nancy B.; The Chapel Service; 1927, *29*, 248-249
Mulholland, Ann N.; A Unit on the Bible; 1944, *46*, 81
Peck, Annetta W.; Sunday Evening in an Office Building; 1917, *19*, 570-571
Richardson, Mrs. O. T.; Religion for the Deaf Child; 1954, *56*, 397-399
Robinson, Ruth; What Can the Hard of Hearing Do for the Church?; 1940, *42*, 863-864
Stovel, Laura; A New Avenue of Approach to the General Public; 1929, *31*, 55-57
Treibert, Marjorie; Religion in the Home; 1940, *42*, 710-714
Yeakle, Hannah E.; A Church for the Hard of Hearing; 1944, *46*, 95-96; 124-126

Annals of the Deaf

Anderson, Tom L.; Religious Education in Schools for the Deaf; 1937, *82*, 433-439
Hasenstab, Philip J.; The Religious Training of the Deaf Child; 1892, *37*, 15-23
Henderson, S., and Francis, D. H.; Workshop for Episcopal Workers for the Deaf; 1962, *107*, 232-291
Henderson, S., and Stein, S. P.; Workshop for Catholic Personnel for the Deaf; 1961, *106*, 294-340
Manning, Arthur C.; Religious Education of the Deaf; 1921, *66*, 354-361
Wild, Laura H.; The Religious Education of the Deaf; 1922, *67*, 213, 231

SCIENCE STUDIES

Volta Review

Andrews, Harriet U.; The Deaf Child and Nature; 1913, *15*, 387-393
Andrews, Harriet U.; The Importance of Nature Study for Deaf Children; 1914, *16*, 192-198
Andrews, Harriet U.; In the Woods in August; 1914, *16*, 503-515
Blair, Mary; A Series of Elementary Science Lessons; 1936, *38*, 570-572; 616-618; 644-647; 715-718; 760
Church, Lilian L.; Methods Used in Presenting Practical Science Problems to the Deaf Child; 1925, *27*, 215-217

SCIENCE STUDIES—continued

Volta Review

Church, Lilian L.; Problems Illustrating the Project Method of Teaching Science; 1925, *27*, 379-381
Church, Lilian L.; The Project Method of Teaching Practical Science; 1926, *28*, 46-48; 94-96; 338-340
Church, Lilian L.; The Project Method of Teaching the Science of Common Things; 1925, *27*, 539-541; 711-713
Eckstrom, Faith F.; Studying Science in the Lower Grades; 1956, *58*, 75-76
Elias, Hans; A Method of Teaching Science to the Deaf; 1941, *43*, 584-587
Howes, Annette S.; Science As It Is Taught in the Grammar Department of Clarke School; 1926, *28*, 149-150
Howson, James W.; Some Aspects of Science Teaching; 1926, *28*, 652-654
Kennard, M., and Fitzgerald, E.; Outline of Nature Study for Deaf Children; 1941, *43*, 429; 448-452
Phillips, F. I., and Peterson, W.; A Planetarium Visit; 1953, *55*, 435-438
Shiels, Katherine; General Science; 1930, *32*, 139-141
Willson, Amy E.; Nature Study in the Primary Grades; 1931, *33*, 442-443

Annals of the Deaf

Carter, W. H.; Nature Study; 1916, *61*, 127-132
Clarke, F. D.; Science For the Deaf and Dumb; 1871, *16*, 97-110
Day, Herbert E.; Nature Study in Schools for the Deaf; 1908, *53*, 113-118
Day, Herbert E.; Science Teaching in Schools for the Deaf; 1901, *46*, 183-186
Fowler, Frances Ellis; Nature Study; 1909, *54*, 166-172
Greenberger, D.; Object Lessons in Science; 1886, *31*, 254-259
Owsley, Peter J.; Teaching Science to Deaf Children; 1963, *107*, 339-342
——————; Suggestions for the Study of Nature in Primary Grades; 1934, *79*, 255-260

SOCIAL STUDIES

Volta Review

Arnold, Allie; Beginning History; 1934, *36*, 647-649; 694
Beattie, Grace M.; Geography; 1920, *22*, 648-654
Blish, Isabel S.; Creating Social Awareness Through Social Studies; 1959, *61*, 366-373

Clatterbuck, M. B.; Social Studies in the Oregon School; 1939, *41*, 136-138
Coffey, M. Adelaide; Fourth Grade Geography; 1928, *30*, 806-809
Collins, Marcella; A Spin Around the World; 1936, *38*, 573-575; 615
Cowles, Katherine; Vitalizing Geography; 1926, *28*, 585-586
Dickey, Dorothy B.; Place Geography; 1936, *38*, 510; 546-547
Donaldson, Elizabeth M.; Geography for Young Minds; 1929, *31*, 252-254
Fouts, Mildred; Vitalizing the Geography Dosage; 1947, *49*, 456; 490-492
Freck, Phyllis; Geography in the Grammar Grades; 1933, *35*, 249-251
Fullington, Angeline; A History Project; 1931, *33*, 316-318
Gawith, Frances W.; Geography and History for Intermediate Grades; 1907, *9*, 135-142
Harris, James C.; The Heavens; 1921, *23*, 284-292
Harwood, Viola; History for the Deaf; 1928, *30*, 340-341
—————; History (Virginia Teachers); 1928, *30*, 625-629
Jones, Anne; A Holland Project; 1933, *35*, 390-392
King, Kate L.; Making Geography the Most Interesting Subject; 1926, *28*, 708-710
Kirkley, J. R.; Outline Maps and Current Events; 1936, *38*, 332; 368-369
Long, T. Schuyler; The Teaching of History; 1920, *22*, 550-557
Miller, Ada R.; A Seventh Grade Study of Europe; 1933, *35*, 25-26
Moore, Helen T.; Methods and Devices for Teaching Current Events and History; 1931, *33*, 128-129
Morrison, Jessie S.; Geography in Departmental Grades; 1929, *31*, 254-256
O'Connell, Agnes; A History Project in Sixth Grade; 1928, *30*, 33-34
Olanoff, Rose S., and McCormick, Margaret; The House I Live In (Unit on Brotherhood); 1953, *55*, 75-76
Poulos, T. H.; Planning a Social Studies Program for the Deaf; 1954, *56*, 443-446
Renard, Ella S.; Some Suggestions for Teaching History; 1926, *28*, 206-207
Savage, Julia W.; Current Events in Advanced Classes; 1926, *28*, 251-253
Sister M. Albert; Seventh Grade Geography; 1932, *34*, 109-110
Smith, James L.; Current History in the Schoolroom; 1903, *5*, 112-118
Strickland, Elizabeth H.; Geography Notes; 1927, *29*, 750-754; 1928, *30*, 101-106; 168-172; 232-234; 291-294; 391-393; 436-439; 482-485; 809-814; 1929, *31*, 201-204; 322-325; 427-444; 1930, *32*, 37-40; 147-149
Strickland, Elizabeth H.; Hints on How to Teach Geography; 1911, *13*, 403-409
Timberlake, Josephine B.; History Is a Continuous Process; 1953, *55*, 337-339
Wood, Doris E.; A Language-Geography Project in 2B; 1934, *36*, 524-526

SOCIAL STUDIES—*continued*

Annals of the Deaf

Adams, Mabel E.; History Teaching; 1920, *65*, 414-424

Adams, Mabel E.; A Lesson in Preparatory History in a Fifth Grade in a School for the Deaf; 1915, *60*, 273-277

Curtiss, Louise A.; History in the Grammar Grades; 1928, *73*, 246-248

Driggs, Frank M.; Geography Teaching; 1897, *42*, 299-316

Ervin, Annie M.; Teaching Current History; 1923, *68*, 134-142

Fletcher, Katharine; Some Reasons for Teaching History; 1892, *37*, 177-182

Fletcher, Katharine; Text-Books in History; 1897, *42*, 179-198

Goggin, Anne P.; The Cultivation of the Reading Habit and of a Taste for History in the Primary Grades; 1900, *45*, 441-445

Goggin, Anne P.; Teaching Geography; 1912, *57*, 369-379

Jenkins, Weston; About Teaching Geography; 1886, *31*, 101-107

Jenkins, Weston; The Place of History Study; 1907, *52*, 213-223

Mashburn, Arthur G.; Geography Teaching; 1903, *48*, 440-451

Newcombe, F. C.; Introduction to the Study of Geography; 1886, *31*, 107-110

Read, Elmer D.; Geography; 1905, *50*, 502-509

Read, Elmer D.; Objective Tests in History; 1930, *75*, 252-273

Read, Elmer D.; Problems Met in Teaching History; 1908, *53*, 202-207

Read, Elmer D.; Subject-Matter Plan for Teaching History; 1932, *77*, 211-231

Reed, Katharine F.; Suggestions for Geography Teaching; 1906, *51*, 136-141

Rhodes, Elizabeth; Illustrative Charts for Geography Teaching; 1915, *60*, 137-139

Robinson, Warren; History; 1903, *48*, 18-22

Sister M. Constantia; The Teaching of Social Studies in Schools for the Deaf; 1934, *79*, 310-314

Smith, Minnie E.; Projects in Geography—Grade 4A; 1928, *73*, 254-256

Sutton, Estella V.; History-Teaching—Facts or Philosophy?; 1895, *40*, 130-137

White, Henry C.; How History May Be Taught; 1889, *34*, 185-190

Whitcher, Cora M.; Devices Used in Teaching Geography; 1916, *61*, 408-411

SPEECH

Volta Review

Alcorn, Kate; Speech Developed Through Vibration; 1938, *40*, 633-637
Alcorn, Sophia; Speech in the Detroit Day School; 1949, *51*, 163; 192-194
Alcorn, Sophia; The Tadoma Method; 1932, *34*, 195-198
Alcorn, Sophia; The Use of Touch; 1930, *32*, 452-453
Allen, Anna C.; Voice Culture; 1900, *2*, 219-230
Angelocci, Angelo A.; Some Observations on the Speech of the Deaf; 1962, *64*, 403-405
——————; Auricular Instruction; 1900, *2*, 481-488
Avondino, Josephine; The Babbling Method; 1918, *20*, 667-671; 767-771; 1919, *21*, 67-71; 142-145; 224-228; 273-282
Avondino, Josephine; Fluency; 1930, *32*, 454-455
Bailey, Jane D.; The Value of Vibration in Teaching Speech to the Deaf; 1932, *34*, 200; 230-231
Bell, Alexander G.; French Pronunciation in the Melville Bell Symbols; 1909, *11*, 537-542
Bell, Alexander G.; Historical Notes Concerning the Teaching of Speech to the Deaf; 1900, *2*, 33-68; 113-115; 257-272; 385-409; 489-519; 1901, *3*, 131-140; 329-357; 428-452; 1902, *4*, 19-41; 139-151; 438-454; 1903, *5*, 369-378; 1905, *7*, 49-70
Bell, Alexander G.; Reminiscences of Early Days of Speech-Teaching; 1912, *14*, 579-581
Bell, Alexander M.; Phonetic Syllabication; 1915, *17*, 97-102
Bell, Alexander M.; Principles of Speech and Dictionary of Sounds; 1914, *16*, 65-78; 128-142; 217-227; 303-308; 403-408; 486-488; 555-558; 667-670; 731-735; 830-838; 1915, *17*, 31-40; 79-80; 116-118; 161-163; 204-206; 248-249; 283-292; 335-336; 405-420; 494-504
Bell, Mrs. Alexander G.; Speech-work in New Zealand; 1911, *12*, 677-682
Benedict, A. L.; English Spelling and Pronunciation; 1920, *22*, 303-306
Benedict, A. L.; Notes on the Sequence of Elementary Sounds in English; 1916, *18*, 393-397
Benedict, A. L.; Pronunciation of "th" in English; 1917, *19*, 696-698
Benedict, A. L.; Speech with Reference to Delicacy of Auditory Sensations; 1917, *19*, 419-425
Benedict, A. L.; Vowel Incidence in English; 1917, *19*, 97-101
Benedict, A. L.; Vowel Pronunciation in English; 1916, *18*, 495-498
Bingham, Katherine T.; Speech Is as Natural to the Deaf as to the Hearing Child; 1915, *17*, 25-26
Black, John W.; Experimental Phonetics; 1960, *62*, 313-315
Bodycomb, Margaret; The Speech of the Deaf and the Normal Speaker; 1946, *48*, 637-638
Booth, Iris, et al.; The Practical Use of Speech in Holding a Job; 1940, *42*, 600-606

SPEECH—continued

Volta Review

Breckwoldt, Gerhart H.; The Use of the Artificial Palate for Visual Control and Improvement of Articulation; 1948, *50*, 301-303

Brill, Richard G., and Gordon, Anne; The Special Speech Teacher in a School for the Deaf; 1949, *51*, 549-550, 588-590

Bruce, Wallace; Social Integration and Effectiveness of Speech; 1960, *62*, 368-372

Burke, Mary M.; Making Speech More Interesting; 1929, *31*, 789-790

Butler, A. Evelyn; Corrective Work in Speech; 1909, *11*, 408-410

Calvert, Donald R.; Deaf Voice Quality: A Preliminary Investigation; 1962, *64*, 402-403

Calvert, Donald R.; Speech Sound Duration and the Surd-Sonant Error; 1962, *64*, 401-402

Carr, Josephine; The Use of Spontaneous Speech; 1955, *57*, 20-21

Carter, A. E.; Teaching Speech to the Deaf; 1915, *17*, 315-317

Christmas, Jeannette J.; P, T, and K As Breath Stops; 1926, *28*, 195-197

Clapp, John M.; What Good Speech Can Do for the Business Man; 1917, *19*, 611-613

Cloud, Daniel T.; Touch and Hearing in Speech Work; 1935, *37*, 350; 381

Connery, Julia M.; A Demonstration in Voice Training; 1919, *21*, 108-109

Crouter, A. L.; The Development of Speech in the Deaf Child; 1910, *12*, 288-298

Cruttenden, Mary E.; The Value of the Speechmaster; 1953, *55*, 294; 316-318

Dawes, Rachel E.; Articulation at the Western Penn. School; 1927, *29*, 772-780

DeLand, Fred; Give Your Child the Best Educational Advantages; 1918, *20*, 329-333

DeLand, Fred; The Melville Bell Symbols for Recording Speech Sounds; 1919, *21*, 617-621

DeLand, Fred; The Pioneer Pictorial Presentation of Mouth Positions for Use in Teaching Speech and Speech-Reading to the Deaf; 1914, *16*, 455-465

De L'Epee, Abbe; The Only Method of Completely Restoring the Deaf and Dumb to Society; 1900, *2*, 68-69

————; Demonstration of How NOT to Teach Speech; 1935, *37*, 585, 617

————; The Development of Pitch in the Voice of Congenitally Deaf Children; 1918, *20*, 258-261

Di Carlo, Louis M.; Speech and Communication for the Deaf; 1960, *62*, 317-319

Driggs, Frank M.; Speech Problems in Combined-System Schools; 1914, *16*, 631-635

Drum, Philip R.; How Speech Therapy Feels; 1963, *65*, 74-75
Duff, Jessie; Gaining the Speech Habit; 1919, *21*, 479-483
Duff, Jessie; The Use of Speech and Speech-Reading; 1916, *18*, 1-2
Dunbar, Evelina; Articulation, Voice and Speech; 1925, *27*, 5-8
Dyer, Helen L.; Need A Deaf Child's Speech Be Expressionless?; 1914, *16*, 85-87
Eccleston, Mary M.; How We Learn Speech in the Beginning; 1928, *30*, 279-280
─────────; Editorial Comment. De L'Epée, The Great Advocate of Speech; 1918, *20*, 801-803
Elliott, Sarah L.; Speech in Our Advanced Department; 1927, *29*, 457-459
Ersner, Matthew S.; Defective Speech and Some of Its Phases; 1918, *20*, 392-395
Farman, J. J.; Speech Intelligibility Test (Farman-Phillips); 1954, *56*, 168-170
Ferreri, Giulio; Teaching Speech to the Deaf; 1911, *13*, 225-227
Fish, Kate H.; Speech Work for Older Pupils; 1907, *9*, 250-255
Fleitz, Mildred, and Dacey, Edward; A Game with the Vowel Sounds; 1929, *31*, 373-374
Frisina, D. Robert, and Bernero, R. J.; A Profile of the Hearing and Speech of Gallaudet College Students; 1958, *60*, 316-321
Froeschels, Emil; A New Method in the Oral Education of the Deaf Child; 1940, *42*, 664-666
Fuller, Sarah; The Melville Bell Symbols as an Aid in Correcting Stammering; 1915, *17*, 214-216
Gardiner, M.; The Story of "Visible Speech"; 1910, *12*, 99-102
Gardner, Mark B.; Speech We May See; 1956, *58*, 149-155
Garns, John S.; Why the Deafened Should Have Vocal Training; 1929, *31*, 757-759
Garrett, Mary S.; Helps and Hindrances of Deaf Children in Acquiring Speech and Language at the Natural Age; 1908, *10*, 274-276
Gault, R. H.; The Use of the Sense of Touch in Developing Speech; 1934, *36*, 82-83
Glenn, Frances L.; Speech: Its Place in Child Culture; 1910, *12*, 418-419
Glenn, Frances L.; Speech and Speech Reading in Primary Classes; 1907, *9*, 98-104
Goetzinger, Cornelius P.; Effects of Small Perceptive Losses on Language and on Speech Discrimination; 1962, *64*, 408-414
Greene, James S.; National Hospital for Speech Disorders; 1922, *24*, 223-227
Gregg, F. M.; The Psychology of Speech; 1943, *45*, 138-139; 178
Grussing, Florence P.; Speech as a Subject; 1932, *34*, 271-272

SPEECH—continued

Volta Review

Gruver, Margaret H.; The Tadoma Method; 1955, *57*, 17-19
Gutzmann, Albert; Care of the Speech of Children in the Family and the School; 1902, *4*, 107-112
Hancock, E. Frances; Use of Diagnostic Speech Charts; 1934, *36*, 645, 690
Harris, G. T.; A Study in the Sound "S"; 1927, *29*, 298-299
Hector, Elizabeth R.; Speech Defects; 1928, *30*, 173-174
Hedrick, Jennie; A New Nomenclature for Nasality; 1919, *21*, 538-540
Heider, Fritz, and Sykes, Jean L.; A Study of the Spontaneous Vocalizations of Fourteen Deaf Children; 1941, *43*, 10-14
Henderson, Jennie M.; Outline of a Speech Lesson; 1930, *32*, 134-136
Henderson, Jennie M.; The Teacher's Voice; 1930, *32*, 609-610
Houchins, Rollie R.; Pitch Discrimination; 1962, *64*, 424-426
Hubbard, Elbert; Stutterers and Stammerers; 1917, *19*, 627-629
Hudgins, Clarence V.; Concerning the Validity of Speech Tests; 1943, *45*, 271-272; 316
Hudgins, Clarence V.; A Method of Appraising the Speech of the Deaf; 1949, *51*, 597-601; 638
Hudgins, Clarence V.; The Research Program in Speech at the Clarke School; 1952, *54*, 355-362
Hudgins, Clarence V.; Speech Breathing and Speech Intelligibility; 1946, *48*, 642-644
Hudgins, Clarence V.; Speech Intelligibility Tests: A Practical Program; 1943, *45*, 5-6; 52-54
Hudgins, Clarence V. (moderator, panel); Speech and Speech Perception; 1953, *55*, 20-38
Hudgins, Clarence V.; A Study of Respiration and Speech; 1936, *38*, 341-343; 373
Hudson-McKuen, G.; Obstructions to Speech-Development; 1911, *13*, 286-291
Hudson-McKuen, G.; The Physiology and Psychology of Hearing with Special Reference to the Development of Speech; 1910, *12*, 267-272
Hurd, Anna C.; The Use of Speech in All Activities; 1930, *32*, 455-457
Joiner, Enfield; How We Rehabilitated the Speech of Soldiers; 1920, *22*, 245-248
Joiner, Enfield; Speech Contests; 1938, *40*, 628-630
Joiner, Enfield, and Lewis, Sarah; Speech Correction in the Primary Grades; 1926, *28*, 620-624
Joiner, Enfield; Our Speech Teaching Heritage; 1948, *50*, 417-422
Jones, Eleanor P.; Details of Work in Beginning Class from February to June, 1913; 1914, *16*, 110-114

Kenyon, Elmer L.; Psychophysiologic Principles Underlying Improvement in Vocal Pitch, Tension and Quality in the Deafened, With the Presentation of an Effectual Physiologic Substitute for Lost Hearing in Vocal Management; 1929, *31*, 129-141
Kenyon, Elmer L.; Stammering as a Disorder of Speech Dependent on Conditions of Child Development; 1920, *22*, 39-45
Kidder, Charles W.; The Serviceability of Visible Speech; 1919, *21*, 589-593
Kinsey, Eveline I.; On the Management of the Voice; 1904, *6*, 206-210
Knight, Marian; Making the Elements Fun to Learn; 1955, *57*, 360-361
Koester, Diedrich; Visible Speech; 1955, *57*, 255-256
Kopp, George A.; The Application of Recent Findings in the Field of Speech Correction; 1938, *40*, 638-640
Kopp, George A., and Green, Harriet C.; Visible Speech; 1948, *50*, 60-62; 264-266
Lack, A.; Speech Problems Throughout the School; 1937, *39*, 72-75; 123-124
Lamb, Helen D.; Drill Exercises on One Hundred Difficult Words of Common Speech; 1923, *25*, 100-105
Lamb, Marion H.; Some Suggestions for Corrective Speech Work; 1935, *37*, 133-136
Larr, Alfred L., and Stockwell, Robert P.; A Test of Speech Intelligibility; 1959, *61*, 403-407; 437
Lauritsen, Marné; Methods and Results of Training with the Teletactor; 1928, *30*, 604-609
Leonard, Eleanor C.; School-room Ethics in Speech Teaching; 1913, *14*, 651-653
Lewin, Lucie M.; The Speech Habit; 1927, *29*, 242-244
Long, J. Schuyler; Poetry as an Aid to Pronunciation; 1920, *22*, 448-450
Lore, James I.; A System of Recording American-English Speech Sounds; 1961, *63*, 433-434
Lore, James I.; A Technique for Developing Adequate Post-Plosive Aspiration; 1957, *59*, 351
Lucas, Frances; Corrective Work in Speech; 1909, *11*, 408-410
McCalmont, Phyllis; A Departure from Formal Classroom Teaching of Communication Skills; 1956, *58*, 61-63
McCowen, Mary; How Best To Secure Intelligent Speech for Deaf Children; 1907, *9*, 256-261
McKendrick, John G.; Experimental Phonetics; 1902, *4*, 327-343
Makuen, G. Hudson; A Study of 1,000 Cases of Stammering; 1915, *17*, 268-273
Mangan, Kenneth R.; Speech Teaching for Older Children; 1960, *62*, 319-321

SPEECH—continued

Volta Review

Mannen, Grace; Speech for Outside Activities; 1958, *60*, 391-395

Martin, Frederick; A Method of Raising a Low-Pitched Voice and Lowering a High-Pitched Voice; 1925, *27*, 19-24

Martin, Frederick; The Prevention and Correction of Speech Defects; 1919, *21*, 434-438; 1923, *25*, 281-284

Monaghan, Alice; The Need for a School to Have a Philosophy of Teaching Speech; 1958, *60*, 386-391

Monro, Sarah J.; The Music of Speech; 1913, *15*, 127-130

Monro, Sarah J.; Phonetics and Word Study; A Plan for Pronunciation and Speech Drill; 1919, *21*, 213-216; 286-289; 360-363; 604-606; 669-672; 1920, *22*, 15-18; 94-97; 233-235; 383-384

Monro, Sarah J.; Preliminaries To Speech-Teaching; 1912, *13*, 468-472

Monro, Sarah J.; Rhythm in Speaking; 1917, *19*, 641-645

Monro, Sarah J.; Some "Don'ts" and Their "Whys"; 1904, *6*, 116-121

Monsees, Edna K.; Experiences with Children Who Failed to Learn to Talk When Taught as Deaf or Hard of Hearing; 1958, *60*, 328-330

Mulholland, Ann M.; Communication: A Review of Current Research; 1963, *65*, 513-522

Muyskens, John H.; The Building and Maintenance of Clear Speech for the Deaf; 1938, *40*, 655-657

Nelson, Boyd E.; Building a Speech Vocabulary; 1943, *45*, 74-75

New, Mary C.; Color in Speech Teaching; 1942, *44*, 133-138; 199-203

New, Mary C.; The Deaf Child's Speech Vocabulary; 1954, *56*, 105-108

New, Mary C.; Speech for the Young Deaf Child; 1940, *42*, 592-599

New, Mary C.; Speech in Our Schools for the Deaf; 1949, *51*, 61-64; 98-102

Nitchie, Edward B.; A Study of Vowel Positions; 1905, *7*, 412-415

Nitkin, Nathaniel; Improving Your Speech; 1940, *42*, 35-39

Numbers, Fred C.; Is Speech Teaching a Failure?; 1946, *48*, 264-266; 316

Numbers, Fred C.; The Versatile Consonant; 1946, *48*, 638-640

Numbers, Mary E.; The Place of Elements Teaching in Speech Development; 1942, *44*, 261-265

O'Connor, Clarence D.; Better Speech for Better Living; 1946, *48*, 624-627

O'Connor, Clarence D.; That the Deaf May Speak; 1952, *54*, 418-420; 466

Osborne, Caroline A.; Speech Defects in the School Child; 1918, *20*, 517-521

Oswald, Mabel V.; Stammering and Voice Defects; 1919, *21*, 708-711

Peterson, Gordon E., et al. (Panel discussion); Effective Speech for the Deaf; 1962, *64*, 369-378

Peterson, Gordon E.; The Influence of Voice Quality; 1946, *48*, 640-641
Pittinger, Priscilla; Speech and the Deaf Adult; 1954, *56*, 449-451
Poulos, Thomas H.; Improving the Intelligibility of Deaf Children's Speech; 1952, *54*, 265-267, 284
Poulos, Thomas H.; A Speech Improvement Program in a Large Residential School for the Deaf; 1962, *64*, 405-408
Power, Sue B.; The Difficulties of Speech in Acquired Deafness; 1920, *22*, 670-672
Pratt, George T.; Oral Education for Deaf Children: Why and How; 1961, *63*, 480-483
Presto, Marya; An Experiment in Voice Control; 1943, *45*, 490-493
Pugh, Bessie; Clarifying Speech Problems for the Deaf; 1963, *65*, 15-21
Pugh, Bessie; The Speech Vocabulary of Young Children; 1946, *48*, 267; 312-313
Quick, Marian; A Speech Program for Advanced Pupils; 1955, *57*, 22-23
Raph, Jane B.; Problems and Issues in Teaching Speech; 1960, *62*, 302-306
Reed, Mrs. Frank A.; The Practical Correction of Impediments in Speech; 1913, *15*, 11-18
Reed, Mrs. Frank A.; Speech Impediments and Their Correction in the Public Schools of Detroit; 1915, *17*, 7-8
————; Report on the Progress of Speech Teaching in America; 1904, *6*, 264-279; 1906, *8*, 270-283; 1907, *9*, 370-383
————; Resolutions Relating to Speech Teaching (1868-1900); 1900, *2*, 520-526
Richardson, Paul C.; Developing Fundamental Speech Patterns; 1959, *61*, 276-282
Roberts, Emma; To Speak or Not To Speak; 1914, *16*, 697-698
Roe, W. Carey; The "Explosive" Sounds; 1915, *17*, 457-459
Rooney, Alice G.; Voice Work for the Young Deaf Child; 1944, *46*, 558-560; 608
Rotter, Paul; The Development of Speech in Young Children; 1955, *57*, 53-57; 82
Russell, G. Oscar; "Uncanny Deaf Speech"; 1928, *30*, 566-572
Scott, Ella; How to Correct Defective Articulation; 1900, *2*, 457-462
Scripture, E. W.; The Analysis of Vowel Curves; 1921, *23*, 99-102
Scripture, E. W.; Inscriptions of Speech; 1920, *22*, 427-434
Scripture, E. W.; The Mechanism of Breathing; 1921, *23*, 403-406
Scripture, E. W.; The Nature of Stuttering; 1917, *19*, 297-298
Scripture, E. W.; The Organ of Voice, 1920, *22*, 571-575
Scripture, E. W.; The Physical Nature of a Vowel; 1921, *23*, 149-150
Scripture, E. W.; The Physics of Speech; 1921, *23*, 366-368

SPEECH—continued

Volta Review

Scripture, E. W.; Tracing from Speech Records; 1920, *22*, 480-485
Scripture, E. W.; The Voices of the Deaf; 1913, *15*, 77-80; 141-145; 269-275; 314-316
Scripture, E. W.; The Vowel Siren; 1921, *23*, 75-76
Silverman, S. Richard; The Report on Speech Teaching; 1943, *45*, 622-623; 662
Silverman, S. Richard; The Speech Program of Central Institute; 1943, *45*, 12-15; 56-57
Silverman, S. Richard; Teaching Speech to the Deaf—The Issues; 1954, *56*, 385-389; 417
Simon, Arthur B.; Why Take Time Out for Speech Teaching?; 1945, *47*, 326; 378-380
Sister Mary Laurentine, et al.; Effective Speech for the Deaf (panel discussion); 1962, *64*, 374-378
Sister Mary Laurentine; The Speech Program at St. Joseph Institute for the Deaf; 1964, *66*, 459-463
Sister Marianna; How to Improve the Speech of Older Deaf Children; 1950, *52*, 61-62; 100-102
Sister St. Esther; Common Sense and Speech Teaching; 1945, *47*, 485-486; 542
Smith, Sherman K.; Can We Improve the Voice Quality of the Congenitally Deaf?; 1932, *34*, 528-534
Smith, Sherman K.; Speech Patterns; 1933, *35*, 160-161; 188
Smith, Sherman K.; Voice and Speech Problems; 1931, *33*, 438-439
————; Speech Diagrams Showing Positions of Vocal Organs; 1914, *16*, 207-215
————; Speech Teaching in Schools for the Deaf; An Association Committeee Report; 1943, *45*, 7-11; 50
Spyker, Sally; The Development of Speech in the Case of a So-Called Deaf-Mute; 1917, *19*, 61-63
Stedman, Anne B.; An Outline of the Elements and Treatment of Stammering; 1917, *19*, 71-72
————; Statistics of Speech Teaching in American Schools for the Deaf; 1899, *1*, 84-106; 1900, *2*, 298-315; 1901, *3*, 156-160; 280-297; 1902, *4*, 134-138; 292-311; 1903, *5*, 190-194; 300-316; 1904, *6*, 270-281; 1905, *7*, 282-293; 1906, *8*, 270-283; 1907, *9*, 370-383; 1908, *10*, 290-302; 1909, *11*, 234-246; 1910, *12*, 246-258; 1911, *13*, 104-116; 1912, *14*, 108-121; 681-683; 1913, *15*, 92-103; 1914, *16*, 79-81; 310-322; 1915, *17*, 190-202; 1916, *18*, 200-213; 1917, *19*, 240-252; 1918, *20*, 368-381; 1919, *21*, 392-405; 1920, *22*, 362-375
Steed, Lyman; Visible Speech; 1925, *27*, 54-57
Steinberg, John C.; The Teaching of Speech; 1929, *31*, 408-409

Stetson, R. H.; Contributions of Teachers of the Deaf to the Science of Phonetics; 1943, *45*, 19-20; 54-56

Stevens, J. E.; Stammering; 1923, *25*, 532-535

Stobschinski, Robert; The Jena Method Applied to Speech; 1933, *35*, 325-328

Stokoe, Agnes; Vibration in Speech Teaching; 1948, *50*, 422-423

Stoner, Marguerite; The Development of Early Speech with Emphasis on the Synthetic Method; 1955, *57*, 15-17

Story, Arthur J.; The Development of "Natural" Speech; 1910, *12*, 613-621

Story, Arthur J.; The Importance of Consonants in Speech and Speech-Reading; 1909, *11*, 479-488

Story, Arthur J.; Some Practical Points; 1915, *17*, 155-158

Story, Arthur J.; The Speaking Mouth; 1909, *11*, 13-19

Story, Arthur J.; "Strange Voices" in the Deaf; 1912, *14*, 531-533

Story, Arthur J.; Talks to Young Teachers of Speech: The Development of Voice for Speaking; 1917, *19*, 68-70

Story, Arthur J.; Talks to Young Teachers of Speech: Errors in the Consonantal Sounds; 1916, *18*, 315-317

Story, Arthur J.; Talks to Young Teachers of Speech: The Mouth in Speech; 1918, *20*, 320-322

Story, Arthur J.; Talks to Young Teachers of Speech: The Synthetic Method; 1916, *18*, 397-399

Swift, Walter B.; Discussion of the Emotional Theory of Stuttering; 1920, *22*, 510-518

Swift, Walter B.; How to Begin Speech Correction in the Public Schools; 1919, *21*, 585-589

Swift, Walter B.; A Reasonable Objection to Unscientific Methods in Speech Correction; 1920, *22*, 166-168

Taylor, Harris; Oralism in Oral Schools; 1910, *12*, 349-353

Taylor, Harris; Progress of Speech-Teaching in the United States; 1912, *13*, 531-533

Taylor, Harris; Speech Diagrams; 1914, *16*, 389-399

Taylor, Harris; Speech-teaching in American Schools for the Deaf; 1915, *17*, 56-58

Thomason, Pattie; An Experiment in Voice Culture; 1914, *16*, 441-444

Thomason, Pattie; Suggestions for Improving the Quality of the Voice; 1917, *19*, 361-364

Thomason, Pattie; Voice and Speech; 1919, *21*, 484-485

Thomason, Pattie; Voice Training for Deaf Children; 1918, *20*, 311-314; 387-388

Thomason, Pattie; Voice Training in the Intermediate Grades; 1921, *23*, 88-90

SPEECH—*continued*

Volta Review

Thompson, Iza; Modernism in Forming a Basis of Intelligible Rhythmic Speech for the Deaf-Born Child; 1927, *29*, 343-349

Thompson, Iza; The Sensitive Flame of the Bunsen Burner as an Aid to Voice Production and Speech for the Congenitally Deaf Child; 1921, *23*, 397-399

Tilly, William; The International Phonetic Alphabet; 1925, *27*, 57-59

Timberlake, Josephine B.; A Tool for Speech Teaching; 1940, *42*, 10-12; 56-57

Timberlake, Josephine B.; Voice Training for the Deafened; 1923, *25*, 351-354

Tompkins, Ernest; Is Stammering Emotional?; 1920, *22*, 752-754

Tompkins, Ernest; Stammering and Amnesia; 1920, *22*, 85-88

Tompkins, Ernest; Stammering and the Scientific Attitude; 1923, *25*, 483-485

Tompkins, Ernest; Stammering: A Reasonable Answer to a Reasonable Objection; 1920, *22*, 450-452

Utley, Jean, and Walker, N. F.; Are the Northampton Charts Outmoded?; 1942, *44*, 485-490

———; Vocal Physiology, the Principles of Speech, etc.; 1914, *16*, 66-78

Voelker, Charles H.; A Sound Count for the Oral Curriculum; 1935, *37*, 155-156

Vorce, Eleanor R.; Teaching Speech at Lexington School; 1955, *57*, 11-13

Walker, Hazel W.; Dr. Frederick Martin's Speech Methods as Applied to the Deaf and the Hard of Hearing Child; 1931, *33*, 171-174

West, Robert; Speech and Hearing; 1935, *37*, 573-578; 626-629

Wettstein, Frances; Articulation in the Intermediate Grades; 1907, *9*, 153-159

Wolf, Edna L.; A Questionnaire for the Oral Teacher; 1939, *41*, 328; 376

Wood, Margaret; Speech in Our Upper School; 1958, *60*, 382-386

Worcester, Alice E.; Pronunciation at Sight; 1915, *17*, 85-93

Wright, John D.; Desk Work in Speech; 1917, *19*, 105-106

Wright, John D.; A Friendly Talk; 1919, *21*, 203-209

Wright, John D.; Fundamentals in Teaching the Deaf to Speak; 1916, *18*, 132-135

Wright, John D.; Interest: Another Fundamental in Speech Teaching; 1916, *18*, 437-439

Wright, John D.; Natural Speech; 1916, *18*, 401-403

Wright, John D.; On Nasality; 1954, *56*, 408-409

Wright, John D.; Some Homely Suggestions in Speech Teaching; 1926, *28*, 614-616

Wright, John D.; Was the Ultimate Elimination of Oralism Foreseen?; 1914, *16*, 639-641

Yale, Caroline A.; Dr Bell's Early Experiments in Giving Speech to the Deaf; 1927, *29*, 293-295
Yale, Caroline A.; Formation and Development of Elementary English Sounds; 1902, *4*, 240-244; 323-326; 424-427; 1903, *5*, 12-15; 140-142; 231-240
Yale, Caroline A.; Phonetic Notation (the Northampton Charts); 1925, *27*, 49-54
Zaliouk, A., Cohen, S., and Zaliouk, D.; Intelligible Speech Through a Visual-Tactile System of Phonetical Symbolization; 1957, *59*, 426-435; 454

Annals of the Deaf

Adams, Mabel E.; The Intelligibility of the Speech of the Deaf; 1914, *59*, 451-460
Arnold, Thomas; The Functions of Touch in Learning to Speak; 1886, *31*, 120-130
Arnold, Thomas; Mr. Thomas Arnold's Method of Teaching Articulation; 1882, *27*, 90-98
Bell, Alexander G.; Visible Speech as a Means of Communicating Articulation to Deaf-Mutes; 1872, *17*, 1-21
Blanton, Smiley; Treatment of Stutterers; 1922, *67*, 371-385
Brehm, F. Elizabeth; Speech Correction; 1922, *67*, 361-370
Buell, Edith M.; Easy and Natural Speech; 1914, *59*, 379-386; 443-451; 1915, *60*, 129-137
Butler, A. Evelyn; Advanced Work in Articulation; 1907, *52*, 349-354; 1916, *61*, 333-338
Carhart, Raymond; A Method of Using the Gault-Teletactor to Teach Speech Rhythms; 1935, *80*, 260-263
Christmas, Jeannette J.; Articulation Work in the Primary Grades; 1907, *52*, 320-330; 1916, *61*, 306-315
Clark, A. S.; "The Elements of Human Speech" Reviewed; 1874, *19*, 21-26
Coats, G. Dewey; Characteristics of Communication Methods; 1950, *95*, 486-490
Curtis, John H.; Organs of Speech and Hearing; 1849, *2*, 158-164
Davidson, Emma F.; Voice Culture for Advanced Pupils; 1907, *52*, 354-372; 1916, *61*, 339-360
Elliot, Richard; Speech for the Deaf; 1869, *14*, 129-145
Fay, Edward A.; The Hygenic Value of Speech; 1892, *37*, 80
Fowler, Frances E.; Articulation Drill; 1909, *54*, 416-420

SPEECH—continued

Annals of the Deaf

Fusfeld, Irving S.; How the Deaf Communicate—Speech; 1958, *103*, 243-254

Garrett, Emma; A Plea That The Deaf "Mutes" of America May Be Taught to Use Their Voices; 1883, *28*, 15-20

Gillespie, Frances E.; The Theory and Practice of Instruction for an Oral Class of Beginners; 1901, *46*, 492-507; 1902, *47*, 233-242

Grandgent, Charles H.; Vowel Measurements; 1891, *36*, 11-38

Greenberger, D.; The Organs of Speech; 1883, *28*, 1-14; 226-234; 1885, *30*, 259-270

Greenberger, D.; Visible Speech as a Means of Communicating Articulation to the Deaf and Dumb; 1874, *19*, 65-74

Greene, David; Breath and Voice; 1901, *46*, 477-487

Hedgecock, Le Roy D.; Speech and Hearing Problems of the Young Deaf Child; 1955, *100*, 435-485

Hotchkiss, J. Burton; Articulation for Semi-Mutes; 1870, *15*, 136-149

Houser, Bessie; Pioneer Oral Work; 1933, *78*, 374-376

Hudgins, Clarence V.; Voice Production and Breath Control in the Speech of the Deaf; 1937, *82*, 338-363

Hudson-Makuen, G.; The Physiology & Psychology of Hearing with Special Referencee to the Development of Speech; 1910, *55*, 325-332

Joiner, Enfield; Teaching of Speech; 1922, *67*, 397-404

Kelley, Noble H., and Guilmartin, Mary D.; The Kelley-Guilmartin Speech Test for Deaf Children; 1941, *86*, 225-226

Lucas, Frances; Articulation and Lip Reading in the Advanced Department; 1907, *52*, 344-349

Mangan, Kenneth R.; Speech Improvement Through Articulation Testing; 1961, *106*, 391-396

Mason, Marie K.; Individual Deviations in the Visual Reproduction of the Speech of Two Speakers; 1939, *84*, 408-424

Mason, Marie K., and Bright, Margaret; Tempo in Rhythmic Speech Education; 1937, *82*, 385-401

Meyer, Max F.; What Retards Speech Teaching to the Deaf Parvel?; 1938, *83*, 153-168

Monro, Sarah A.; The Piano as an Aid to Speech; 1901, *46*, 166-169

Montgomery, Ida; The Practical Value of Articulation; 1870, *15*, 133-136

Noyes, Marion; Articulation Work in Intermediate Grades; 1907, *52*, 330-337; 1916, *61*, 315-322

Paul, W.; Entrance into School and Exercises Preliminary to Articulation; 1893, *38*, 8-14

Peet, Harvey P.; Analysis of Bonet's Treatise on the Art of Teaching the Dumb to Speak; 1851, *3*, 200-211

Peet, Isaac L.; A Method of Teaching Articulation to Every Pupil; 1893, *38*, 281-291

Phillips, John; The Elements of Human Speech, as Applied to the Instruction of Deaf-Mutes in Articulation; 1873, *18*, 241-254
Pintner, Rudolf; Speech and Speech Reading Tests for the Deaf; 1929, *74*, 480-486
Potter, Ralph K.; Visible Speech; 1946, *91*, 447-452
Pybas, Adelaide H.; Articulation Work in the Intermediate Grades; 1916, *61*, 323-329
Rawlings, Charles G.; A Comparative Study of the Movements of Breathing Muscles in Speech and Quiet Breathing of Deaf and Normal Subjects; 1935, *80*, 147-156; 1936, *81*, 136-150
Rio, Armand; The Mysteries of Speech Unveiled; 1919, *64*, 402-420
Russell, G. Oscar; Visualizing Speech for the Deaf; 1927, *72*, 329-340
Shaffer, Chester M.; The Kinesthetic Method of Speech Development and Speech-Reading; 1942, *87*, 421-442
Shaw, M.; A Study in the Analysis and Correction of the Speech of the Hard of Hearing; 1936, *81*, 255-268
Sister M. Emmanuel; Speech Work with the Deaf Child; 1926, *71*, 135-141
Sister Sylvania; Correlation of Comprehension and Speech in the Education of the Deaf; 1934, *79*, 306-309
Steinke, Elsie M.; Justification of Speech Teaching and Speech Reading; 1902, *47*, 345-349
Stone, Collins; Articulation as a Medium for the Instruction of the Deaf and Dumb; 1849, *2*, 105-112; 232-242
Storr, R. S.; Articulation in Deaf-Mute Instruction; 1882, *27*, 160-162
Story, Arthur J.; The Development of Voice for Speaking; 1918, *63*, 285-292
Story, Arthur J.; Errors in Consonantal Sounds; 1916, *61*, 443
Story, Arthur J.; The Mouth in Speech; 1918, *63*, 440-446
Story, Arthur J.; The Synthetic Method; 1916, *61*, 449
Story, Arthur J.; Talks to Young Teachers of Speech; 1916, *61*, 443-453
Taylor, Harris; Oralism in Oral Schools; 1910, *55*, 379-385
Taylor, Harris; The Phonograph as an Aid in Articulation Teaching; 1914, *59*, 337-339
Thompson, Iza; The Use of the Sensitive Flame for Voice Production and Speech for the Congenitally Deaf Child; 1926, *71*, 185-189
Throckmorton, Helen; Preparatory Work and First Steps in Articulation; 1916, *61*, 289-306
Trask, Cornelia; Articulation and Lip-Reading; 1869, *14*, 146-156
Turvey, T. M.; The Importance of Voice Culture in Teaching the Deaf; 1909, *54*, 126-140
Vinson, Marietta R.; The Production of a Tone by the Human Vocal Mechanism; 1933, *78*, 211-219

SPEECH—continued

Annals of the Deaf

Voelker, Charles H.; Demonstration Apparatus to Teach Natural Speech to the Deaf; 1940, *85*, 500-503
Voelker, Charles H.; An Experimental Study of the Comparative Rate of Utterance of Deaf and Normal Hearing Speakers; 1938, *83*, 274-284
Voelker, Charles H.; The Occurrence of Homophenous Articulations in American Usage; 1934, *79*, 210-213
Voelker, Charles H.; A Preliminary Strobophotoscopic Study of the Speech of the Deaf; 1935, *80*, 243-259
Voelker, Charles H.; The Schwa and Other Indefinite Vowels in Deaf Oralism; 1937, *82*, 253-255
Voelker, Charles H.; The Usage of Vowel Positions; 1935, *80*, 5-6
Wolf, E. L.; New Methods for the Development of Words in Speech; 1931, *76*, 442-448
Worcester, Alice E.; How Shall Our Children Be Taught to Pronounce at Sight the Words of Our Written Language?; 1885, *30*, 6-25
Wright, John D.; Combined But Not Commingled; 1917, *62*, 209-210
Wright, John D.; The Fair Chance Column; 1921, *66*, 5-7
Wright, John D.; The Necessity of a Speech Environment; 1916, *61*, 137-141
Wright, John D.; Retention of Speech; 1921, *66*, 462-475
Wright, John D.; The Speech Method of Educating the Deaf; 1910, *55*, 439-452
Wright, John D.; Why Speech Teaching Fails Sometimes; 1915, *60*, 322-323
Yale, Caroline A.; The Teaching of Elementary English Sounds; 1918, *63*, 425-435

SPEECHREADING

Volta Review

Albright, M. Arline; Ear, Eye, or Both; 1944, *46*, 11-13
Amsler, Fridette; The Jena Method of Teaching Lip-Reading; 1927, *29*, 107-109
Anderson, Marian J.; Getting the Words from the Thought and Not the Thought from the Words; 1919, *21*, 283-284
Anderson, Marian J.; Paying My Family Debts; 1922, *24*, 201-204
Andrews, Harriet U.; First-Aid to Our Relatives; 1919, *21*, 15-19
Andrews, Harriet U.; Of Lip-Reading Adults; 1909, *11*, 179-183

Becker, Margaret R.; With the Lip Reading Class; 1944, *46*, 360; 366-368
Bell, Mabel G.; The Subtile Art of Speech-Reading; 1917, *19*, 109-116
Bell, Mabel H.; Speech Reading; 1940, *42*, 607-610
Bell, Martha C.; Lip-Reading in the First Year; 1929, *31*, 307-309
Bennett, Josephine; Lip Reading for the Deaf Child; 1944, *46*, 489-494; 546
Berger, Emma; A Speech Reading Lesson for Victory Gardeners; 1944, *46*, 519-520; 530
Bickler, Mary H.; How a Deaf Child Was Taught Speech-Reading and Speech; 1921, *23*, 382-388; 424-430; 455-470
Bigelow, Jane K.; Changing Etiquette, Adapted for Lip-Reading Practice; 1930, *32*, 87-88
Birge, Marguerite S.; Teaching A Child; 1922, *24*, 212-214
Blake, Clarence J.; Speech-Reading for the War Deaf; 1918, *20*, 361-363; 385-387; 465-470; 557-560
Brand, Elizabeth; What's the Difference?; 1918, *20*, 701-703
Brand, Elizabeth; With the Lip Reading Class; 1939, *41*, 653-654; 713-714; 722-723
Brauckmann, Karl; Speechreading in America, A German View of America's Work; 1934, *36*, 103-104; 126
Breckinridge, Mary S.; Lip-Reading; 1917, *19*, 281-287
Brintnall, Mrs. Arthur W.; Lipreading Is Fun; 1955, *57*, 115-116
Bruce, Lula M.; Giving Lip Reading Its Fair Share of Time; 1938, *40*, 665-668
Bruce, Lula M.; Suggestions for Teaching Speech Reading; 1942, *44*, 5-9; 93-98; 114
Bruhn, Martha E., et al.; The Conference on Lip Reading; 1925, *27*, 68-73
Bruhn, Martha E.; Enseignement Pratique de la Lecture sur Les Levres; 1918, *20*, 308-309; 357-360; 421-427; 528-534; 651-653; 698-700; 792-796
Bruhn, Martha E.; Exercise on Proper Nouns; 1919, *21*, 487-495
Bruhn, Martha E.; First Report on My Lecture Courses; 1918, *20*, 553-555
Bruhn, Martha E.; Is Lip Reading a Science or an Art?; 1926, *28*, 476-478
Bruhn, Martha E.; Learning Lip-Reading by the Müller-Walle Method; 1917, *19*, 389-394
Bruhn, Martha E.; Manual of Lip-Reading; 1917, *19*, 464-478; 545-553; 595-599; 667-672; 1918, *20*, 3-7
Bruhn, Martha E.; Methods in Lip-Reading; 1914, *16*, 747-748
Bruhn, Martha E., et al.; Methods of Teaching Lip Reading to Adults—A Symposium; 1942, *44*, 636-641; 658; 701-707; 722; 1943, *45*, 30-35; 94-96

SPEECHREADING—*continued*

Volta Review

Bruhn, Martha E.; The Müller-Walle Method; 1920, *22*, 536-539
Bruhn, Martha E.; Bruhn Lip-Reading System (Müller-Walle Method); 1916, *18*, 65-69
Bruhn, Martha E.; The Müller-Walle Method of Lip-Reading; 1915, *17*, 293-295
Bruhn, Martha E.; Relative Skill in Lip-Reading; 1917, *19*, 220-222
Bruhn, Martha E.; What Is the Secret of Success?; 1918, *20*, 73-75
Buell, Edith M.; Speech-Reading in the Classroom; 1928, *30*, 94-99
Bunger, Anna M.; On Being Converted to the Jena Method; 1929, *31*, 705-708
Bunger, Anna M.; Speech Reading in College; 1937, *39*, 569-572; 601
Carr, Josephine; A Limited or Limitless Vocabulary Through Speechreading; 1954, *56*, 109-113
Case, Lucy E.; Symposium on Conversation-Class Work in Lip-Reading; 1915, *17*, 2-4
Chambless, Elizabeth; Class Lessons and Private Lessons; 1935, *37*, 34-36
Chandler, Flora; Lip Reading as a Federal Project; 1936, *38*, 416; 425
Chandler, Flora; With the Lip Reading Class; 1938, *40*, 582-583; 602
Clark, Juliet D., and Walker, Jane B.; Lessons in Lip-Reading for Deaf Soldiers; 1918, *20*, 129-133; 205-212; 282-289; 443-450; 493-498; 655-657; 681-684; 730-732
Clark, Juliet D.; Lipreading for the Slightly Deafened, Harmful or Beneficial?; 1921, *23*, 302-304
Conklin, Edmund S.; A Method for the Determination of Relative Skill in Lip-Reading; 1917, *19*, 216-219
Cook, M. Alleyne; With the Lip Reading Class; 1941, *43*, 139-140; 202-203; 1942, *44*, 230-231
Corlett, Juliet C.; Lip Reading Practice Material for Older Deaf Pupils; 1932, *34*, 411-412
Costello, Mary R.; Language Development Through Speechreading; 1958, *60*, 257-259, 272
Davies, Laura A.; For the Practice Class; 1923, *25*, 536-539
Davies, Laura A.; He That Overcometh; 1922, *24*, 252-256
Davies, Laura; The Practise Class; 1919, *21*, 432-434
DeLand, Fred; Ancient and Modern Methods of Teaching Lip Reading; 1924, *26*, 327-328
DeLany, Elizabeth G.; The Lip-Reader as a Beginner; 1917, *19*, 541-543
DeLany, Elizabeth G.; Lip-Reading Hundreds of Years Old; 1916, *18*, 442-445
Denmark, F. L.; Speech-Reading as a Basis for Language Development; 1920, *22*, 278-281
de Vries, J. G.; A Commandment That Should Not Be Obeyed; 1904, *6*, 283-287

Di Carlo, Louis M.; With the Lip Reading Class; 1940, *42*, 375-376
Disher, Dorothy R.; Lip Reading in Tallahassee; 1936, *38*, 352-353; 371-372
Downing, Nora; Elements of Success in Speech-Reading; 1922, *24*, 335-339
Drake, Margaret L.; Practice Material for the Teacher of Hard-of-Hearing Children; 1927, *29*, 76-78
Dunn, Margaret; Lip Reading in the Elementary Grades; 1936, *38*, 533-535
Dupuis, L., and Legrand, A.; Lip-Reading for Deaf Children; 1911, *13*, 298-302; 353-357; 412-416
Durfee, Marion; Practice Class Material; 1926, *28*, 80-83
Dyer, Helen Louise; The Speech-Reading Teacher's Opportunity; 1915, *17*, 175-176
Ellis, Vaughn E.; Lip-Reading at Northwestern; 1950, *52*, 26-27
Evers, Louise S.; With the Lip Reading Class; 1941, *43*, 741-742; 758; 1943, *45*, 231-232; 584
Farrar, A.; The Relative Value of Speech and Lipreading; 1903, *5*, 429-435
Fearon, J.; Oral Spelling; 1900, *2*, 30-32
Feilbach, Rose V.; With the Lip Reading Class; 1940, *42*, 175-176; 188-189
Ferrall, John A.; Let the Context Twins Do Your Work; 1918, *20*, 188-190
Ferrall, John A.; Linger Longer—Do!; 1922, *24*, 387-391
Ferrall, John A.; Lip-Reading—"Happiness Insurance"; 1918, *20*, 433-437
Ferrall, John A.; The Manifold Advantages of Soundless Speaking; 1922, *24*, 262-264
Ferrall, John A.; A Sense of Humor; 1922, *24*, 97-100
Ferrall, John A.; Speed Practise; 1918, *20*, 774-777
Ferreri, Giulio; Speech-Reading; 1910, *12*, 161-165
Foss, Bertha M.; Advanced Lip Reading; 1940, *42*, 694-696
Frankenthal, Sybil; With the Lip Reading Class; 1941, *43*, 439-440
Fuller, Sarah; Speech-Reading: A Guide for Self-Instruction Where Trained Teachers are Not Available; 1913, *15*, 253-265; 1918, *20*, 428-431; 579-580; 744-749; 1919, *21*, 147-149; 209-213
Gault, Robert H.; Interpretation of Spoken Language When the Feel of Speech Supplements Vision of the Speaking Face; 1928, *30*, 379-386
Gebhart, Helen M.; The Müller-Walle Method; 1919, *21*, 771-776
Geer, Alleyne C.; With the Lip Reading Class; 1943, *45*, 166-168; 188; 1945, *47*, 572-574; 599

SPEECHREADING—*continued*

Volta Review

Goldberg, Herman R.; Lip Reading for the Baseball Fan; 1947, *49*, 223; 238-240

Goldberg, Herman R.; What Do You Think of the Marshall Plan? A Lipreading Practice Exercise; 1948, *50*, 216

Goldstein, Max A.; The Practical Value of Lip-Reading; 1911, *13*, 220-224

Gordon, Avondale N.; Lip-reading for the Adult Deaf; 1915, *17*, 365-368

Hansen, A.; A Series of Tests in Lip-Reading; 1908, *10*, 381-384

Haspiel, George S.; A Rationale for Lipreading Therapy; 1965, *67*, 684-687

Haycock, C. Sibley; Lip-Reading, the Art of Judith Lee; 1912, *14*, 9-14

————; Hearing with the Eyes; 1918, *20*, 278-280

Hearty, Mary G.; Practice Class Material: Flower Show; 1926, *28*, 403-406

Heider, Fritz, and Grace M.; An Experimental Investigation of Lip Reading; 1940, *42*, 821-825; 882

Heider, Grace M.; Psychological Research in Lip Reading and Language; 1934, *36*, 517-520; 568

Heider, Grace M.; The Utley Lip Reading Test; 1947, *49*, 457-458; 488-490

Hill, Elsie; Lip-Reading Practice Material, A Cat Show; 1928, *30*, 386-387

Holt, Laura D.; The Practice Class; 1927, *29*, 123-126

Hood, C. A.; Kaleidoscopic English and a Lipreader; 1953, *55*, 11-14

Howell, Louise; Lip-Reading for the Hard-of-Hearing Adult; 1917, *19*, 15-16

Howes, Esther C.; Giving Our Children Speech Reading Which They Can Use at Home; 1940, *42*, 610-614

Hull, Susanne E.; Lip-reading as a Remedy for Deafness; 1912, *14*, 129-133

Hutchinson, Enid; With the Lip Reading Class; 1939, *41*, 589-590; 602

Hutman, Florence E.; The Experience of a Public-School Teacher; 1917, *19*, 523-525

Ives, Annie M.; Beautiful Islands of Everywhere; 1925, *27*, 695-698

Ives, Annie M.; Practice Class Material; 1930, *32*, 126-129

Ives, Annie M.; With the Lip Reading Class; 1939, *41*, 362-363; 379; 415; 421; 467; 476; 524-525

Jewell, Grace H.; Lip-Reading Practice Material; 1927, *29*, 410-412

Jewell, Grace H.; Practice Class Material; 1924, *26*, 182-184

Jones, Carrie L.; The Development of Lip Reading as a Useful Tool; 1940, *42*, 372-374; 395

Jones, Mary D.; Some Suggestions About Lip-Reading; 1908, *10*, 160-165

Kane, Edith B.; Helpful Practice Material; 1923, *25*, 323-325

Kane, Edith B.; Illustrated Proverbs; 1918, *20*, 229-230
Kane, Edith B.; Questions and Answers for Practise Classes; 1918, *20*, 484-486
Kane, Edith B.; Superstitions for the Practice Class; 1922, *24*, 429-430
Kane, Edith B.; Variety Is the Spice of Lip-Reading; 1919, *21*, 194-196
Kane, Edith B.; Wisps of Humor for the Practice Class; 1922, *24*, 94-96
Keeler, Sarah W.; A Method of Teaching Speech-Reading to the Adult Deaf; 1905, *7*, 1-22
Keith, John; Has Lip Reading Missed the Bus?—Yes; 1943, *45*, 286-288
Kenfield, Coralie N.; The Education or Re-education of the Deafened Adult; 1924, *26*, 100-102
Kenfield, Coralie N.; The Lip-Reading Practice Class; 1928, *30*, 486-488
Kenfield, Coralie N.; The Practice Class, Material for Teachers of Lip-Reading; 1928, *30*, 432-435
Kenfield, Coralie N.; The Public School Class; 1935, *37*, 32-34
Kenfield, Coralie N.; What the General Public Should Know Concerning Lip-Reading; 1917, *19*, 562-565
Kennedy, Mildred; How the Study of Speech-Reading May Be Pursued by One Living at a Distance from School or Teacher; 1918, *20*, 135-137
Kennedy, Mildred; An Incident; 1919, *21*, 386-389
Kennedy, Mildred; Lip-Reading and the Ear-Trumpet; 1917, *19*, 583-585
Kennedy, Mildred; Mirror Practice as an Aid to Lip-Reading; 1908, *10*, 155-159
Kessler, Emma B.; For the Practice Class; 1923, *25*, 278-281; 1929, *31*, 36-38
Kessler, Emma B.; Lip-Reading for the Adult Hard of Hearing; 1918, *20*, 355-357
Kessler, Saul N.; Seventeen and More; 1922, *24*, 32-35
Kimball, Caroline F.; What the Study of Lip-Reading Means; 1917, *19*, 536-538
Kinzie, Cora E.; The Kinzie Method of Instruction in Speech-Reading; 1920, *22*, 609-620; 1923, *25*, 66-68
Kinzie, Cora E., and Rose; The Kinzie Method of Speech-Reading for the Deaf; 1918, *20*, 249-258; 403-411; 499-509; 593-599; 627-630
Kinzie, Cora E.; Simplified Material for School Use; 1926, *28*, 509-513
Kinzie, Cora E.; The Value of Speech-Reading for the Deaf; 1917, *19*, 365-367
Kitson, H. D.; The Role of Association in Lip-reading; 1914, *16*, 619-620
Kline, Louise T.; The Value of Play in the Practise Class; 1919, *21*, 750-754

SPEECHREADING—continued

Volta Review

Knight, Augustus C.; Devices for Teachers of Lip-Reading; 1924, *26*, 623-625
Knowles, Elizabeth; With the Lip Reading Class; 1941, *43*, 680
LaCrosse, Edwin L.; Corrective Speech with Older Pupils; 1925, *27*, 16-19
Ladd, Alice; For the Practice Class; 1923, *25*, 85-90
Lamb, Helen Davis; Drill Exercises; 1923, *25*, 29-34
Lambert, C. G.; A Teacher of Lipreading; 1954, *56*, 212-213
Lane, Dorothy H.; First Year Lip-Reading; 1930, *32*, 142-143
Larr, Alfred; Speechreading Through Closed Circuit TV; 1959, *61*, 19-21
Leonard, Bessie N.; The General Aspects of the Teaching of Speech and Lip-Reading to the Deaf; 1928, *30*, 140-143
Lindquist, Ida P.; Adventures in Lip-Reading; 1917, *19*, 515-517
Lindquist, Ida P.; Is It Worth While?; 1918, *20*, 513-516
Lindquist, Ida P.; Practice Class Material; 1927, *29*, 229-233
Lindquist, Ida P.; Practice Material for Teachers of Lip-Reading Classes; 1928, *30*, 342-344
Lindquist, Ida P.; Rehabilitation Through Lip-Reading; 1927, *29*, 741-744
Lux, Alta M.; Stories for the Practice Class; 1927, *29*, 415-417
MacBeth, Madge; The Gateway to the Silent World; 1918, *20*, 509-511
McCowen, M.; The Development of Speech Reading in the Deaf Child; 1910, *12*, 307-312
McDonald, Alice; Practice Class Material; 1927, *29*, 130-132
McKenna, Alice; Adventures in Lip-Reading; 1921, *23*, 213-215
McKerral, Lena & Wilton; The Adaptation of Practise Exercises for Lip-Readers; 1918, *20*, 262-270; 323-328; 390-392; 525-528; 575-577; 708-709; 1919, *21*, 60-62; 149-153; 197-200; 291-294; 406-410; 556-559
McLean, Marjorie; The Development of Speech-Reading Power; 1920, *22*, 485-494
Macnutt, Ena G.; Lip-Reading Practice Material, 1929, *31*, 311-333
Macnutt, Ena G.; Practice Material; 1924, *26*, 360-363
Maigetter, Elizabeth; An Activity Program for Primary Grades; 1938, *40*, 23; 54-55
Mason, Marie K.; Objective Scoring in Tests of Visual Hearing; 1937, *39*, 576-581; 593
Matlock, Gladys D.; The Improvement of Lip-Reading Through Better Care of the Children's Eyes; 1938, *40*, 668-675
Maxson, Kathryn P.; Story Telling; 1933, *35*, 289, 314
Meredith, Anna; Lip-Reading Practice Material; 1927, *29*, 339-340
Milesky, Samuel D.; Testing Lipreading Potential; 1960, *62*, 372-375

Misra, Surya Kant, and Palmer, Martin F.; A Comparison of Speech Reading in Hindi and English in a School for the Deaf; 1964, *66*, 615-617
Monro, Sarah J.; The Speech-Reader's Duty to Himself; 1918, *20*, 276-278
Montague, Harriet; Lip-Reading—A Continuing Necessity; 1944, *46*, 91-94; 114-116; 159-162
Montague, Harriet; With the Lip Reading Class; 1940, *42*, 868-869
Morgenstern, Louise I.; Advanced Methods of Studying and Teaching Lip-Reading; 1917, *19*, 529-531
Morgenstern, Louise I.; The Conscientious Objector; 1918, *20*, 270-272
Morgenstern, Louise I.; Fifty Lessons in Lip-Reading; 1917, *19*, 479-488; 501-509; 631-639
Morgenstern, Louise I.; Lip-reading for Class Instruction; 1916, *18*, 188-190; 1918, *20*, 144-146
Morgenstern, Louise I.; The Mental Factor in Lip-Reading; 1918, *20*, 14-17
Morgenstern, Louise I.; None So Deaf As Those Who Won't See. A "Lipodrama" in One Act; 1918, *20*, 81-83
Morgenstern, Louise I.; Present-Day Methods of Teaching Lip-Reading; 1917, *19*, 599-601
Morgenstern, Louise I.; The Role of Words in the Practise of Lip-Reading; 1919, *21*, 52-54
Morgenstern, Louise I.; The Significance of the Study of Lip-Reading for the Hard-of-Hearing Adult; 1917, *19*, 127-129
Morgenstern, Louise I.; Teaching Lip-reading to the Adult Hard of Hearing in Public Evening School Classes; 1915, *17*, 255-257; 297-299; 391-393
Morgenstern, Louise I.; Words and Their Affinities; 1918, *20*, 551-553; 642-644; 692-694; 749-753; 1919, *21*, 265-271; 323-329; 410-411; 552-554
Morris, Dorothy M.; Humor in the Speech-Reading Period; 1939, *41*, 5-8; 51
Morris, M. Esther; With the Lip Reading Class; 1940, *42*, 44-45; 50; 109-110; 121-123
Müller-Walle, Julius; The Müller-Walle Method of Speech-Reading; 1912, *13*, 526-528
————; N.E.A. Conference on Lipreading; 1926, *28*, 64-69
Nelson, Boyd E.; A Lip Reading Program for a School; 1944, *46*, 5-10, 56
Neville, Virginia; Lipreading Material for Adult Beginners; 1952, *54*, 71; 76
Nitchie, Edward B.; Class Instruction in Lip-Reading; 1917, *19*, 177-179
Nitchie, Edward B.; The Detective Possibilities of Lip-Reading; 1915, *17*, 81-83

SPEECHREADING—*continued*

Volta Review

Nitchie, Edward B.; An Educational Neglect; 1903, *5*, 415-420
Nitchie, Edward B.; The "Experience System" Plus; 1914, *16*, 744-746
Nitchie, Edward B.; The Eye as a Substitute for Deaf Ears; 1910, *12*, 597-601
Nitchie, Edward B.; "Grasping the Meaning as a Whole" 1904, *6*, 198-201
Nitchie, Edward B.; How to Practise Lip-reading; 1912, *14*, 141-145
Nitchie, Edward B.; Lip-Reading, an Art; 1913, *15*, 276-278
Nitchie, Edward B.; Lip-reading for the Hearing; 1915, *17*, 435-436
Nitchie, Edward B.; The Lip-Reading Teacher's Equipment and Opportunities; 1914, *16*, 801-803
Nitchie, Edward B.; The Physiological Basis of the Visible Movements in Lip-Reading; 1913, *15*, 56-68
Nitchie, Edward B.; Principle and Methods of Teaching Lip-Reading; 1916, *18*, 269-280
Nitchie, Edward B.; Synthesis and Intuition in Lip-Reading; 1913, *15*, 311-314
Nitchie, Edward B.; Training Plus Experience; 1915, *17*, 66-72
Nitchie, Edward B.; The Use of Homophenous Words; 1916, *18*, 85-93
Nitchie, Edward B.; What a Deaf Adult Should Do to Acquire the Art of Lip-reading; 1915, *17*, 251-254
Nitchie, Edward B.; Why Not Lip-reading?; 1915, *17*, 178-179
Nitchie, Elizabeth H.; The Hard-of-Hearing or Deafened Teacher of Lip-Reading; 1921, *23*, 97-99
Nitchie, Elizabeth H.; The Nitchie Method of Teaching Lip-Reading; 1920, *22*, 621-629
Nitchie, Elizabeth H.; The Psychology of Teaching Unusual Pupils; 1926, *28*, 516-520
Nitchie, Elizabeth H.; The Synthetic Method and Why I Believe in It; 1919, *21*, 764-771
————; The Normal Training of Teachers of Lip-Reading; 1924, *26*, 66-73; 107-110; 195-201
Nowlin and Kinnier; Suggestions for Practise Classes; 1919, *21*, 545-549
Numbers, Mary E.; An Experiment in Lip Reading; 1939, *41*, 261-264
Olin, Caroline L.; The Müller-Walle Method of Speech-Reading; 1911, *13*, 23-26
Ordman, Theodore; Has Lip Reading Missed the Bus?—No; 1943, *45*, 288-290; 316-318
————; Over 500 War-Deafened Veterans Able to "Hear" Through Lip-Reading; 1922, *24*, 107-108
Paxon, Ruth; Giving Lip Reading Its Share of Attention in the Teaching Program; 1938, *40*, 663-664
Pierce, Jerry A.; The Experience System of Speech-Reading; 1914, *16*, 739-744

Pierce, Jerry A.; The Psychology of Speech-Reading; 1914, *16*, 56-59; 1923, *25*, 522-527

Pierce, Jerry A.; Theory Minus; 1915, *17*, 61-65

Pomeroy, Wilmer; Better Speech for Better Speech-Reading; 1919, *21*, 429-432

Pomeroy, Wilmer; God's Gift to the Speech-Reader; 1919, *21*, 601-603

Pomeroy, Wilmer; Have You Trained Lips?; 1919, *21*, 262-265

Pomeroy, Wilmer; The Speech-Reader's Alphabet; 1921, *23*, 236-238

Porter, Mrs. Nathan T., Jr.; Exercises for Teaching of Lip-Reading; 1920, *22*, 208-209; 434-437

Prall, Josephine; Lipreading and Hearing Aids Combine for Better Comprehension; 1957, *59*, 64-65

Pratt, Emily A.; The Importance of Determining the Need for Lip Reading among Deafened School Children; 1927, *29*, 558-563

Prelutsky, Louis; Using Cross-Word Puzzles in the Lip Reading Class; 1937, *39*, 586; 602

Ranson, Ethel O.; With the Lip Reading Class; 1939, *41*, 173; 178

Reiter, Frank H.; Profiting by the Findings of Research Workers; 1938, *40*, 658-661

Roberts, Emma; A Privilege to Enjoy; 1914, *16*, 257-259

Rogers, Mary; Picking Cherries, a Lip-Reading Game; 1923, *25*, 135-136

Ruffin, Henrietta H.; "Out of the Slough of Despond"; 1925, *27*, 525-526

Russell, Lillian E.; Beginning Lip Reading; 1940, *42*, 687-693

Samuelson, Estelle E.; The Lip-Reading Tournament at the New York League; 1921, *23*, 368-370

Samuelson, Estelle E., and Fabregas, Minnie B.; A Treasure Chest of Games for Lip Reading Teachers; 1936, *38*, 592-595; 614; 666-668; 737-740; 1937, *39*, 42-44; 56; 106-108; 117; 168-169; 187

Schumann, Dr. Paul; Ninety-nine Theses on Seeing Speech for the Deaf, the Deafened, and the Hard of Hearing; 1921, *23*, 246-250

Schwarz, Carrie K.; Conversation—Intermediate Work; 1929, *31*, 115-116

Scriver, Helen; The Art of Lip Reading; 1925, *27*, 422-424

Scriver, Helen; A Class Menu; 1935, *37*, 27-29

Scriver, Helen; Ship Ahoy! Practice Material for Lip-Reading Class; 1926, *28*, 398-402

Scriver, Helen; The Value of Play in Teaching Deafened Adults; 1929, *31*, 175-177

Scriver, Helen; With the Lip Reading Class: A Place for Homonyms; 1938, *40*, 296-298

Simonds, Elsie H.; Achieving Success with Lip-Reading; 1917, *19*, 401-403

SPEECHREADING—continued

Volta Review

Smith, Mathilda W.; Lip-Reading Practice Class Material, A Bell Program; 1927, *29*, 414-415

———; Speech Reading in Schools for the Deaf; 1942, *44*, 614-617; 656-658

Staples, Anna L.; Suggestions for Practise Classes; 1919, *21*, 5-7

Steed, Eleanor L.; Speech Reading and How It Grows; 1946, *48*, 69-74, 122-124

Steffey, Mary E.; Humor in the Practice Class; 1925, *27*, 120-122

Story, Arthur J.; The Development of Speech Reading; 1914, *16*, 13-19

Story, Arthur J.; Lip-reading; 1915, *17*, 389-391

Story, Arthur J.; Speech-Reading Depends More Upon Use Than Actual Teaching; 1915, *17*, 185-188

Story, Arthur J.; Speech-Reading for the Deaf—Not Dumb; 1910, *12*, 671-676

Strickland, Florence I.; Lipreading Practice Material; 1927, *29*, 412-414

Strickland, Florence I.; Practice Class Material; 1924, *26*, 185-187

Taber, Frank A.; With the Lip Reading Class; 1942, *44*, 360-361; 374

Tallman, Mary L.; Lip Reading in an Unusual School; 1935, *37*, 36-37

———; The Teaching of Speech-reading to the Adult Deaf; 1912, *14*, 540-544

Thomason, Pattie; The Müller-Walle Method Adapted to Children; 1917, *19*, 417-419

Torrey, Gertrude; Lip-reading for the Adult Deaf; 1914, *16*, 535-538

Torrey, Gertrude; Lip-reading for the Slightly Deaf; 1915, *17*, 51-53

Transue, Hannah W.; A Lip Reader's Views of Lip Reading; 1942, *44*, 161-164; 184; 204-206; 252

Trask, Alice N.; Correcting Misstatements; 1918, *20*, 197-198

Trask, Alice N.; Graded Practice Class: An Outstanding Feature of the Kinzie Method; 1925, *27*, 472-475

Trask, Alice N.; Material for Practice Class; 1918, *20*, 721-724; 1921, *23*, 21-24

Trask, Alice N.; More About Lip-Reading and Then Some; 1917, *19*, 567-569

Trask, Alice N.; Riddles for Lip-Reading Practise; 1921, *23*, 408-411

Trask, Alice N.; Similes; 1919, *21*, 248-250

Trask, Alice N.; Variety Is the Spice of Practice; 1918, *20*, 535-538

Trill, Ellen M.; How to Help One Who Is Studying Lip-Reading; 1917, *19*, 705-707

Turley, Ethel J.; With the Lip Reading Class; 1941, *43*, 53-55

Van Adestine, et al.; Presenting the Problem to the Public; 1917, *19*, 511-513

VanPraagh, William; Lip-Reading: What It Ought to BE; 1902, *4*, 45-47

Van Wyk, Mary K.; Beginning Speechreading; 1957, *59*, 165-168
Vonderheit, Esther C.; Lip-Reading Practice Material; 1929, *31*, 263-267
Vose, Persis; Qualities Necessary for Good Lip-Reading; 1924, *26*, 281
Wadleigh, Grace K.; Concerning the Psychology of the Müller-Walle Method; 1918, *20*, 705-707
Wadleigh, Grace K.; The Exercise Story; 1918, *20*, 470-472
Walker, Jane B.; Material for the Practice Class; 1923, *25*, 241-245
Walker, Jane B.; With the Lip Reading Class; 1946, *48*, 226; 240-242; 285; 291-292
Walker, Jane B.; With the Speech Reading Class; 1938, *40*, 43-44; 55; 108-109; 169-170; 182; 359-361; 412-414; 424-426; 1939, *41*, 40-42; 103-105; 1941, *43*, 620-621; 1942, *44*, 39-40; 60
Washington, Margaret L.; Constructive Class Management; 1935, *37*, 30-32
Weston, Cora C.; Stumbling Blocks and Pitfalls; 1922, *24*, 286-289
Whildin, Olive A.; Is Lip Reading Education or Training?; 1935, *37*, 751-752; 779-780
Whildin, Olive; Graded Devices for Hard of Hearing Children; 1927, *29*, 233-235
Whitaker, Bessie L.; If You Want to be a Good Lip-Reader, Settle Down to Business; 1917, *19*, 432-439
Whitaker, Bessie L.; The Possibility of Making a Complete Success of Speech-Reading, Applied in Large Part to the Adult; 1922, *24*, 127-141
Whitaker, Bessie L.; Speech-Reading and Its Value; 1918, *20*, 637-640
Witherspoon, Elizabeth; Problems of the Lip Reading Teacher; 1936, *38*, 101-103
Wolf, Rena; Speech-Reading in the Evening High School in Philadelphia; 1920, *22*, 92-97
Wright, Florence F.; With the Lip Reading Class; 1940, *42*, 238-239; 253
Wright, John D.; A Swiss Pioneer in Speech Reading for Deafened Adults; 1925, *27*, 465-467
Wright, John D.; Where Lip-Reading Reaches Its Maximum Efficiency; 1912, *14*, 257-259
Yenrick, D. E.; Speechreading Materials for the Primary Public School Grades; 1951, *53*, 249-251
Young, Mrs. Arthur J.; With the Lip Reading Class; 1941, *43*, 393; 399
Young, Leo H.; What I Get Out of Lip Reading; 1939, *41*, 37-39; 53-54
Ziegler, Clara M.; Graded Class Practice; 1923, *25*, 386-389
Ziegler, Clara M.; Practice Class Material; 1929, *31*, 377-379
Ziegler, Clara M.; With the Practice Class; 1945, *47*, 357-358

SPEECHREADING—continued

Annals of the Deaf

Bell, Alexander G.; Speech Reading for the Partially Deaf; 1907, *52*, 28-30
Bell, Mabel G.; Success in Speech Reading; 1890, *35*, 127-130
Booth, Edmund; A Genius for Lip-Reading; 1884, *29*, 17-24
Boudin, Etienne; The Conditions of Success in Speech Reading; 1912, *57*, 187-197
Bruhn, Martha E.; The Müller-Walle System of Lip-Reading; 1917, *62*, 353-364
Chapin, Alma L.; Lip-Reading Commands; 1920, *65*, 499-508
Cobb, Jennie L.; Speech Reading; 1921, *66*, 266-271
Davidson, Emma F.; Lip-Reading Lessons; 1912, *57*, 437-453; 1913, *58*, 5-15; 239-249; 1914, *59*, 181-193; 264-274; 480-505
Fonner, Mary D.; Lip-Reading: How to Improve It; 1916, *61*, 87-91
Fusfeld, Irving S.; Factors in Lipreading as Determined by the Lipreader; 1958, *103*, 229-242
Gordon, Anne; Lip-Reading in the Primary Department of the California School; 1939, *84*, 350-362
Gutzmann, Herm.; Facial Speech-Reading; 1899, *44*, 272-285; 317-335; 412-419
McCowen, M.; The Development of Speech Reading in the Deaf Child; 1910, *55*, 364-370
Marichelle, H.; A Practical Test of Lip-Reading; 1911, *56*, 324-331
Miller, J., Rousey, C., and Goetzinger, C.; An Exploratory Investigation of a Method of Improving Speechreading; 1958, *103*, 473-478
Moffat, L.; Lipreading for the Adult Deaf; 1889, *34*, 263-271
Nelson, Boyd E.; Co-ordinating Lip-Reading and Speech with Current Events; 1944, *89*, 132-141
Neuschutz, Louise I.; The Standardization of Methods of Teaching Lip-Reading and Training Teachers; 1926, *71*, 219-221
Olin, Caroline L.; The Müller-Walle Method of Teaching Speech-Reading; 1911, *56*, 335-337
Palen, Imogen B.; Methods Used in Teaching Lip-Reading to Speaking Children; 1926, *71*, 190-197
Reamy, Olive L.; The Teaching of Speech Reading; 1893, *38*, 4-8
Reid, Gladys; A Preliminary Investigation in the Testing of Lip-Reading Achievement; 1946, *91*, 403-413
Robinson, Warren; Speech-Reading—A Study; 1905, *50*, 169-173
Steinke, Agnes; Lip-Reading; 1901, *46*, 277-285
Stobschinski, Robert; Lip-Reading: Its Psychological Aspects and Its Adaption to the Individual Needs of the Hard of Hearing; 1928, *73*, 234-242; 355-365
Stone, Elizabeth A.; Story Telling; 1909, *54*, 1-7
Wiedemer, A.; How Can Speech Reading Be Brought to a Higher State of Perfection?; 1912, *57*, 254-278

TEACHER TRAINING

Volta Review

———; A Bibliography for Teachers of the Deaf Compiled by the Association's Committee on the Use of Professional Literature; 1944, *46*, 17-20; 85-86; 102

Booth, F. W.; Normal Training for Oral Teachers of the Deaf; 1907, *9*, 206-212

Bruce, Wallace T.; Orientation for New Teachers; 1964, *66*, 456-459

Bruhn, Martha E.; Theory Minus Versus Training Plus Experience; 1915, *17*, 143-145

Carney, Mary V.; Qualifications for Teachers of Lip Reading; 1938, *40*, 93-96; 124

Connor, Frances F., and Leo E.; Future Directions in Teacher Education for Teachers of the Deaf; 1958, *60*, 67-74; 93

Connor, Leo E.; Child Study in the Education of Deaf Children; 1962, *64*, 72-76; 103

Costello, Mary R.; The Teacher of the Deaf—Circa 1964—and Onward; 1964, *66*, 445-449

Craig, Sam B.; Recruitment of Teachers; 1946, *48*, 701-704

———; An Examination for Teachers of the Deaf: The 1943 Examination for the Diploma Issued by the National College of Teachers of the Deaf, England; 1943, *45*, 617-619

Fellendorf, George W.; Teacher Recruitment; 1962, *64*, 452-456

Flint, Richard W.; Survey Shows Need for Better Teacher Recruitment Program; 1957, *59*, 66-71

Groht, Mildred A.; Basic Qualifications of a Teacher of the Deaf; 1957, *59*, 13-16

Hall, Percival; What Must Be the Required Training of Normal Students Previous to Their Special Training?; 1928, *30*, 573-577

Henderson, Jennie M.; Voice Training and Rhythm: Their Application to the Teaching of Speech to the Deaf; 1914, *16*, 435-439

Hilliard, Ethel M.; Modern Tendencies in Speech Teaching; 1926, *28*, 616-620

Johnson, Evan V., and Frisina, D. Robert; A Study of the Need for Academic Classroom Teachers of the Deaf; 1960, *62*, 500-503

Kelly, Elizabeth; The Recruiting of Teachers; 1946, *48*, 698-701

Lane, Helen S.; Preparation of Teachers for the Handicapped; 1937, *39*, 558-561; 592

Lane, Helen S. (moderator); Teacher Recruitment and Training; 1952, *54*, 491-500; 512-514

Moore, Lucile M.; Teacher Training; 1923, *25*, 356-358

Numbers, Mary E.; What Training Should Be Required for the Teacher?; 1938, *40*, 718-721

Pearson, Frank B.; Teacher Training; 1929, *31*, 519-521

TEACHER TRAINING—*continued*

Volta Review

Pratt, George T.; Planning and Organizing a Teacher Recruitment Program; 1957, *59*, 9-12; 40
Quigley, Stephen P.; Major Problems in Teacher Education and Recruitment; 1958, *60*, 366-370
Rotter, Paul; A Study for Improving Programs for the Preparation of Teachers of the Deaf; 1962, *64*, 481-486
Rowell, Hugh G.; The Opportunities Which the University Offers for the Training of Teachers of Handicapped Children; 1929, *31*, 613-618
Rudloff, Joseph S.; Recruiting Teachers for the Deaf; 1960, *62*, 541-542; 564
Stoner, Marguerite; What the Inexperienced Teacher Needs in the Way of Supervision; 1946, *48*, 692-694
Winnie, A. J.; Normal Training of Teachers of Deaf Children; 1919, *21*, 30-31; 153-155
Wright, John D.; Normal Training of Teachers; 1918, *20*, 727-729
Yale, Caroline A.; How Can We Best Fit Ourselves to Teach Speech to the Deaf; 1940, *42*, 589-592

Annals of the Deaf

Brill, Richard G.; The Educational Preparation of Oral Teachers of the Deaf; 1952, *97*, 313-327
Brill, Richard G.; A Survey of Credential Requirements for Teachers of the Deaf in the U.S; 1955, *100*, 321-329
Crosby, Laura; The Classroom Teacher; 1953, *98*, 362-368
Crouter, A. L.; The Training of Teachers of the Deaf; 1917, *62*, 293-304
Jones, John W., et al.; The Training and Certification of Teachers; 1929, *74*, 244-315
McManaway, Howard M.; Proper Training of Shop Teachers; 1925, *70*, 424-429
Numbers, Fred C.; Advantages and Disadvantages in Conducting a Normal Training Class in Connection with School Work; 1927, *72*, 341-349
Streng, Alice H.; Educating Teachers of the Deaf for the Schools for Tomorrow; 1964, *109*, 348-355
—————; U.S. Office of Education Study of Training Courses for Teachers of the Deaf; 1938, *83*, 428-441

VISUAL AIDS

Volta Review

Alcorn, Alice; Visual Education As An Aid to Geography; 1926, *28*, 707-708
Burdge, Alice V.; The Value and Administration of Visual Education; 1932, *34*, 496-502
Cavanagh, Anita; A New Audio-Visual Aid for Speech; 1951, *53*, 12-13; 40-42
Cole, Roy; Television for Deaf Children; 1960, *62*, 256-259; 281
Cory, Patricia B.; Films and Filmstrips; 1959, *61*, 71
Cory, Patricia B.; Filmstrips for Deaf Children; 1957, *59*, 451-454; 1961, *63*, 299; 1962, *64*, 507-508
Cory, Patricia B.; Materials Center; 1956, *58*, 15-19
Crane, Norman, and Evans, Betty; The Talking Dictionary; 1962, *64*, 125-127
Cypreansen, Lucile, and McBride, Jack; Lipreading Lessons on Television; 1956, *58*, 346-348
Davenport, Virginia H.; Cross-Word Puzzle; 1936, *38*, 641-642; 679
David, Edward E., Jr.; Speech in the Computer Age; 1962, *64*, 394-397
Deannard, Elizabeth; The Sand Table; 1933, *35*, 125-126
Dommisse, Elsa J.; Visual Material for Language Teaching; 1947, *49*, 84-86
Drennen, Genevieve; Make It Pretty; 1956, *58*, 337-340
Falconer, George A.; Teaching Machines for the Deaf; 1960, *62*, 59-62; 76
Falconer, George A.; Teaching Machines for Teaching Reading; 1962, *64*, 389-392
————; Films and Filmstrps Pertaining to Deafness; 1956, *58*, 158-160
————; Films on Hearing and Deafness; 1962, *64*, 77-83; 104
Finn, Betsy A.; Pictures in Lower Intermediate Grades; 1933, *35*, 367-369
Gough, John A.; Captioned Films for the Deaf; 1963, *65*, 24-25; 50
Gough, John A.; Visual Aid Back-up Service for Teachers of the Deaf; 1964, *66*, 548-551
Grey, Howard A., et al.; Cinefluorography As An Aid to More Intelligible Speech; 1961, *63*, 323-327; 357
Heider, Grace M., and Fritz; Motion Pictures in Classroom Work; 1935, *37*, 71-75
Hester, M. S.; A Program of Visual Educaton for a Residential School; 1932, *34*, 503-506
Hester, M. S.; The Use of Educational Films; 1932, *34*, 51-55
Hudgins, Clarence V.; Visual Aids in the Correction of Speech; 1935, *37*, 637-643; 703-704
Kennard, Marie S.; Pictures Used with Drill Verbs; 1935, *37*, 157; 186-187

VISUAL AIDS—*continued*

Volta Review

Kennedy, Lydia B.; Pictures in the Primary Grades; 1933, *35*, 376-377
Kraft, Dorothy G.; Presentation of Visual Aids Materials to the Upper Grades; 1956, *58*, 247-250; 255
Lane, Helen S.; Television for the Deaf; 1951, *53*, 345; 392
Larr, Alfred; Speechreading Through Closed Circuit TV; 1959, *61*, 19-21
LaRue, Sarah J.; Correlating Motion Pictures With Classroom Work; 1927, *29*, 253-254
McLaughlin, Marjorie; Uses of the Flannelgraph; 1952, *54*, 317; 326-328
McLeod, Frances; A Pictionary; 1955, *57*, 59-60
Mackin, Helen; Hand Work Helps Language Work; 1938, *40*, 761-762
Mason, Marie K.; Personal Experience in Teaching Lip Reading Through Motion Pictures; 1946, *48*, 661-663
Montague, Harriet; Non-Reading Aid Project in Wisconsin; 1941, *43*, 15-17; 30
Moore, Lucelia; Television as a Medium for Teaching Speechreading and Speech; 1955, *57*, 263-264
Nelson, Wilma I.; Advancing the Use of Visual Aids; 1942, *44*, 11-12; 60
Nelson, Wilma I., et al.; The Use of Visual Aids in Teaching; 1939, *41*, 499-502; 534; 566-568; 600; 631-633; 668-669
Nitchie, Edward B.; Moving Pictures Applied to Lip-Reading; 1913, *15*, 117-125
Olson, Christine; Using the Opaque Projector; 1958, *60*, 267-268
Ostern, Beatrice; Use of Movie Films in a Class of the Deaf; 1953, *55*, 247; 276
Oyer, Herbert J.; Teaching Lipreading by TV; 1961, *63*, 131-132; 141
Peterson, Gordon E.; Technological Frontiers in Communication; 1962, *64*, 369-374
Purdy, Martha E.; An Experiment in Visual Education with the Deaf; 1943, *45*, 201; 248-249
Romero, Emerson; Sound Films for the Deaf; 1948, *50*, 259-260; 288-290
Schowe, Ben M., Jr.; Projecting Books as an Aid to Teaching Reading; 1962, *64*, 421-422
Scott, Elizabeth V.; The Use of Slides in the Primary Classes; 1932, *34*, 56-58
Sigurdson, Haldora K.; Films For Speech and Hearing Instruction; 1949, *51*, 224-226; 240-242
————; Television for Deaf Children in Chicago; 1962, *64*, 30
Thornton, Joyce; Pictures Make Words; 1959, *61*, 18; 43
Utley, Jean, et al.; Lip Reading and Motion Pictures; Factors Involved in the Teaching and Testing of Lip Reading Ability Through the Use of Motion Pictures; 1946, *48*, 657-663
Van Wyk, Mary K.; A New Visual Aid Trainer; 1955, *57*, 347-348

Annals of the Deaf

Boatner, Edmund B.; Captioned Films for the Deaf; 1951, *96*, 346-352
Bower, Dolores; Comics—A Meaningful Teaching Experience in the Language Arts; 1960, *105*, 230-231
Carpenter, Lula E.; Teaching From Objects; 1903, *48*, 424-435
Earle, Carrie W.; The Use of Pictures in the Primary Grades; 1896, *41*, 357-370
Falconer, George A.; A Mechanical Device for Teaching Sight Vocabulary to Young Deaf Children; 1961, *106*, 251-257
Fessant, John M.; Application of Programmed Learning for Deaf Children to Industrial Arts; 1963, *108*, 241-245
Gay, Ruth C.; A Doll House Unit of Work; 1938, *83*, 425-426
Kiesel, Theodore A.; Picture Teaching; 1902, *47*, 403-439
McAloney, Thomas S.; The Value of Pictures in Teaching the Deaf; 1893, *38*, 196-203
McClure, William J.; Visual Education and the Deaf; 1941, *86*, 166-180
Peterson, Edwin G.; Testing Deaf Children with Kohs Block Designs; 1936, *81*, 242-254
Ross, Louise; Vitalizing Object Work for Beginning Classes; 1928, *73*, 248-249
Smith, James L.; Visual Education by Use of the Blackboard; 1933, *78*, 257-262
Vermillion, Frances F.; Visual Aids in Arithmetic; 1940, *85*, 487-493
Walker, E. W.; Instruction by Means of Pictures; 1906, *51*, 276-280

VOCATIONAL—REHABILITATION

Volta Review

Adams, Mabel E.; Welfare Work at Horace Mann School; 1911, *13*, 381-386
Alpiner, Jerome G., and Walker, Richard A.; A Residential Vocational Rehabilitation Program for Young Adults With Severely Impaired Hearing; 1964, *66*, 118-121; 163
Alsberg, Julia; Vocational Guidance; 1955, *57*, 119-120
Amato, David; The District of Columbia's Rehabilitation Program; 1947, *49*, 79; 94-96
Andrews, Harriet U.; Deaf Girls as Hospital Nurses; 1910, *12*, 471-476
Becker, V. A.; California's Rehabilitation Program for the Deaf; 1956, *58*, 73-74
Bluett, Charles G.; Objective Analysis in Vocational Placement; 1939, *41*, 133-135; 179

VOCATIONAL—REHABILITATION—*continued*

Volta Review

Bluett, Charles G.; Objective Tests in Vocational Interviews; 1937, *39*, 636-638; 657-658
Bluett, Charles G.; Selecting Vocations for the Deaf; 1937, *39*, 677-679
Bluett, Charles G.; Vocational Survey of the Graduating Class of the California School for the Deaf; 1939, *41*, 549-555; 615-620; 662
Branson, Helen K.; For the Handicapped, What Kind of Job?; 1951, *53*, 247-248
Breese, Estelle; Vocational Language Problems; 1936, *38*, 695; 748
Brown, Donald W.; Vocational Preparation for the World of Tomorrow; 1964, *66*, 368-372
Bruhn, Martha E.; The Hard of Hearing as Wage-Earners and Home-Makers; 1919, *21*, 574-576
Carter, E.; The Training of Girls; 1914, *16*, 187-192
Chambless, Elizabeth; Rehabilitation Can Rehabilitate; 1938, *40*, 345-346; 371
Chambless, Elizabeth; Rehabilitation is a Two-Sided Affair; 1938, *40*, 584-585
Cogswell, Frank H.; Co-operation Between School and Shop; 1913, *15*, 137-139
Connor, Leo, and Rosenstein, Joseph; Vocational Status and Adjustment of Deaf Women; 1963, *65*, 585-591
Davidson, S. G.; A Vocation School for Deaf and Hearing Boys; 1905, *7*, 32-43
De La Bat, G.; Vocational Interchange; 1937, *39*, 615-617; 662-663
DeLand, Fred; The Rearranging of Affairs After Hearing Vanishes; 1919, *21*, 320-323
DeLand, Fred; War Deafness; 1917, *19*, 493-496
De Young, Dirk P.; What Can't a Deaf Man Do?; 1925, *27*, 136-138
Duff, Jessie; Triumph Over Handicap; 1922, *24*, 242-246
Dyer, Helen L.; Aiming Toward Independence; 1915, *17*, 465-470
Dyer, Helen L.; Vocational Suggestions for the Adult Deaf; 1915, *17*, 9-11
Elstad, Leonard M.; Vocational Competence Through Academic Preparation; 1964, *66*, 372-376
Etter, Carl L.; Philosophy of Vocational Rehabilitation; 1941, *43*, 251-254; 276-278
Ferrall, John A.; Cast Down Your Bucket Where You Are!; 1919, *21*, 12-15
Ferrall, John A.; The Employment Question; 1919, *21*, 704-706
Finch, Wallace J.; The Use of Language in Industry; 1938, *40*, 688-689
Flange, C. S.; Selecting a Career; 1944, *46*, 72-74; 126
Garrett, Charles W.; Quo Vadis. A Pilot Study of Employment Opportunities for the Hearing Impaired; 1964, *66*, 669-677

Green, Ruth; Employment Counseling for the Hard of Hearing; 1954. *56*, 209-212
Greenmun, Robert M.; A Deaf Newspaper Editor; 1937, *39*, 140-142; 181-182
Hays, Harold; The Social and Economic Importance of Deafness; 1913, *15*, 303-310
Hicker, H. D.; Vocational Rehabilitation and the Deaf; 1932, *34*, 487-491
Howard, Jay C.; The Deaf and the Deafened in Industry; 1940, *42*, 845-846; 874
Howard, Petra F.; A Deaf Person Learns From His Job; 1956, *58*, 201-204
Jenks, Monica K.; Guidance and Rehabilitation; 1960, *62*, 411-412
Khan, Evelyn; The Economic Rehabilitation of the Educated Deaf; 1964, *66*, 562-565
Krol, S. T.; Blessing in Disguise; 1949, *51*, 604-605; 628-630
Lee, John J.; Time and Tide in Developing Services for the Handicapped; 1960, *62*, 403-409
Lemley, Herman A.; Relationship Between Vocational and Academic Departments; 1936, *38*, 696-697
Lindquist, Ida P.; Rehabilitation of the Hard of Hearing; 1940, *42*, 95-99; 115
McDermott, Valeria D.; Vocational Studies for the Deafened; 1923, *25*, 503-505
Montague, Harriet; Jobs for the Hard of Hearing; 1939, *41*, 219-222; 250-251
Morrison, J. Stuart; Industrial Training: What Shall We Subtract and What Shall We Add in the New Century of the Education of the Deaf; 1920, *22*, 222-231
Murphy, Albert T.; Personal Relations in a Profession; 1954, *56*, 261-262
Nace, John G.; A Superintendent Looks Ahead at the Future of Vocational Technical Education; 1965, *67*, 688-692
Nelson, Boyd E.; Objectives of Vocational Training; 1944, *46*, 389-390; 428-432
Nitchie, Edward B.; Unemployment, the Tragedy of Deafness; 1911, *13*, 217-219
Nitkin, Nathaniel; Rehabilitation and Personality; 1939, *41*, 17-19, 56
Owsley, Peter J.; Academic-Vocational Education of Hearing Handicapped Children; 1964, *66*, 551-555
Patterson, Alpha W.; Printing as a Trade for the Deaf; 1926, *28*, 649-654
Peterson, P. N.; Principles of Vocational Guidance; 1930, *32*, 572-576
Phillips, Wendell C.; The Re-Education of Deaf Soldiers; 1919, *21*, 89-91
Pierce, J. A.; The Economic Efficiency of the Deaf; 1914, *16*, 260-266
——————; The Plan of Reconstruction of the Defects in Hearing and Speech; 1918, *20*, 457-460

VOCATIONAL—REHABILITATION—continued

Volta Review

Pope, Alvin E.; Correlation of Industrial and Academic Work; 1920, 22, 539-546

Reid, Harry W.; New Offerings and Trends in Vocational Education; 1961, 63, 287-288; 301

Richardson, Charles W.; Re-Education of Soldiers with Defective Hearing and Speech; 1918, 20, 511-513

Rosenstein, Joseph; Social and Vocational Assessment; 1963, 65, 542-547

Rosenstein, Joseph; Social and Vocational Planning for the Adolescent; 1962, 64, 433-442

Salade, Robert F.; Printing: An Ideal Vocation for the Deaf; 1916, 18, 59-63

Samuelson, Estelle E.; Employment Services for the Deafened; 1923, 25, 488-498

Sullivan, Oscar M.; Vocational Training of the Deafened; 1929, 31, 107-110

Turner, Wallace R.; Starting a Print Shop; 1935, 37, 196-197

Washington, Margaret L.; Rehabilitation and the Hard of Hearing; 1938, 40, 36-37

Woodburg, Max W.; The Placement of the Graduates of the Utah School for the Deaf; 1926, 28, 762-766

Wright, John D.; The Economic Significance of Deafness; 1914, 16, 28-31

Annals of the Deaf

Altschulor, David, and Zabell, Emil; Cooperative Arrangement between Division of Vocational Rehabilitation and a Private Agency; 1958, 103, 399-402

Anderson, Tom L.; The Need for Occupational Studies in Relation to Vocational Guidance for Boys; 1929, 74, 407-410

Anderson, Tom L.; Vocational Needs of Today; 1935, 80, 105-115

Balis, Sylvia C.; Industrial Education; 1893, 38, 15-20

Barnes, Harvey B.; The Need for Separating Advanced Vocational Training from the Elementary School Atmosphere; 1940, 85, 449-451

Barnes, Harvey B.; Public Employer Relations and a Job Training Center for the Deaf; 1941, 86, 134-136

Betts, Otis A.; Vocational Training for the Deaf; 1930, 75, 115-124

Boatner, Maxine T.; Vocational Education Under the Gallaudets; 1957, 102, 300-311

Butler, Stahl; Agricultural Training for the Deaf; 1937, 82, 262-271

Cooke, Jaye H.; Training and Placing the Deaf in Industry; 1944, 89, 160-166

Crammatte, Alan B.; Vocational Guidance in Schools for the Deaf; 1939, *84*, 381-390; 392-404

DiMichael, S. G.; Understanding and Counseling the Adult Deaf: An Overdue Mission of Our Time; 1958, *103*, 393-398

Divine, L. R.; The Finishing Touches to Vocational Education; 1934, *79*, 238-243

Doane, Ray C.; Suggestions for Improving Vocational Training; 1957, *102*, 356-358

Driggs, Frank M.; Deafness as a Social Problem—the Industrial Side; 1929, *74*, 113-127

Euritt, Guilford D.; Technical Training for the Deaf; 1905, *50*, 365-370

Falberg, Roger M.; An Adventure Into Adult Education of the Deaf; 1962, *107*, 329-338

Fessant, John M.; Application of Programmed Learning for Deaf Children to Industrial Arts; 1963, *108*, 241-245

Friedman, Max; The Feelings and Attitudes of the Deaf Towards Vocational Rehabilitation Counselors and Their Programs; 1958, *103*, 403-408

Fusfeld, Irving S.; A Study of the Vocations Taught in American Schools for the Deaf; 1934, *79*, 377-382

Fusfeld, Irving S.; Suggestions Regarding Failure to Follow the Trade Learned in School; 1959, *104*, 277-281

Grady, Theodore; The Deaf in the Legal Profession; 1901, *46*, 429-434

Griffin, Mary E.; Industrial Training for Deaf Girls; 1925, *70*, 340-350

Hanson, Olof; The Industrial Problem Among the American Deaf; 1904, *49*, 363-369

Helmle, Margarette B.; Employment, Replacement Training, and Vocational Counseling for the Deaf; 1937, *82*, 411-424

Hicker, H. D.; Coordination of Services for Vocational Adjustment of the Deaf; 1939, *84*, 322-331

Hjorth, Ernst; A Few Remarks on Vocational Education; 1934, *79*, 244-254

Hopson, A. B.; Effects of Trade Training on the School Life and After—School Life of Our Deaf Girls; 1920, *65*, 481-486

Jones, Uriel C.; A Critical Survey of Vocational Guidance in Schools for the Deaf; 1940, *85*, 471-486

Kennedy, W. Richard; Rehabilitation for the Deaf; 1958, *103*, 389-392

Knievel, William R.; A Vocational Aptitude Test Battery for the Deaf; 1954, *99*, 314-319

Lauritsen, Wesley; Helping Our Graduates Secure Positions; 1936, *81*, 126-135

Lavos, George, and Jones, Earl W.; The Deaf Worker in Industry; 1946, *91*, 154-176

VOCATIONAL—REHABILITATION—*continued*

Annals of the Deaf

McClure, William J.; Accomplishments of the Deaf; 1958, *103*, 365-371
Manning, A. C.; Reconstruction of Deafened American Soldiers; 1920, *65*, 74-85
Orr, John P.; The Deaf and Their Vocational Problems; 1939, *84*, 124-131
Parrish, O. G.; The Vocational Training Program of the New Jersey School for the Deaf; 1943, *88*, 122-126
Peterson, P. N.; The Influence of Manual Training Upon the Mental Development of the Deaf; 1915, *60*, 119-129
Phillips, Richard M.; A Career Information Program for Schools for the Deaf; 1952, *97*, 301-309
Phillips, Richard M.; Community Obligations to the Deaf; 1958, *103*, 378-381
Porter, George S.; The Deaf in Business; 1901, *46*, 141, 149
————; Positions for Which Deaf-Mutes May be Considered; 1942, *87*, 288-294
Richardson, P. L.; The Industrial Training of the Deaf; 1904, *49*, 260-268
Schowe, B. M.; The Deaf at Work; 1958, *103*, 283-292
Seal, Albert G.; Maximum Use of Community Resources in the Rehabilitation of the Deaf; 1958, *103*, 414-423
Shortley, Michael J.; Rehabilitation for the Deaf and the Hard of Hearing; 1948, *93*, 42-47
Simpson, Emmette W.; Agricultural Education for the Deaf; 1912, *57*, 305-313
Stelle, Roy M.; Vocational Rehabilitation As Opportunity for the Deaf; 1958, *103*, 424-433
Stephens, Alfred E.; Labor Legislation Affecting the Deaf; 1939, *84*, 132-136
Stutsman, Grace T.; Farming for the Deaf; 1916, *61*, 142-150
Sullivan, Oscar M.; Vocational Guidance for the Deaf; 1929, *74*, 386-389
Switzer, Mary E.; Identification of Researchable Rehabilitation Problems of the Deaf; 1960, *105*, 337-370
Thompson, Hazel N.; Vocational Training for Girls; 1928, *73*, 393-419
Underhill, Odie W.; The Deaf Man and the Printing Trade; 1923, *68*, 317-330
Williams, Boyce R.; Cooperative School and Rehabilitation Programs, Their Organization and Factors of Effectiveness; 1948, *93*, 165-173
Williams, Boyce R.; Essential Characteristics (Qualifications) of a Rehabitable Deaf or Hard of Hearing Individual; 1947, *92*, 215-226
Williams, Boyce R.; Guidelines for the Establishment of Rehabilitation Facilities for the Deaf; 1961, *106*, 341-364
Williams, Boyce R.; Resource Needs of the Deaf and Ways to Resolve Them; 1958, *103*, 293-299
Williams, Boyce R.; Vocational Rehabilitation; 1953, *98*, 383-387

AUTHOR INDEX

A

Abernathy, E. R. 78
Abernathy, Edward B. 57
Acker, Lela 1
Adametz, Josef 34
Adams, Bradford C. 17
Adams, Ida H. 1, 51
Adams, Mabel E., 14, 43, 51, 67, 71, 92, 103, 123
Addison, W. H. 34
Adelson, L. 68
Adler, Edna P. 57
Adrain, E. D. 72
Albright, Arline 11, 106
Alcorn, Alice 121
Alcorn, Kate 93
Alcorn, Sophia 14, 93
Allabough, B. R. 86
Allen, Anna C. 93
Allison, Margaret G. 73
Alpiner, Jerome G. 123
Alsberg, Julia 123
Altschulor, David 126
Altshuler, K. Z. 78
Amato, David 123
Amsler, Fridette 106
Anderson, Effie W. 83
Anderson, J. Scott 4
Anderson, Mrs. J. Scott . 11, 63, 68
Anderson, Marian J. 88, 106
Anderson, Norman O. 14
Anderson, Robert M. 59
Anderson, Tom L., 27, 57, 67, 89, 126
Anderson, William A. 63
Andrews, Harriet E. 3
Andrews, Harriet U., 12, 63, 72, 73, 89, 106, 123

Angelocci, Angelo A. 93
Anselmini, Andrew A. 4
Appel, Catherine R. 68
Arbaugh, Laura L. 17
Archer, Tunis V. 1, 17, 51
Armstrong, Lola M. 73
Arnold, Allie 73, 90
Arnold, Mercer 14
Arnold, Thomas 103
Asals, Frances B. 4
Ashby, Madelyn T. 43
Ashley, J. B. 51
Askew, Louise M. 27
Aurell, Ernest 27
Avery, Charlotte B. 63, 68
Avery, Elizabeth B. ... 27, 43, 51
Avondino, Josephine 83, 93
Ayres, J. A. 27

B

Babcock, E. J. 43
Bailey, Jane D. 93
Baldrian, Karl 51
Balis, Sylvia C. ... 16, 27, 73, 126
Ballenger, Lula 73
Baltzer, Susanna 43
Bangs, Jack L. 59
Bangs, Tina E. 4
Banks, Marjorie S. 43
Barley, Kenneth 4
Barnard, F. A. 51
Barnes, F. G. 17, 43, 51, 59
Barnes, Harvey B. 126
Barrett, E. M. 16
Barrett, Katherine 38
Barrows, Albert L. 17
Barrows, C. M. 4
Bartlett, Bertha L. 64

Bartlett, D. E. 51
Bates, Laura M. 71
Beard, Richard O. 68
Beattie, Grace M. 90
Beattie, Mary B. 62
Beatty, Mary M. 43
Becker, Margaret R. 107
Becker, V. A. 123
Beckmeyer, Theodore 83
Beebe, Helen H. 4
Bell, Alexander G., 11, 12, 17, 27, 42, 43, 51, 64, 83, 86, 93, 103, 118
Bell, Mrs. Alexander G. 12
Bell, Alexander M. 93
Bell, Mabel G. 107, 118
Bell, Mabel H. 107
Bell, Martha C. 107
Bellefleur, Philip A. 4
Bellows, Howard P. 37
Bemis, Luna M. 3
Bender, James F. 73
Bender, Ruth E. 4, 38
Benedict, A. L. 43, 93
Bennett, Josephine ... 43, 83, 107
Benning, Doris B. 71, 86, 87
Bentley, Keilor 13
Berg, Lloyd E. 87
Berger, Emma 107
Berry, Amelia E. 4
Berry, Gordon 4, 17, 37
Berry, Helen 43
Berryman, Florence S. 61, 73
Betterly, E. J. 17
Betts, Otis A. 126
Bickler, Mary H. 64, 107
Bickley, Celia 17
Bigelow, Jane K. 107
Bilger, Robert 73
Bindon, D. 27
Binet, A. 27
Bingham, Cornelia D. 71
Bingham, Katherine T. ... 17, 93
Birch, Jack W. 51

Birch, Jane R. 78
Bird, William L. 3
Birge, Marguerite S. 107
Birkenshaw, Lois 61
Bishop, Helen M. 73
Black, John W. 93
Blair, Cora L. 43
Blair, Francis X. 27
Blair, Mary 17, 89
Blake, Clarence J. 4, 107
Blankenhorn, M. D. 14
Blankenship, Ota C. 43
Blanton, Smiley 103
Blattner, J. W. 27
Blish, Isabel S. 90
Blish, Stanford C. 17, 73
Bliss, Susan E. 43
Bluett, Charles G. .. 17, 123, 124
Boatner, Edmund B., 17, 27, 123, 126
Bodensiek, Gustav 34
Bodycomb, Margaret, 4, 17, 68, 93
Bollbach, Betty L. 4, 44
Bolton, Thaddeus L. 16
Boone, Daniel R. 44
Booth, Edmund 118
Booth, Frank W., 1, 3, 17, 44, 51, 59, 119
Booth, Iris 93
Bopst, E. G. 73
Boshler, Irene E. 73
Boudin, Etienne 118
Bower, Dolores 2, 123
Bowman, Dorothy L. 14
Bown, Jesse C. 44
Boyd, Hypatia 73
Boyd, John 11
Braddock, Mary J. 4
Bradford, Charles A. 38
Bradway, Katherine P. 78
Brady, Wilma S. 61
Braly, Kenneth 4, 38
Brand, Elizabeth 107
Brandon, Wallace R. 51

Branson, Helen K. 124
Brauckmann, Karl 107
Breckinridge, Mary S. . 27, 59, 107
Breckwoldt, Gerhart H. 94
Breese, Estelle 124
Brehm, F. Elizabeth 103
Breitwieser, J. V. 17
Breunig, H. Latham 18, 64
Bridgman, Olga 78
Brill, Richard G., 18, 42, 87, 94, 120
Brill, Tobias 27, 44, 78
Brintnall, Mrs. Arthur W. ... 107
Brockman, Seymour J. 42
Broderick, Thomas G. 4
Brown, Donald W. 124
Brown, J. 44
Brown, Ruth 37, 73
Bruce, Lula M. 83, 107
Bruce, M. Ethel 44
Bruce, Wallace T. 94, 119
Bruhn, Martha E., 37, 44, 107, 108, 118, 119, 124
Buchanan, Nancy 4
Buchli, M. J. 34
Buchman, Martha 44
Buell, Edith M., 18, 44, 51, 87, 103, 108
Bull, J. C. 28
Bunch, C. C. 11
Bunger, Anna M. 108
Burchard, Edward M. 78
Burdge, Alice V. 121
Burger, Richard 39
Burke, Mary M. 94
Burnet, John R. 16, 51
Burnett, Alice 68
Burns, Margaret A. 28
Butler, A. Evelyn 94, 103
Butler, Stahl 78, 103, 126

C

Caldwell, Elizabeth H. 44
Caldwell, William A. ... 3, 44, 51

Calkins, Ernest E. 73
Calvert, Donald R. 4, 94
Cambon, K. G. 68
Camp, Anna R. 11
Cardwell, W. A. 78
Carhart, Raymond 103
Carney, Mary V. 119
Caroll, David H. 87
Carpenter, Lula E. 123
Carr, Josephine 73, 94, 108
Carter, A. E. 94, 124
Carter, E. 124
Carter, Howard A. 39
Carter, Maud 62
Carter, W. H. 90
Case, Lucy E. 108
Casey, Sally L. 83
Cavaliere, R. A. 39
Cavanagh, Anita 61, 121
Cayley, Stephanie 64
Chamberlain, Naomi H. ... 18, 68
Chambless, Elizabeth ...108, 124
Chandler, Flora 108
Chapin, Alma L. 118
Chaplin, Joyce W. 18
Chapman, W. C. 14
Charles, Edna N. 73
Christian, Harvey T. 2
Christmas, Jeannette J. ... 94, 103
Church, Lilian L. 83, 89, 90
Clapp, John M. 94
Clark, A. S. 103
Clark, Alice E. 59
Clark, Juliet D. 108
Clarke, Francis D. 28, 62, 90
Clatterbuck, M. B. 91
Clayton, Nellie C. 18
Cleary, E. P. 44
Cloud, Daniel T. 37, 71, 94
Coakley, Estelle L. 4
Coats, G. Dewey 57, 103
Cobb, Jennie L., 2, 28, 43, 51, 60, 79
Cochrane, W. A. 57

131

Coffey, M. Adelaide 91
Cogswell, Elaine Ward 73
Cogswell, Frank H. 124
Cohen, Sonya S. 14
Cole, Robert H. 64
Cole, Roy 121
Coleman, G. D. 79
Collins, Helen M. 4
Collins, Marcella 91
Collins, Virginia E. 73
Conklin, Edmund S. 108
Connally, Eileen E. 28
Connery, Julia M. 94
Connor, Frances F. 119
Connor, Leo E. 18, 119, 124
Cook, M. Alleyne 108
Cooke, Jaye H. 126
Cooper, Helen M. 18
Corlett, Juliet C. 108
Corliss, Edith L. 39
Cornell, Louise E. 61
Cory, Patricia B. 69, 83, 121
Costello, Mary R. 5, 108, 119
Costello, Patrice 59, 61
Cota, Agnes 44
Cotton, Jack C. 5
Cowles, Katherine 91
Cox, Ian 28
Cox, Jerome R. Jr. 5
Cox, Mary R. 44, 51
Craig, Sam B. 37, 119
Craig, William N. 51, 71
Crammatte, Alan B. 127
Cramp, Arthur J. 42
Crandell, Marian P. 44, 84
Crane, Norman 121
Crawford, May T. 44
Crawford, N. T. 73
Croker, Gertrude W. 51
Crosby, Laura L. 52, 87, 120
Crouter, A. L. ... 18, 28, 94, 120
Crouter, Alan Y. 39, 44, 52
Crouter, John Y. 69
Crowther, A. E. 88

Crum, Carole 18, 64, 73
Crutchett, Ralph 39
Cruttenden, Mary E. 94
Cuddy, Nelle M. 5
Curry, Lorre 64
Curtis, John H. 103
Curtiss, Louise A. 92
Cutler, Elizabeth M. 79
Cypreansen, Lucile 121
Czily, Prof. A. 15

D

Dalgarno, Geo. 28
Dallet, Jean 18
Daly, Margaret A. 18
Danger, O. 18, 34, 42, 73
Daniel, Elizabeth 18
Davenport, Virginia H. 121
David, Edward E. 121
Davidson, Emma F. 103, 118
Davidson, Helena M. 69
Davidson, S. G. .. 18, 45, 52, 124
Davies, Gladys B. 5
Davies, Laura A. 108
Davies, Rachel D. 45, 84
Davis, M. V. 84
Davis, Samuel G. 52
Davis, W. M. 28
Dawes, Rachel E. 45, 94
Day, Herbert A. 28, 52, 90
Dean, Katherine S. 84
Dean, Louise E. 28
Deannard, Elizabeth 121
DeCondillac, Etienne B. 36
Deem, Harriet L. 3
DeHaven, Mabel 19
DeHearne, D. 57
De La Bat, G. 39, 124
DeLand, Fred, 13, 15, 19, 42, 94, 108, 124
De Lany, Elizabeth G. . 37, 73, 108
De L'Epee, Abbe 94
DeMotte, Amelia 52, 73

Denison, James 3, 87
Denmark, F. L. 108
DeVries, J. G. 19, 108
Dewar, Dorothy G. 19
De Young, Dirk P. 124
Dibos, Lucille 45
Di Carlo, Louis M., 1, 5, 39, 94, 109
Dickey, Dorothy B. 91
Dickinson, Myrle E. 73
Dietrich, Rose I. 52
DiMichael, S. G. 127
Dinsmore, Annette B. 16
Disher, Dorothy R. 109
Divine, L. R. 28, 127
Doane, Ray C. 127
Doctor, Powrie V., 28, 45, 60, 61, 87
Dodds, P. 52
Doerfler, Leo G. 5
Dombro, Robert H. 59
Dommisse, Elsa J. 121
Donald, Dora 15
Donald, Ida M. 45
Donaldson, Elizabeth M. 91
Doneghy, Lucy 45
Downing, A. U. 2
Downing, Nora 109
Doyle, F. W. 5
Doyle, John B. 5
Dozier, J. D. 28
Drake, Margaret L. 109
Draper, Amos G. 57
Drennan, George L. 79
Drennen, Genevieve .. 14, 37, 121
Driggs, Frank M., 19, 28, 42, 45, 92, 94, 127
Driscoll, Anita 2
Drouot, E. 28
Drum, Philip R. 95
DuBard, Etoile 59, 74
Dudley, D. C. 57
Duff, Jessie 14, 95, 124
Dunbar, Evelina 95

Duncan, R. C. 39
Dunlap, Mary M. 19
Dunlap, S. C. 45
Dunn, Margaret 109
Dupuis, L. 109
Durfee, Marion A. 37, 109
DuToit, J. M. 79
Dyer, Helen L. ... 61, 95, 109, 124

E

Earhart, E. K. 19
Earle, Carrie W. 123
Eccleston, Mary M. 95
Eckstrom, Faith F. 90
Eddy, Jonathan H. 3
Eddy, L. 79
Edgar, Lucille S. 74
Edge, Lillie K. 84
Effler, Louis R. 74
Egan, Ann R. 19
Eickhoff, Arlington J. 84
Eiseman, Marie H. 45
Elias, Hans 90
Elkan, Dorothea 1
Elliot, Richard 103
Elliott, A. Edwina 28
Elliott, C. Evangeline 2
Elliott, Ida D. 28
Elliott, Sarah L. 5, 95
Elliott, Shirley S. 45
Ellis, Vaughn E. 109
Elstad, Leonard M., 5, 11, 28, 29, 124
Ely, Grace D. 79
Empey, Margaret 5
English, Sandra 64
Erd, Robert 29
Ersner, Matthew S. 95
Ervin, Annie M. 45, 84, 92
Etter, Carl L. 124
Eubank, Earle E. 37
Euritt, Guilford D. 127
Evans, Florence L. 37

133

Evans, Mildred 19, 45, 64
Evers, Louise S. 109
Ewing, Alexander W. 45
Ewing, Ethel C. 74
Ewing, Irene 36, 69

F

Fagan, E. 61
Falberg, R. 29, 127
Falconer, George A. . 29, 121, 123
Fant, Louie 57
Farman, J. J. 95
Farquhar, Grover C. 84, 87
Farrant, Roland H. 79
Farrar, A. 15, 19, 109
Farrell, Gabriel 16
Fauth, Bette L. 29
Fauth, La Verne 29
Favors, A. 61
Fay, Edward A., 16, 18, 43, 52, 69, 103
Fay, G. O. 29
Fay, Helen 29, 64
Fay, O. Gilbert 57
Fearon, J. 15, 109
Fechheimer, A. Lincoln 19
Fehr, Joann D. 45
Feilbach, Rose V. 109
Fellendorf, George W. . 39, 64, 119
Ferrall, John A. 74, 109, 124
Ferreri, Giulio, 5, 15, 19, 20, 29, 34, 37, 74, 95, 109
Fessant, John M. 87, 123, 127
Fetterly, H. B. 34
Field, Lois G. 5, 64
Finch, Wallace J. 124
Finn, Betsy A. 121
Finney, Mariette E. 74
Fish, Anna G. 16
Fish, Kate H. 95
Fiske, Stella A. 63
Fitzgerald, Edith .. 45, 52, 57, 88
Fitzgerald, Margaret H., 5, 52, 84, 87

Flanders, Gwendolyn A. 61
Flange, C. S. 124
Flaxman, Mrs. G. D. 74
Flegel, Elynor 20
Fleitz, Mildred 95
Fletcher, Harvey 5
Fletcher, Katharine 52, 92
Flint, Richard W. 84, 119
Florence, Geneva 79
Fogel, Howard H. 39
Foley, Julia A. 59
Fonner, Mary D. 52, 118
Forchhammer, G. 34
Ford, Catherine 45
Fordyce, Charles 84
Fornari, P. 20
Forrester, T. C. 5, 11
Forsythe, Kathrin B. 69
Fort, Berneice 5
Fosmark, Laura B. 84
Foss, Bertha M. 20
Fouts, Mildred 91
Fowler, Edmund P. 43
Fowler, Frances Ellis 90, 103
Fox, Thomas F. 16, 29, 52
Foy, Robert E. 45
Frackelton, Berneda P. 79
Frankenthal, Sybil 109
Franz, Shepherd I. 74
Freck, Phyllis 91
Freeman, Samuel M. 3
Frick, Kathryne M. 16
Friedman, Max 127
Frisina, D. Robert 11, 95
Fritz, Katherine 84
Froeschels, Emil 95
Frohn, W. 74
Frueh, Frank 5, 11
Fruewald, E. 37
Fuller, Carl W. 67
Fuller, Millicent B. 63
Fuller, Sarah, 13, 16, 64, 67, 95, 109
Fullington, Angeline 3, 20, 91

Funk, Stanton C. 64
Fusfeld, Irving S., 20, 29, 52, 57, 104, 118, 127

G

Gale, Edward P. 52
Gallaudet, Edward M. . 29, 57, 79
Galloway, James H. 39, 41
Gantenbein, Andrew 45
Garbett, Arthur S. 61
Gardiner, M. 95
Gardner, I. B. 79
Gardner, Mark B. 95
Gardner, W. Morton 6
Gardner, Warren H. 6, 69
Gare, Marion W. 45
Garns, John S. 95
Garrett, Charles W. 124
Garrett, Emma 104
Garrett, Mary S. 95
Gates, A. I. 84
Gault, R. H. 29, 95, 109
Gawith, Frances W. 84, 91
Gay, Ruth 63, 74, 79, 123
Gebhart, Helen M. 109
Geddes, Kathleen R. 61
Geer, Alleyne C. 109
Gemmill, W. H. 29
Gentilli, Amadeo 6
George, D. W. 57
Gesell, Arnold 69, 74
Gesner, Elizabeth T. 84
Giangreco, Joseph 52, 64
Giangreco, Marianne 45
Gibian, Rose 74
Gildston, Phyllis 37
Gile, Ben C. 6
Gill, Dorothy 6
Gillespie, Frances E. 29, 104
Gillespie, John A. 52
Gillet, H. S. 52
Glasser, Mrs. Mac 88

Glenn, Frances L. 88, 95
Glenn, Sallie 3
Glowatsky, Edward 79
Goda, Sidney 64, 84
Goetzinger, Cornelius P., 11, 30, 37, 45, 79, 95
Goggin, Anne P. 92
Goldberg, Herman R. 20, 110
Goldberg, Rose E. 74
Goldstein, Hyman 30
Goldstein, Max A., 6, 11, 20, 42, 110
Goldstein, Robert 6, 30, 39
Goodwin, Elizabeth 45
Göpfert, E. 52
Gordon, Anne 118
Gordon, Avondale N. 110
Gordon, Mary L. 46
Gough, John A. 30, 67, 121
Grady, Theodore 127
Grammatico, Leahea 46
Grandgent, Charles H. 104
Gratz, Leola A. 74
Graves, Frank P. 6
Green, Grace G. 20
Green, Ruth 125
Green, Samuel A. 30
Greenaway, E. S. 69
Greenberger, D. ... 3, 53, 90, 104
Greene, David 104
Greene, James S. 95
Greenmun, Robert M. 30, 125
Gregg, F. M. 95
Grey, Howard A. 121
Griffin, Barbara 84
Griffin, Mary E. 127
Griffing, W. T. 30
Griffith, Mary J. 84
Griffiths, Ciwa 6, 69
Groff, Marné L. 53
Groht, Mildred A. . 20, 46, 84, 119
Grosvenor, Elsie B. 13
Grosvenor, Elsie M. 13
Grosvenor, Mrs. Gilbert 13

135

Grosvenor, Melville B. 13
Grussing, Florence P. 95
Gruver, Elbert A. ... 20, 46, 60, 74
Gruver, Margaret H. 20, 96
Guedel, A. E. 30
Guilder, Ruth P. 6
Guilmartin, Mary D. 46
Guinness, S. 46
Gulick, Mabel 84
Gusow, F. 64
Guthrie, Virginia S. 20, 69
Gutzmann, Albert 96
Gutzmann, Herm. 118

H

Haeseler, Charlotte 6
Hagens, E. W. 20
Hall, G. Stanley 16
Hall, Grace D. 64
Hall, Inis B. 15
Hall, Percival 20, 30, 53, 119
Haller, G. L. 39
Hamel, Clara A. 46
Hammer, Helen L. 20, 61, 84
Hancock, E. Frances 96
Haney, Mary R. 64
Hanna, Elizabeth 88
Hansen, A. 110
Hansen, Anders ... 15, 20, 35, 74
Hansen, M. R. 64
Hanson, Earl C. 39
Hanson, Olof 30, 57, 127
Hardy, William G. ... 6, 20, 39, 74
Harkness, Margaret M. 46, 74
Harman, Augusta 20, 64
Harrell, Hattie 20
Harrington, Donald A. 39, 46
Harris, G. T. 96
Harris, Grace M. 6, 64
Harris, James C. 91
Harris, Lena 15
Harris, Nathan P. 30
Harris, Norma 65

Hart, Beatrice O. 46
Harvey, A. 3
Harwood, Viola 91
Hasenstab, Philip J. 87, 89
Haskins, C. N. 3, 57
Haskins, Harriet 39
Haspiel, George S. 110
Haug, O. 39
Haycock, C. Sibley 110
Haycock, George S. 20, 34
Haynes, Carrie A. ...., 20
Hays, Harold 74, 125
Hearty, Mary G. 110
Hector, Elizabeth R. 71, 96
Hedgecock, Leroy D. .. 11, 67, 104
Hedley, Arthur 74
Hedrick, Jennie 96
Heider, Fritz 6, 46, 96, 110
Heider, Grace M., 15, 69, 75, 110, 121
Heinl, S. S. 87
Hinrichs, Eunice L. 69
Helmle, Margarette 127
Hembrook, Margaret 2
Henderson, Jennie M., 20, 61, 71, 96, 119
Henderson, Myrtle L. 65
Henderson, Myrtle W. 53
Henderson, S. 30, 89
Henderson, Sara C. 12
Herrick, Helen 6, 59
Hester, M. S. 121
Heward, H. 21
Hicker, H. D. 125, 127
Hickernell, W. F. 42
Hickey, Marshall S. 79
Higgins, F. C. 30
Higgins, Lydia F. 46
Hill, A. C. 21
Hill, Elsie 110
Hill, Miss W. 84
Hillard, Ethel M. 21, 46, 119
Hines, Edward J. 21
Hirsch, D. 30, 68

Hiskey, M. S. 75
Hitz, John 13
Hjorth, Ernst 127
Hobart, Elsa L. 47
Hodgson, E. A. 53
Hoffmann, Hugo 21, 35
Hoffman, Virginia 69
Hofmarksrichter, R. 79
Hogsteater, H. T. 79
Holley, Minnie C. 47
Hollister, H. H. 57
Holowach, Jean 42
Holt, Laura D. 110
Hood, C. A. 110
Hooper, Mrs. J. C. 65
Hopson, A. B. 127
Horowitz, Leola S. 21
Hotchkiss, J. Burton 104
Houchins, Rollie R. 96
Houser, Bessie 104
Howard, Caroline M. 30
Howard, Evelyn S. 69
Howard, Jay C. 125
Howard, Petra F. 125
Howe, Alice G. 37
Howe, Samuel G. 16
Howell, Louise 110
Howes, Annette S. 90
Howes, Esther C. 69, 85, 110
Howson, James W. 30, 53, 90
Höxter, Richard 36
Hubbard, Elbert 96
Hudgins, Clarence V., 6, 39, 96, 104, 121
Hudson, Alice F. 71
Hudson-McKuen, G. 96, 104
Hull, Susanna E. 53, 110
Humason, Thomas A. 53
Hunt, J. F. 35, 79
Hunter, Annie R. 88
Hurd, Anna C. . 21, 30, 53, 69, 96
Hurst, Fannie D. .. 47, 53, 75, 87
Hutchinson, Enid 110
Hutman, Florence E. 110
Hutton, Charles 6
Hutton, George 57

I

Iandoli, Edward A. 69
Ingle, Helen F. 47, 53
Ingram, Christine P. 21
Ingvarsson, Ivar M. 47, 53
Irion, Theo. W. 53
Ives, Annie M. 110

J

Jackson, Anne W. 47
Jacobs, J. A. 58, 79
Jacoby, Beatrice 65
James, William 82
Jayne, Gladys G. 61, 63
Jelks, Mrs. F. W. 65
Jenkins, Weston G., 3, 21, 53, 58, 75, 92
Jenkins, William G. 53, 79
Jenks, Monica K. 125
Jennings, Gertrude J. 21
Jesseman, Victoria C. 12, 68
Jewell, Grace H. 110
Johansen, Donald 21
Johnson, Clyde W. 12
Johnson, Elizabeth H., 12, 30, 40, 79
Johnson, Evan V. 119
Johnson, Jeanette N. 65
Johnson, Marion C. 6
Johnson, Richard O. 72
Joiner, Enfield . 21, 47, 85, 96, 104
Jolly, Faith 21
Jones, Anne 91
Jones, Carrie L. 110
Jones, Christina C. 21
Jones, Eleanor P. 96
Jones, John W., 16, 30, 47, 53, 87, 120
Jones, Kate-Helen 21, 47
Jones, Lilian G. 35

137

Jones, Mabel K.	47
Jones, Mary D.	110
Jones, Miss Ogwen	7
Jones, Uriel C.	127
Jordan, Sarah A.	61
Justman, Joseph	21

K

Kane, Edith B.	110, 111
Kaufman, Maurice	85
Kawakami, Marcia	61
Kawamoto, Unosuke	47
Kearns, C. W.	21
Keaster, Jacqueline	7, 21
Keefer, M. B.	47
Keeler, Sarah W.	111
Keep, John R.	3, 53, 58
Keith, John	111
Keller, Helen	16
Keller, Lillian	47
Kelley, J. C.	37
Kelley, Noble H.	104
Kelly, Elizabeth	119
Kelly, Emma	53
Kelly, J. B.	7
Kendall, David C.	7
Kendall, Elsie P.	87
Kenfield, Coralie N.	111
Kennard, Marie S.	85, 90, 121
Kennedy, Eloise	87
Kennedy, Lydia B.	122
Kennedy, Mildred	7, 75, 111
Kennedy, W. Richard	127
Kenner, Marcus L.	30
Kent, Alice	85
Kent, Eliza	2, 3
Kent, Margaret	30, 53, 61
Kenwood, John C.	40
Kenyon, Elmer L.	97
Kerr, A. M.	7
Kerr, M. M.	30
Kessler, Emma B.	111
Kessler, Saul N.	111
Ketcham, Margaret B.	61
Khan, Evelyn	125
Kharasch, Ethel N.	61
Kidder, Charles W.	97
Kidder, K. B.	85
Kiesel, Theodore A.	31, 72, 123
Kilpatrick, W. M.	72
Kimball, Caroline F.	111
Kimber, W. J.	75
King, Gordon	79
King, Kate L.	91
Kinsey, Eveline I.	97
Kinsley, Grace	21
Kinzie, Cora E.	111
Kirk, Louise	47
Kirk, Samuel A.	80
Kirkhuff, J. D.	31
Kirkley, J. R.	87, 91
Kitson, H. D.	75, 111
Kleffner, Frank R.	1
Klienfeld, L.	65
Kline, Louise T.	111
Kline, Thomas K.	80
Kling, Gertrude N.	7
Klopfer, Stephen	35
Knievel, William R.	127
Knight, Augustus C.	61, 112
Knight, Marian	97
Knight, Maude H.	75
Knowles, Elizabeth	112
Knox, Addie C.	47
Knudsen, Vern O.	40, 41
Koch, Albert	7
Koester, Diedrich	97
Kopp, George A.	97
Kopp, Harriet G.	21
Kraft, Dorothy G.	87, 122
Krohn, Emmylou	15
Krol, S. T.	125

L

LaBenz, Paul J.	7
Lack, A.	97

LaCrosse, Edward 59	Lloyd, James H. 1
LaCrosse, Edwin L. ... 7, 12, 112	Long, E. Florence 2
Lacy, Mabel V. 47	Long, J. Schuyler, 31, 54, 58, 72,
Ladd, Alice 112	80, 91, 97
Lamb, Helen D. 97, 112	Longwill, Mrs. J. B. 69
Lamb, Marion H. 7, 97	Lore, James I. 97
Lambert, C. G. 112	Lorge, Irving 41
Lampard, Marie T. 63	Love, James K. 22, 42, 70
Lamprecht, Emil 72	Lowry, Charles D. 75, 80
Landis, Kate S. 31	Lucas, Frances 87, 97, 104
Lane, Dorothy H. 112	Ludlow, Fitz H. 63
Lane, Helen S., 21, 59, 65, 69, 75,	Lux, Alta M. 112
119, 122	Lynndelle, Vivian 7
Langdon, Marcia A. 59	Lyon, V. W. 80
Lange, Paul 15	
Larr, Alfred L. ... 75, 97, 112, 122	Mc
Larsen, Laila L. 7	McAlister, Grace W. 61
LaRue, Mary S. 31, 60	McAloney, Thomas S. . 47, 72, 123
LaRue, Sarah J. 122	McArdle, S. M. 70
Lassman, Grace 40, 65, 69	McCabe, Brian F. 42
Latham, W. H. 31	McCalmont, Phyllis 97
Lauritsen, Marné 97	McClellan, Grace A. 65
Lauritsen, Wesley 54, 127	McClure, George M. 31, 54
Lavos, George 75, 80, 127	McClure, William J. 123, 128
Lee, John J. 21, 125	McConnell, Freeman 7
Lehmann, Mrs. Floyd 65	McCowen, M. 112, 118
Leigh, Jean W. 75	McCowen, Mary 22, 61, 97
Leighton, Etta V. 37	McDaniel, Nettie 22
Lemley, Herman A. 125	McDermott, Valeria D. 125
Leonard, Bessie N. 112	McDonald, Alice 112
Leonard, Eleanor C. .. 22, 47, 97	McDowell, Evelyn 22
Leonard, Myrtle H. 22	McFarlane, J. H. 22
Leshin, George J. 22, 60	McGee, T. Manford 7, 42
Letzter, Margaret C. 54	McGinnis, Mildred A. 1
Levine, Edna S., 40, 65, 69, 75, 80	McGrady, Harold J. 47
Lewin, Lucie M. 97	McGroskey, Robert L. 7
Lewis, Bertha 31	McIntire, W. F. 31
Lewis, Dorothy N. 40	McIntire, Wayne 22
Lewis, Sarah E. 2, 47	McKendrick, John G. 97
Liebman, Jeffrey 75	McKenna, Alice 112
Lindquist, Ida P. 112, 125	McKenzie, Lilla B. 7
Lindstrom, Thure A. 47	McKerral, Lena 112
Ling, Daniel 40	McKenney, Lettie W. 61
Lloyd, Glenn T. 12, 54	McLaughlin, Clayton L. 2

139

McLaughlin, Harriet F. ... 22, 85
McLaughlin, Marjorie 122
McLean, Marjorie 112
McLeod, Frances 122
McManaway, Howard M., 7, 22, 31, 120
McMillan, K. 2
McNeil, Marie T. 85
McNeill, Naomi 70
McPherson, Jane G. 80

M

MacAuley, Dorothy 65
MacBeth, Madge 112
MacDonald, Nellie V. 70, 85
MacFarlan, Douglas 7
Mackie, Romaine P. 31
Mackin, Helen 122
Macloingsigh, Peadar 22
MacMillan, Betty 47
Macnutt, Ena G. 38, 112
MacPherson, James R. 60
Madden, Anne M. 7
Madison, J. L. 22
Magner, Marjorie E. ... 35, 68, 85
Maigetter, Elizabeth 112
Makuen, G. Hudson 97
Mangan, Kenneth R., 22, 85, 97, 104
Mannen, Grace 47, 65, 98
Manning, Arthur C. 89, 128
Manning, Clarence A. 22
Manz, Fred M. 22
Marage, R. 7
Marbut, Musa 54
Marichelle, H. 118
Markell, Alan 61
Martin, Frederick 98
Martineau, Harriet 76
Margulies, Mrs. A. R. 70
Mashburn, Authur G. 92
Mason, Marie K., 8, 104, 112, 122
Matlock, Gladys D. 112

Maxon, Kathryn P. 47, 112
May, Elizabeth 61
Mayer, Jonas H. 76
Mayne, Richard E. 13
Mays, Lenable 89
Mendelson, N. 70
Menninger, K. A. 76
Meredith, Anna 112
Merkl, W. 8
Merklein, Richard A. 8
Merry, Ralph V. 15
Meyer, Max F. 54, 104
Milesky, Samuel D. 112
Miller, Ada R. 91
Miller, Alfred L. 8
Miller, Anne S. 22
Miller, Bertha 62
Miller, E. O. 76
Miller, James R. 42, 118
Miller, June B. . 22, 31, 38, 65, 70
Miller, Linda K. 80
Miller, Malinda K. 72
Miller, Marjorie 48
Miller, Reid C. 22
Mills, Mary M. 63
Mira, Mary P. 80
Mirrielees, Ruchiel 48
Misra, Surya K. 113
Mitchell, Dorothy 48
Moffat, L. 54, 118
Monaghan, Alice 60, 98
Monro, Sarah J., 62, 63, 98, 104, 113
Monsees, Edna K. 1, 98
Montague, Harriet, 8, 13, 15, 23, 31, 40, 68, 70, 113, 122, 125
Montgomery, Ida 104
Moore, Charles E. 40
Moore, Grace 70
Moore, Helen T. 48, 80, 91
Moore, Lucelia 122
Moore, Lucile M., 8, 31, 76, 89, 119
Moore, Mrs. Sidney M. 65
Morgan, Lucia C. 8

140

Morgenstern, Louise I. ... 76, 113
Morkovin, Boris V. 35, 76
Morley, D. E. 8
Morris, Dorothy 2, 113
Morris, M. Esther 48, 113
Morris, Minnie E. 16, 31, 54
Morrison, Jessie S. 91, 125
Morrow, Elizabeth 85
Morsh, Joseph E. 31
Moseley, Nancy B. 89
Mosely, T. F. 54
Mosley, C. C. 31
Moss, Margery 85
Mossel, Max N. 3, 54
Motto, Joseph 23
Mulholland, Ann M. .. 48, 89, 98
Müller-Walle, Julius 113
Murphy, Albert T., 13, 23, 76, 125
Murphy, Margaret 8, 48
Muyskens, John H. 98
Myklebust, Helmer R., 1, 31, 41, 60, 76, 80

Newlee, Clara E. . 2, 23, 76, 85, 87
Newman, Lawrence 3
Newton, Mary G. 85
Neyhus, Arthur I. 76
Nicholas, Georgia C. 65
Nicoll, Mildred G. 85
Nielsen, Dorothy V. 62
Nilson, Roy F. 8
Nitchie, Edward B., 76, 98, 113, 114, 122, 125
Nitchie, Elizabeth H. 114
Nitkin, Nathaniel 98, 125
Nober, E. Harris 8
Norris, Anne C. 23
Norris, Mrs. James F. 38
Northcott, Winifred N. 65
Northrop, Helen 87
Nowlin, Louise S. 114
Noyes, J. L. 31
Noyes, Marion 104
Nordin, Elizabeth A. 16
Numbers, Fred C. 23, 98, 120
Numbers, Leona P. 2
Numbers, Mary E., 8, 23, 48, 98, 114, 119

N

Nace, John G. 125
Naiman, Doris 85
Nall, Frances 35
Neas, B. Jack 14
Nelson, Boyd E., 12, 23, 38, 98, 113, 118, 125
Nelson, Max 8, 60
Nelson, Myrthel S. 54
Nelson, William 35
Nelson, Wilma I. 122
Neuschutz, Louise I. 16, 118
Nevile, Miss B. 23
Neville, Virginia 113
Nevinson, Elizabeth 76
New, Mary C. . 38, 48, 62, 70, 98
Newcombe, F. C. 92
Newell, Nettie 15
Newhart, Horace 8, 42

O

O'Connell, Agnes 91
O'Connor, Clarence D., 8, 23, 31, 40, 65, 80, 98
O'Donnell, Elizabeth K. 65
O'Donnell, Francis H. 3
O'Halloran, Dorothy M. 70
Olanoff, Rose S. 59, 91
Oléron, Pierre 81
Olin, Caroline L. 114, 118
Olson, Christine 122
Olson, Florence 40
O'Neill, Veronica 2
Ordman, Theodore 114
Orman, James N. 54, 81
Orr, John P. 128
Orr, Marie P. 48

141

Osborne, Caroline A. 98
Osler, Sonia F. 76
Ostern, Beatrice 65, 85, 122
Oswald, Mabel V. 98
Owsley, Peter J. . . . 23, 76, 90, 125
Oyer, Herbert J. 122

P

Paddleford, Lillian 54
Pagenstecher, Adelyn 65
Palen, Imogen B. 23, 118
Palva, Tauno 8
Panconcelli-Calzia, G. 23
Parks, Roy G. 87
Parrish, O. G. 128
Pascoe, D. 35
Paterson, Donald G. 31
Patten, H. T. 72, 88
Patterson, Alpha W. 125
Patterson, Robert 31
Patton, Livingston 54
Paul, W. 104
Pauls, Miriam 8, 48
Paxson, Ruth 8, 114
Pearson, Frank B. 119
Peck, Annetta W. 38, 89
Peck, B. J. 23
Peet, Edward 32
Peet, Elizabeth 38, 54
Peet, Harvey P. 38, 58, 104
Peet, Isaac L. 38, 58, 104
Pence, Helen W. 60
Perelló, Jorge 35
Perry, Charles S. 23, 54
Peters, E. F. 81
Peterson, Edwin G. . . 48, 81, 123
Peterson, Gordon E., 24, 98, 99, 122
Peterson, P. N. 54, 125, 128
Pettengill, B. D., 38, 54, 58, 68, 72
Pettingell, J. H. 54
Pharis, Dorothy M. 8
Philbrick, William A. 1
Phillips, F. I. 90
Phillips, John 105
Phillips, Richard M. 81, 128
Phillips, Wendell C. 125
Pierce, Jerry A. . . 76, 114, 115, 125
Pintner, Rudolf, 24, 38, 48, 54, 63, 76, 81, 105
Pitrois, Yvonne 15, 35
Pittenger, Priscilla 38, 48, 99
Pless, Marie A. 40
Poitras, Bonnie 24
Pollack, Doreen 8, 40, 65
Pollard, Nannie A. 55
Pomeroy, Wilmer 115
Poore, Mrs. H. T. 70
Pope, Alvin E. 41, 126
Porter, George S. 128
Porter, Mrs. Nathan T., Jr. . . 115
Porter, Samuel 16, 55
Porter, Sarah H. 38, 55, 63
Porter, Van C. 60
Potter, Ralph K. 105
Poulos, Thomas H., 2, 9, 38, 91, 99
Power, Sue B. 99
Powers, Margaret H. 38
Poyntz, Leonidas 72
Praagh, William 115
Prall, Josephine 40, 41, 115
Pratt, Emily A. 115
Pratt, George T., 24, 76, 99, 115, 120
Presto, Marya 99
Prettyman, Eileen 35
Probyn, June Y. 9
Proctor, Dorothy M. 9
Pugh, Bessie . . . 24, 48, 76, 85, 99
Pugh, Gladys S. 85, 88
Purdy, Martha E. 122
Putnam, G. H. 55, 81
Pybas, Adelaide H. 105

Q

Quick, Marian 24, 66, 77, 99
Quigley, Howard M. 38

Quigley, Stephen P. 9, 120
Quill, Leonora 14
Quinn, Josephine 48, 55, 77

R

Rachlin, Carol 9
Radcliffe, Edith 62
Ralston, Patricia 66
Rankin, C. E. 32, 70
Ranson, Ethel O. 115
Raph, Jane B. 99
Rau, E. F. 35
Raubicheck, Letitia 77
Rawlings, Charles G. 55, 105
Ray, Luzerne 32, 81
Read, Elizabeth 85
Read, Elmer D. 81, 92
Read, Utten 32
Reamy, Olive L. 118
Reay, Edward W. 55
Reed, Mrs. Frank A. 99
Reed, Katharine F., 3, 24, 55, 66, 92
Reed, Nell D. 24
Reeve, Jesse W. 38
Reeves, J. K. 40
Reid, Gladys 118
Reid, Harry W. 126
Reineke, Mary E. 66
Reinhardt, Anna C. 24, 42
Reiss, Mrs. K. 66
Reiss, Madeline 85
Reiter, Frank H. 24, 41, 115
Remnitz, Annabel 24
Renard, Ella S. 91
Resnick, Libby 9
Rhodes, Elizabeth 92
Richards, Edith 48, 88
Richards, George L. 9
Richardson, Beatrice E. 62
Richardson, Charles W. 126
Richardson, Mrs. O. T. 89
Richardson, P. L. 128

Richardson, Paul C., 24, 48, 70, 86, 99
Rider, Edward C. 70
Riemann, G. 15
Rierdon, Beatrice 9
Righter, George J. 40
Rio, Armand 105
Rittenhouse, Marion F. 24
Roach, Robert E. 9, 70
Roberts, Emma .. 24, 66, 99, 115
Roberts, Linnaeus 42, 86, 88
Roberts, M. 48
Robinson, Anna E. 14
Robinson, Geoffrey C. 70
Robinson, Mary W. 55
Robinson, Ruth 89
Robinson, Stanley 16
Robinson, Warren, 48, 49, 55, 92, 118
Rocheleau, Corinne 15
Roe, W. Carey 24, 49, 77, 99
Rogers, Francis L. 24
Rogers, Mary 115
Rogers, William B. 88
Romero, Emerson 122
Rooney, Alice G. 1, 66, 99
Roorda, P. 66
Rose, Lillian 49, 55
Rosen, Jack 9
Rosenstein, Joseph 63, 126
Ross, Ellen B. 77
Ross, Louise 123
Rott, O. M. 42
Rotter, Paul, 9, 59, 66, 70, 99, 120
Rowe, Frederick 58
Rowell, Hugh G. 120
Rudloff, Joseph S. 120
Ruffin, Henrietta H. 115
Rupley, Stella 49
Rush, Mary Lou 55
Rushford, Georgina 9
Russell, G. Oscar 99, 105
Russell, Lillian E. 115
Ruthven, Henrietta 86

S

Salade, Robert F. 126
Samuelson, Estelle E., 38, 115, 126
Sandberg, Irene L. 62
Sandberg, Mabel W. 62
Sanders, Mrs. George T. 66
Sanders, K. D. 25
Sank, Diane 42
Sataloff, Joseph 42
Saunders, Nida 77
Savage, Julia W. 91
Sawyer, Mrs. S. E. 66
Scheeline, Mrs. Isaiah 66
Schein, Jerome 32
Schick, H. F. 77
Schick, Helen C. 12, 81
Schilling, B. W. 25
Schmidt, A. 35
Schneider, Matthias 82
Schowe, B. M. 128
Schowe, Ben M., Jr. 86, 122
Schumann, Paul 115
Schunhoff, Hugo F. ... 25, 32, 82
Schwartz, Marcia G. 25
Schwarz, Carrie K. 115
Scott, Elizabeth 9, 49, 122
Scott, Ella 99
Scott, Mrs. Elmer W. 1
Scott, Wirt A. 55
Scouten, Edward L. 55, 58
Scripture, E. W. 35, 99, 100
Scriver, Helen 115
Scyster, Margaret 71, 72
Seal, Albert G. 128
Sellin, Donald F. 60
Sensenig, Anne 9
Sensenig, Barton 2, 3, 55
Serumgard, Inez M. 86
Shaffer, Chester M. 105
Shanahan, Minette 71
Shaw, Janet P. 15
Shaw, M. 105
Shellgrain, Evelyn M. 49

Shepherd, David C. 9
Shere, Marie O. 60
Sheridan, Laura C. 32, 55, 82
Shiels, Katherine 90
Shiflet, Cleta 55
Shinpaugh, Joe R. 82
Shippy, Ardell 66
Shirley, Mary 82
Shontz, Franklin C. 77
Shortley, Michael J. 128
Sievers, A. D. 77
Sigurdson, Haldora K. ... 77, 122
Silver, Rawley 62
Silverman, S. Richard, 13, 25, 32, 41, 100
Simmons, Audrey A. 9, 49
Simon, Adele 66
Simon, Arthur B. 25, 66, 100
Simon, Mrs. Richard 66
Simonds, Elsie H. 115
Simpson, Emmette W. 128
Sinclair, Margaret 86
Sister Anna Rose 25, 86
Sister Anne Bernadine 49, 86
Sister James Lorene 49
Sister Jeanne d'Arc 49
Sister M. Albert 91
Sister M. Constantia 92
Sister M. de LaSalle 86
Sister M. Emmanuel 105
Sister M. Henriella 25
Sister M. Pauline 60
Sister M. Renée 86
Sister M. Therese 49
Sister Marianna 9, 100
Sister Mary A. Burke 32
Sister Mary Fanchea 9
Sister Mary Laurentine 100
Sister Mary Oswald 25
Sister Mary Walter 25, 49, 55
Sister Rose Gertrude 71
Sister St. Esther 100
Sister Sylvania 105
Skyberg, Victor O. 82

Slankard, Harriet 77
Smalley, Lillian D. 9
Smaltz, Warren M. 82
Smith, Alathena J. 66
Smith, Gale M. 9
Smith, Gladys E. 49
Smith, James L., 3, 32, 33, 49, 58, 82, 88, 91, 123
Smith, Margaret C. 49
Smith, Mathilda W. 116
Smith, Meredith J. 62
Smith, Minnie E. 92
Smith, Muriel A. 66
Smith, Rena A. 77
Smith, Sherman K. 9, 100
Sortini, Adam J. 9, 40, 60, 66
Sowell, James W. 3
Spencer, Robert C. 14
Springer, N. Norton 82
Spyker, Sally 100
Stafford, May M. 3
Stahlem, Evelyn M. 25
Staples, Anna L. 116
Stedman, Anne B. 100
Steed, Eleanor L. 116
Steed, Lyman 25, 100
Steffey, Mary E. 66, 77, 116
Stein, Shirley P. 10
Steinberg, John C. 100
Steinke, Agnes 118
Steinke, Elsie M. 82, 105
Stelle, Roy M. 25, 128
Stelling, H. 35
Stephens, Alfred E. 128
Steppuhn 58
Stern, Rose G. 68
Sterne, Lillian C. 86
Stetson, R. H. 101
Stevens, H. C. 82
Stevens, J. E. 35, 101
Stevens, Kelly H. 62
Stevenson, Elwood A., 10, 12, 41, 63
Stevenson, Margaret J. 77
Stewart, Helen L. 55, 82
Stewart, P. 77
Stewart, W. J. 55
Stillson, S. V. 77
Stix, E. F. 77
Stobschinski, Robert 101, 118
Stockdell, Kenneth G. 10
Stokoe, Agnes 101
Stolp, Lauren E. 25
Stone, Collins 33, 105
Stone, Elizabeth A. ... 82, 88, 118
Stoner, Marguerite, 66, 71, 77, 101, 120
Storey, John D. 77
Storrs, Richard S. 3, 33, 105
Story, Arthur J., 25, 35, 55, 77, 101, 105, 116
Stovel, Laura 89
Strauch, Genevieve B. 49
Streeter, Helen M. 49, 55, 88
Streng, Alice .. 25, 49, 56, 82, 120
Strickland, Elizabeth H. 91
Strickland, Florence I. 116
Strickland, Ruth G. 49, 86
Strizver, Gerald L. 10
Strong, Arch 49
Struck, A. N. 56
Stuckless, E. Ross 49
Stunkel, E. 82
Sturdivant, Elizabeth 25
Stutsman, Grace T. 128
Sullivan, Annie M. 16
Sullivan, Oscar M. 126, 128
Sunstrom, Florence 62
Sutermeister, Eugene 57
Sutton, Estella V. 33, 72, 92
Swain, N. G. 59
Swainson, Miss 35
Swayze, Rachel H. 49
Sweet, Marie E. 1
Swift, Walter B. 101
Switzer, Mary E. 128
Sylvester, Elfrieda M. 25, 77
Szanton, Victor L. 10

145

T

Taber, Frank A. 10, 116
Talbot, Benjamin 33
Tallman, Mary L. 116
Tatman, Mrs. Donald 67, 77
Taussig, E. 10, 49
Taylor, Annah S. 2
Taylor, Ellen E. 71
Taylor, Harris, 13, 14, 25, 43, 56, 72, 101, 105
Taylor, Helen 71
Taylor, Mrs. La Verne 33
Taylor, Nellie M. 56, 88
Taylor, Sam D. 33, 36
Taylor, W. W. 36
Templin, Mildred C., 33, 50, 77, 82
Tervoort, Bernard Th. 50, 56
Thollon, B. 33, 56
Thoma, Florence B. 71
Thomas, Alyce 86
Thomas, Donald 25
Thomas, Elizabeth S. 56
Thomas, Margaret L. 58
Thomason, Pattie 101, 116
Thompson, Emma R. 26
Thompson, Etta M. 50
Thompson, Hazel N. 128
Thompson, Iza 102, 105
Thompson, Richard 67, 77
Thompson, William H. 56
Thorne, Bert 26
Thornton, E. 50
Thornton, Joyce 122
Thornton, Marjorie 63
Throckmorton, Helen 105
Tiberio, C. S. 50
Tilden, Douglas 58
Tillinghast, Edward S. . . 26, 33, 56
Tillinghast, Hilda 33
Tilly, William 102
Timberlake, Josephine B., 10, 26, 36, 40, 77, 91, 102
Titsworth, Elizabeth 10

Tomb, John W. 56
Tompkins, Ernest 77, 102
Tonley, Lucia S. 77
Torrey, Gertrude 116
Transue, Hannah W. 116
Trask, Alice N. 38, 116
Trask, Cornelia 105
Treibert, Marjorie 89
Trill, Ellen M. 116
Troll, George D. 38
Tucker, Walter J. 26
Turley, Ethel J. 116
Turner, W. W. 33, 63
Turner, Wallace R. 126
Turvey, T. M. 105
Tylor, Edward B. 58

U

Uden, A. v. 10, 36, 62
Ulmer, Thomas A. 59
Underhill, Odie W. 128
Unholtz, Louise 62
Upham, Louise 10, 50
Urbantschitsch, Victor 10
Utley, Jean 102, 122

V

Vaisse, Leon 33
Valentine, Cristina 77
Van Adestine 116
Van Der Veer, Gladys 10
Van Ingen, Elizabeth 10
Van Nest, Mary R. 50, 62
Van Wyk, Mary K., 26, 67, 78, 117, 122
Varwig, Renate 71
Ventry, Ira M. 40
Vermillion, Frances F. . . 3, 86, 123
Vernon, McCay 60
Vetidz, G. W. 82
Victoreen, J. A. 40
Vinson, Marietta R. . . 50, 78, 105

Voelker, Charles H., 12, 56, 102, 105, 106
Vonderheit, Esther C. 117
Vorce, Eleanor .. 67, 68, 71, 102
Vose, Persis 117

W

Wade, W. 15, 16
Wadleigh, Grace K. 117
Wagner, Mary A. 72
Wait, Selah 3
Walcher, Helen 67
Waldo, Mary S. 72
Waldron, Grace A. 26
Walker, Crayton 40
Walker, E. W. 82, 123
Walker, H. D. 56
Walker, Hazel W. 102
Walker, Jane B. 38, 50, 117
Walker, S. Tefft 3
Wall, Alice P. 26
Wallin, Margaret K. 10, 71
Walter, Jean 36, 56
Ward, R. H. 50
Warfield, Ethel B. 82
Warner, Larae 26
Warren, Nell 71
Warren, Sue A. 60
Wasell, Irene T. 26
Washburne, C. 78
Washington, Margaret L., 117, 126
Watrous, Helen D. 50
Watson, Charles W. 78
Watson, Norman A. 10
Watson, Ruth B. 41
Watson, T. J. 10, 36, 41
Watts, Jo D. 67
Weaver, James A. 50, 56
Wecker, Karl 63
Weil, Clara S. 78
Weir, Robert C. 60
Weisbord, Marvin R. 78
Wells, Anita 71

Welsh, Eugenia T. 50, 71
Welty, Harry L. 2, 26
Wesselius, Sybrant 14
West, Robert 102
Westervelt, Z. F. 33
Weston, Cora C. 117
Wetherill, Stella J. 50
Wettstein, Carl T. 36
Wettstein, Frances 14, 102
Whildin, Olive A., 26, 41, 50, 67, 78, 117
Whitaker, Bessie L. 117
Whitcher, Cora M. 92
White, Harry 58
White, Henry 88
White, Henry C. 58, 92
White, Stella K. 67
Whitehurst, Mary W. 10, 71
Whitman, Mabel P. 86
Whittlesey, Addie 56
Wiedemer, A. 118
Wilcox, Rachel M. 11
Wild, Laura H. 89
Wilkinson, Warring 58
Williams, Boyce R. .. 33, 67, 128
Williams, Howard 36
Williams, Job 16
Williams, Katharine 33
Williams, Mary E. 57
Williams, T. J. 83
Willoughby, J. Evelyn 50
Willson, Amy E. 90
Wilman, M. Catherine 86
Wilson, D. K. 26, 78
Wing, George 34, 56
Winnie, A. J. 26, 120
Winston, Matie E. 50, 67
Winters, L. 86
Winters, Loretta M. 71
Witherspoon, Elizabeth 117
Withrow, Frank B. 26, 50
Withrow, Margaret S. 50, 86
Wojan, Kathleen 62
Wolach, Marvin 3

Wolf, Edna L. 36, 102, 106
Wolf, Rena 117
Wood, Doris E. 91
Wood, M. W. 88
Wood, Margaret 102
Wood, Nancy 50
Woodburg, Max W. 126
Woodruff, Lucius H. 34
Woods, Elizabeth L. 78
Woodward, Helen .. 41, 50, 67, 86
Worcester, Alice E. 102, 106
Worcester, Eleanor B. 50, 67
Work, Robert 67
Worthington, Anna M. 34, 83
Wright, Bruce 86
Wright, Florence F. 117
Wright, John D., 11, 12, 26, 34, 36, 39, 57, 67, 68, 72, 102, 106, 117, 120, 126
Wrightstone, J. W. 88

XYZ

Yale, Caroline A., 13, 27, 60, 86, 103, 106, 120
Yeakle, Hannah E. 89
Yearsley, Macleod . 11, 34, 36, 71
Yelton, D. C. 56
Yenrick, D. E. 11, 41, 117
Yorty, Jeane B. 67
Young, Mrs. Arthur J. 117
Young, Ellery 27
Young, Irene B. 71
Young, Leo H. 117
Young, Louise T. 27
Yunghans, Marian 36
Zaliouk, A. 103
Zander, Alvin 67
Zebrowski, Alexander 36
Zeckel, Adolf 34, 83
Ziegler, Clara M. 117